DANIEL O'CONNELL

DANIEL O'CONNELL.
From an oil painting by George F. Mulvany, R.H.A.

Daniel O'Connell

NINE CENTENARY ESSAYS

Edited by

PROFESSOR MICHAEL TIERNEY

President, University College, Dublin

BROWNE AND NOLAN LIMITED

THE RICHVIEW PRESS DUBLIN

First Published, 1949

FOREWORD

IT is the destiny of politicians to be misrepresented in life and misunderstood after death ; but few among them have suffered this destiny in so extreme a form as the leader who won emancipation for the Catholics of Ireland and set going the movement which through a century's changes and chances vindicated for the Irish people their ancient right to a separate national identity. In his lifetime O'Connell was derided, even by those he had benefited, as " King of the Beggars," and held up to scorn by his enemies as a loathsome agitator battening on the fancied grievances of the lowest in the community. After his death he was represented to his own people as a giant indeed, but one whose faults were more gigantic than his virtues, and as largely responsible by his preaching of a cowardly doctrine for the catastrophe of the Famine and even for the fiasco of 1848.

This condemnation, passed and ratified by men who never had a tithe of the power over their own generation that O'Connell possessed over his, has remained in force down to this day. It even colours the very panegyrics upon him delivered on occasions chosen to celebrate his achievement. The purpose of the present series of essays, planned to appear for the centenary of his death, has been to present his character and his work in a more objective and more truly historical light.

My editorial task has been the easy one of designing the general character of the book and seeing it through the press. I have not attempted to co-ordinate the views of the distinguished writers whose co-operation it has been my good fortune to obtain. Each essay must be read as an independent contribution to the subject. Nevertheless I am not without hope that from the book as a whole there will emerge a fairly well-balanced and accurate picture of O'Connell, and that what it may lack in completeness it will make up in freshness of approach. To my fellow-essayists and to all who have helped in the book's production I offer my sincere thanks.

MICHAEL TIERNEY.

CONTENTS

THE GAELIC BACKGROUND

GERARD MURPHY

WHEN pagan Celtic barbarism gave way to the semi-barbarism of early Christian Ireland, it seemed for a time as though the world might see a new Far Western Christian civilization, as different in quality from the Western Christian civilization that was to come from Italy and France as that civilization was from the Orthodox Christian civilization of the Byzantine east. Sixth- and seventh-century monasteries, such as those of Iona, Derry, Bangor, Armagh, Glendaloch, Monasterboice, Aran, Clonfert, Clonmacnois, Durrow, Terryglass, Clonenagh, and Cork, had been the seed-beds in which that nascent civilization flourished. By the end of the ninth century, however, it was clear that even the monastic soil was out of heart; and before the monasteries had performed their task of truly civilizing the lay *tuatha* from whom they drew their recruits, early promise of a rich harvest was already belied.

Again at the end of the twelfth century a new phase of Gaelic growth met with disaster; for the forcible, but imperfectly achieved, Norman conquest nullified an interesting native effort of the Irish to bring their Gaelic order voluntarily into harmony with the now strong and rapidly-growing Western Christian civilization. A stunted form of Gaelicism, often (and not without some reason) identified by outsiders with barbarism,[1] continued on, however, with little or no signs of decay till the beginning of the seventeenth century, when the defeat of Hugh O'Neill and Red Hugh O'Donnell foretold its doom. Some ninety years later, with the disasters at the Boyne, Aughrim, and Limerick (A.D. 1691), came a definite end to whatever

---

[1] Even that great defender of Gaelic Ireland, Hugh O'Neill, Earl of Tyrone, in a petition dated 23rd December, 1597, did not hesitate to describe the upbringing of the Irishry as barbarous: "Item that it may please Her Majesty, for that the abuses of her bad officers hath been the beginning of all these troubles, and the Irishry cannot away with the rigour of the law upon every small occasion, their bringing up being barbarous, to grant unto his lordship authority that Tyrone may be made a County Palatine, as the like is granted to others in Ireland." (*Calendar of State Papers, Ireland, Elizabeth, 1597*, p. 476.)

prospects there might previously have been of a natural
revival of Gaelicism : from that on the re-Gaelicizing of
Ireland would have required a conscious effort on the part
of a national leader ; for not alone had all official remnants
of the Gaelic political system disappeared, but the Irish
gentry were rapidly coming to look on the Irish language
itself as a patois, useful only for communication with a
peasantry who were deprived by tyrannous laws against
their religion of all school education and all hopes of
material advancement.

Nevertheless even in 1775, when Daniel O'Connell, later
to be known as The Liberator, was born, there were still
many districts in Ireland where Irish was a language commonly used by the Catholic gentry, and where the Catholic
manner of life was still largely Gaelic in tone. Daniel's
grandmother, Máire ní Duibh, descended from the " Dark "
branch of the Glenflesk O'Donoghues, in 1751 keened her
eldest son John in Irish, and reproved a kinswoman for
kneeling in silent prayer by the corpse, after the manner of
city-women, instead of beating her hands and lamenting as
" the dark women of the Glen " would have done.[1] In 1773
Daniel's aunt, Eibhlín Dubh Ní Chonaill, kept up the
tradition by keening her husband, Arthur O'Leary, in what
is undoubtedly the finest poetic lament extant in the Irish
language. In 1795 another aunt, Alice, widow of John
Seggerson, keened Máire ní Duibh herself in a similar
touching lament, only a fragment of which has been preserved.[2] Daniel's uncle " Hunting Cap " (Muiris an
Chaipín), who reared and educated him, exercised for deeds
lawful and unlawful the same sway over tenants and followers as a long line of Gaelic ancestors had exercised
before him, and sgian na coise cuime, " the crooked-hafted
knife " which he used to hand to his representatives as the
symbol of his authority is still remembered in Íbh Ráthach.[3]

---

[1] Mrs. M. J. O'Connell, The Last Colonel of the Irish Brigade, I, p. 24.
[2] Ibid., II, p. 155.
[3] For documents and traditions concerning Hunting Cap see : Mrs. M. J.
O'Connell, Last Colonel, I–II, passim; D. Ó Súilleabháin, Seanchas na
Deasmhumhan, p. 191 ; the same author's Beatha Dhomhnaill Uí Chonaill,
pp. 40-6, and his article in Béaloideas, XV (1945), pp. 10–13, 16.

Daniel himself, having been fostered by one of his father's farm-workers, could speak nothing but Irish when he returned at the age of four to his parents' home, and his first conversations with his father and mother were in that language.[1] All round him in his boyhood were to be found, almost in full strength, that wealth of peasant poetry, song, and folktale, and that Gaelic eloquence and ease of intercourse which, even in a weakened form, have so charmed modern scholars. He himself had listened to and knew these stories and songs, and when at the age of twenty-one he took a passing interest in the Ossianic controversy he could claim with truth that tales about Oscar, Ossian, "Fingal," Gaul, Dermid, and Bran, were known to him from childhood : " The names of Ossian's heroes," he writes in his journal (7th December, 1796), " were familiar to my infancy, and long before I had heard of Macpherson or his translation the characters of the poem were mostly known to me." Whenever in later life he revisited his native Íbh Ráthach he could enter into the Gaelic life of the peasantry with that geniality which at all times characterised him, and which was itself doubtless part of his Gaelic heritage. An old cowherd, for instance, once sang for him Irish verses in which he delicately reminded him of a promise he had made of the gift of a suit of clothes. O'Connell not alone took the hint, but joyously identified the poet whom he guessed to have composed the verses for the occasion : *Mo graidhin thu, a Thomáis*, he said, *níor chaillis riamh é !*[2]

Yet though Dan's first conversations with his father and mother were of necessity in Irish, he must soon have learnt from them that second language which later he was to use with effect in fighting for the rights of his Catholic fellow-countrymen. For the Kerry gentry of those days were perforce bilingual, a command of Irish being necessary for communication with tenantry and servants, while for intercourse with the Protestant ascendancy in Ireland, or

---

[1] See anecdotes recorded (without citation of authority) by M. MacDonagh, *The Life of Daniel O'Connell*, p. 8.
[2] J. Fenton, *The Songs of Tomás Ruadh O'Sullivan*, p. 22.

(in the days of the Pretenders) for advancement even in
Catholic Jacobite circles in France, English was equally
necessary. In the Irish Brigade itself the words of command
were in English : "As I ne'er ventured to speak French
yet to ladies," writes a new recruit, a Clare kinsman of the
O'Connells, in 1779, " the flirts will have it that I have no
tongue except for exercise, where they find my English
commands so boisterous that they think I could never
attune my voice to the soft accents of love."[1]   English,
therefore, was doubtless the language most commonly used
in the eighteenth century by all Irish gentlemen in speaking
to their children : the family correspondence of Daniel
O'Connell's uncles and aunts is in English throughout ;
and though neither the Liberator himself nor his uncle,
General Daniel O'Connell (" The last Colonel of the Irish
Brigade "), ever lost their command of Irish,[2] it is noteworthy that, when talking privately together in 1816 about
the Liberator's proposed duel with Peel, they preferred
French as a medium of communication to Irish, which they
used only when someone who knew French entered the
room.[3]

The Liberator's own views on the Irish language are
well known. Asked in 1833 " whether the use of the Irish
language was diminishing among our peasantry " :

"Yes," he answered, " and I am sufficiently utilitarian
not to regret its gradual abandonment. A diversity of
tongues is no benefit ; it was first imposed on mankind
as a curse, at the building of Babel. It would be of vast
advantage to mankind if all the inhabitants of the earth
spoke the same language. Therefore, although the Irish
language is connected with many recollections that twine
round the hearts of Irishmen, yet the superior utility of
the English tongue, as the medium of all modern communication, is so great that I can witness without a sigh
the gradual disuse of Irish."[4]

[1] Mrs. M. J. O'Connell, *Last Colonel*, I, p. 222.
[2] W. J. O'Neill Daunt, *Personal Recollections of Daniel O'Connell*, I, pp. 14-5;
Mrs. M. J. O'Connell, *Last Colonel*, I, p. 238, II, pp. 261, 299.
[3] Mrs. M. J. O'Connell, *Last Colonel*, II, p. 253.
[4] Daunt, l.c.

Nor could a life devoted to study of the language awaken any enthusiasm in him. Peter O'Connell of Clare died in 1824. He was a man of considerable learning in literary Irish, and a master of the spoken tongue. Shortly after his death, a nephew, Anthony O'Connell, took the manuscript of the Irish-English dictionary upon which his uncle had been working for years to the Assizes of Tralee in Kerry and showed it to Daniel O'Connell, " expecting that he would call public attention to it ; but Mr. O'Connell," we are told, " had no taste for matters of this kind, and he suddenly dismissed his namesake, telling him that his uncle was an old fool to have spent so much of his life on so useless a work."[1]

Forty or fifty years ago if one were to ask a Kerry farmer why he encouraged his children to speak English his answer would have been that Irish would not sell the cow. O'Connell's attitude towards Irish was in essence the same, though it is hardly fanciful to see in his description of his attitude a trace of the Benthamite doctrine of Utility which was in full vogue in his day. Many circumstances, however, commonly influence a practical decision ; and it is therefore probable that neither the advantages of English in selling a cow, nor its utility as a medium of modern communication, adequately describe the complex of motives underlying the gradual abandonment by Irishmen both of their native language and of the Gaelic way of life to which it belonged. For not alone from the utilitarian point of view was it a disadvantage to know no language but Irish ; in addition the Gaelic way of life was undoubtedly more primitive than the English, and there were more obvious relics of barbarism in it. Moreover in the eighteenth century, with the downfall of Gaelic education, Gaelicism had lost much both of its vitality and of its attractive power. O'Connell had no contemporary Ó Bruadair to speak to

[1] Eugene O'Curry's words (written in 1849), quoted by S. H. O'Grady, *Catalogue of Irish MSS. in the British Museum*, I, p. 162. Cf. a similar account of the same incident by O'Curry in his unpublished *Catalogue of Irish MSS. of the Royal Irish Academy, Hodges and Smith's Collection*, Part I (1843), p. 42. Shortly after this incident the manuscript of the dictionary was purchased by James Hardiman, who sold it to the British Museum, where it is now preserved.

him in Gaelic verse as an intellectual equal, judging his actions with full understanding of their motives, as the seventeenth-century Ó Bruadair had judged the actions of his seventeenth-century leaders and their opponents. Indeed had it been possible for an Ó Bruadair, educated in the Gaelic manner, to exist in the nineteenth century, O'Connell could have only imperfectly understood him ; for his language would have been shot through with literary speech-forms, allusions, and mannerisms, to which O'Connell would have been as unaccustomed as a backwoodsman to the language of *Paradise Lost*. A natural tendency to choose what is economically advantageous in preference to what is economically disadvantageous, to choose the mature in preference to the immature, to choose civilization in preference to barbarism, and to choose what is vital and growing in preference to what is decaying, is doubtless, then, what has all along been at the root of the gradual yet consistent abandonment of Gaelicism by those born into it.

There was a time when no leadership was necessary to make the Gael (and many Normans) prefer the Gaelic way of life to the Anglo-Norman way, as exemplified in medieval Ireland. The choice then, however, lay between two likes, two organisms at the same stage of their growth. In O'Connell's day the choice was between a crippled immature thing and a thing highly developed and triumphant. A Gaelic Burke, convinced of the superiority of organic growth and continuity to revolutionary change, might conceivably have advocated vigorous pruning and patient cultivation of the maimed Gaelic tree. But in the late eighteenth century there was no political thinker of Burke's calibre, with a deep understanding of Gaelicism, to teach the principles of such a policy to an Irish leader. From Grattan, on the other hand, and his comrades of the Patriot Party, O'Connell learnt noble principles and a fine ideal which had grown out of that Anglo-Irish civilization to which, by the second side of his upbringing, he belonged. Those principles and that ideal, being readily available, were accepted by him. To them he added a technique of popular agitation, which

was his own contribution to politics ; and that contribution
of O'Connell's has been influential in more ways than one
in forming the Ireland we know to-day, an Ireland such as
neither Grattan nor the hypothetical Gaelic Burke would
have willingly envisaged.

Grattan's Ireland, an Ireland led by English-speaking
Whig landlords, is well known to students of history. Gaelic
Ireland is harder to know intimately : living by custom
rather than thought, the Gaelic world never portrayed
itself to itself, nor discussed its aim or purpose ; it has no
Swift, no Berkeley, no Sterne, no Goldsmith, no collections
of intimate family letters written in Irish. Analogy with
the living present and oral tradition must therefore be our
main guides to understanding it. " I am sorry to learn
that our sister Nelly has taken a step contrary to the will
of her parents, but love will not know or hear reason,"
writes the Liberator's uncle Daniel in sober English in
May, 1768. That document is preserved, for it belongs to
the Anglo-Irish side of O'Connell tradition. Nelly's own
Gaelic version of the incident would have been lost, however, to history, were it not for the retentive memory of
Irish-speaking farmers and cottiers in Cork and Kerry.
Mo ghrá go daingean tu, she said, as in May 1773, some five
years after the elopement, she stood beside her outlawed
husband's bloodstained corpse,

> *Mo ghrá go daingean tu !*
> *Lá dá bhfeaca thu,*
> *Ag ceann tí 'n mharagaidh,*
> *Thug mo shúil aire dhoit,*
> *Thug mo chroí taitneamh doit,*
> *D'éaluíos óm athir leat,*
> *I bhfad ó bhaile leat :*
> *Is dom nárbh atuirseach !* [1]

Already in reading those opening lines do we not feel ourselves transported into a different world ?—a world in
which Nelly is no longer Anglo-Irish Nelly, but Gaelic

---

[1] You are my beloved for ever ! One day that I saw you, at the market-house
gable, my eye perceived you, my heart loved you, I eloped from my father
with you, far from home with you : I never repented it.

Eibhlín Dubh, and in which her husband is no longer
" poor Arthur Leary," whose " violence and ungovernable
temper " were disapproved of by his brother-in-law,[1] but
Art, son of Conchúr, son of Céatach, son of Luíseach
Ó Laoghaire, *Gaol Iarla Antroma, 's Bharraigh ón Amchoill*—
kinsman of Barrys and MacDonalds—and terror of the
Sasanaigh who killed him :

> *Is cuimhin lem aigine,*
> *An lá breá earraigh úd,*
> *Gur bhreá thíodh hata dhoit,*
> *A's bannda óir tairigth' air,—*
> *Cluíomh cinn airigid,—*
> *Lámh dheas chalama,—*
> *Ramsáil bhagarthach—*
> *Fir-chrith-eagala*
> *Ar namhaid chealagach,—*
> *Tu 'gcóir chun falaireacht,*
> *A's each caol ceannann fút :*
> *D'umhluídís Sasanaigh*
> *Síos go talamh doit,*
> *A's ní mar mhaithe leat,*
> *Ach le haon-chorp eagala,*
> *Cé gur leó do cailleadh tu,*
> *A mhúirnín mh'anama.*[2]

---

[1] In a letter dated June, 1773 (Mrs. M. J. O'Connell, *Last Colonel*, I,
p. 173).

[2] My mind remembers, that bright spring day, how well your hat became
you, with a golden band drawn round it,—a silver-hilted sword,—a brave
right hand,—proud menacing gait,—quaking fear on an enemy full of guile,—
and you equipped for pacing, mounted on a slender white-faced steed :
Sasanaigh bowed to the ground before you, out of no love for you, but for
sheer dread, though it is by them you were killed, darling of my soul.

[In 1720 Sir James Cotter was hanged in Cork. His nurse keened him,
and her keen is preserved in a manuscript written in the early nineteenth
century (Maynooth, Murphy MS. 9, p. 345 ; see Maynooth College Library,
Catalogue of Irish Manuscripts, p. 94 ; the complete keen has been published by
Fiachra Éilgeach in the *Irish Press*, 27th April, 1936). Several of the lines
attributed to Sir James Cotter's nurse occur in the passage just quoted from
the keen attributed to Eibhlín Dubh. Eibhlín may have developed and
added to a passage from an earlier keen, or a reciter may have added lines
to Eibhlín's keen. What is important for our present purpose is that the
passage is genuinely Gaelic. Similar doubt about the trustworthiness of
particular points, and similar certainty about their being in keeping with the
Gaelic spirit, must characterize our attitude towards all the records from oral
tradition used in the course of this study.]

We are far here from the poetry of eighteenth-century France or England. For when Eibhlín describes Art in his gold-bound hat terrifying the Sasanach enemy as he rides through Macroom armed with a silver-hilted sword, is her spirit not akin rather to that of Homer when he tells of Alexandros marching " in the front ranks of the Trojans, with a panther-skin, a curved bow and a sword upon his shoulders, brandishing two bronze-headed spears and challenging the best among the Argives to fight him man to man in deadly combat " ?

In the English correspondence of the O'Connell family there is always calculation and caution, never any incitement to violence. But in her Irish poem Eibhlín will not hesitate to call for vengeance on Morris, who had caused her husband to be outlawed and whom she suspected of being directly responsible for ordering the soldier to fire the fatal shot :

> A Mhuirisín, léan ort !
> Fuil do chroí 's t'aé leat !
> Do shúile dá gcaocha !
> Do ghlúine dá raoba !
> Do mharuís mo lao-sa,
> 'S gan éin-fhear i nÉirinn
> A ghreadfadh na p'léir leat ! [1]

Nor was her call for vengeance unheeded ; for soon afterwards Art's brother shot Morris in Cork and then fled to France. [2]

One is tempted to linger over the gentler parts of Eibhlín Dubh's moving lament, the passages in which she describes her orphaned children calling for their father, and his own last leave-taking when he kissed his two children and kissed his wife's finger-tips, prophesying his death :

> Mo ghrá thu 'gus mo thaitneamh !
> Nuair a ghabhais amach a' geata
> D'fhillis tar n-ais go tapaidh,

---

[1] Wretched Morris, sorrow on you ! May your heart's blood flow over you ! May your eyes be blinded and your knees sundered ! You killed my darling ; and is there no man in Ireland to riddle you with bullets ?

[2] Mrs. M. J. O'Connell, *Last Colonel*, I, p. 171.

Do phógais do dhís leanabh,
Do phógais mise ar bharra baise,
Dubhraís, " 'Eibhlín, éir' it sheasamh,
A's cuir do ghnó chun taisge
Go luaimineach a's go tapaidh :
Táim-se 'fágáil a' bhaile,
'S ní móide go deó go gcasfainn."
Níor dhineas dod chaint ach maga :
Bhíthá dá rádh liom go minic cheana.[1]

Such passages, where moments and feelings of eternal human value are perfectly expressed in verse, are as completely Gaelic as the wilder passages we have been considering ; and though they, too, are in their way Homeric— Art's leave-taking being strangely like that of Hector in the sixth book of the *Iliad*—in themselves they would hardly have made the Irish language and Irish ways seem primitive to the generation immediately following Eibhlín Dubh's. Their primitiveness lies rather in the context in which they appear. Such public outpourings of private grief and anger are in the heroic tradition. They are what the Greek expected of a Hecuba or an Andromache mourning over Hector's corpse in the *Iliad*, or of an Electra and an Orestes lamenting Agammemnon in the *Choephoroi*. Already by the sixth century, however, the matrons of Athens employed professional keeners, doubtless because they themselves had outgrown the primitive heroic mould. Professional keeners were forbidden by Solon ; and Athens in its classical maturity knew only the reasoned prose panegyric, which was more suited to a fully civilized community than the emotional metrical outburst of earlier days.

The story of the O'Leary feud with Morris is confused perhaps for modern readers by the fact that Morris belonged to the hated Sasanaigh, while Art Ó Laoghaire was a Gael. But Gaelic turbulence was not confined to situations in which the Sasanach was the enemy. Protection not alone

[1] You are my love and my delight ! When you went out the gate you turned quickly back, you kissed your two children, you kissed the tips of my fingers, you said " Eileen, rise up, and settle your affairs quickly and swiftly : I am leaving home, and it is unlikely that I shall return."—I laughed at what you said : often had you said it to me before.

in his just, but also in his unjust causes, was expected by a Gaelic follower from his lord. In the late seventeenth century Sir Henry Piers writes that the Gaelic lords "were of old, and still are, oppressive of their tenants and followers"; but he adds that those lords go beyond their duty to preserve their tenants from wrongs or injuries and actually aid them to withhold their dues and debts from others, so that "it is a common saying on the mouthes of many farmers, 'What boots me to have a landlord if he defend me not in my just and unjust causes?'"[1] Nor was Sir Henry Piers libelling the Irish, for in the sixteenth century Tadhg Dall Ó hUiginn, asking for help from Cormac O'Hara, declared that to have his patron with him in a rightful cause was no advantage, if he would not also support him in wrong:

> *Bheith aguinn a hucht chóra—*
> *Gá dtú, a mheic mheic Onóra?—*
> *Ní budh éadáil ód dreich dhuinn*
> *gan bheith san éagáir aguinn.*[2]

That this doctrine could still be taken as the rule of life in Gaelic Ireland in the eighteenth century is suggested by an account of an incident in the life of Tadhg mac Tomáis O'Herlihy recently recorded from oral tradition by Pádraig Ó Cruadhlaoich of Macroom, Co. Cork.

"When Tadhg mac Tomáis O'Herlihy was living in Ballyvourney (Pádraig Ó Cruadhlaoich tells us[3]), the Glenflesk people used to cross the border into Ballyvourney to steal, and the Ballyvourney people were tormented by them. Tadhg mac Tomáis gathered a band, about twenty men, I think. They suspected a certain man living in Caol Mór of being the one who used to rob them. Early in the morning they set out to catch the thief. They surrounded the place carefully, but for all their care, the

---

[1] National Library of Ireland, MS. 412, pp. 115, 116.

[2] In short, thou grandson of Onóra, that thou be with me in a rightful cause will be no benefit from thy rosy countenance, if thou do not also support me in wrong (E. Knott, *The Bardic Poems of Tadhg Dall Ó hUiginn* (1550-1591), poem 30, l. 5). I have to thank Professor Knott for directing me to this confirmation of Sir Henry Piers' words.

[3] In his *Cuimhne Sean-leinbh*, pp. 64–5.

thief saw them and ran off to the west, along the side of
Caol Mór, following the course of the river, till he reached
Poll Gorm. Then he turned north along the Cillín road
to Droichead na nGarraí, pursued by the Ballyvourney
men. He reached the castle of Cill Átha. Tadhg
mac Tomáis with some of his men were standing at the
gate. Tadhg asked where he had gone. He was told
that he had gone into the castle. He followed him in ;
and O'Donoghue was there, seated on a chair, with the
robber in underneath the chair.

Tadhg was a very strong man. He seized the robber
by the back of his head and pulled him out from under
the chair, and walked out on to the road. The robber
was tied up, and they made him go in front of them on
the road. They faced for home. They proceeded east-
wards up Poll Gorm and up Cluain Chaoin. As they
were going up the Doire Aimhréidh road, one of them
looked back, and he said at once that they had better
release the prisoner and run, for that more men than they
could deal with were pursuing them. Tadhg mac Tomáis
spoke, saying that if anyone moved any faster, or attempted
to run, he would kill him—for he had a loaded weapon.
It happened that there was a stream of water running
across the road, and they had just crossed the stream.
He heard a horse just behind him. He turned immediately.

' Where are you going, O'Donoghue ? ' he said.

' I have come to fetch that prisoner of yours,' said
O'Donoghue.

' I was surprised that you were so long coming for
him ; for I have always heard that your house is the
refuge of all the robbers in Glenflesk. Your horse's front
feet are in the water. I pledge my word that if you wet
his hind feet I'll fire what's in this through your heart ' ;
and he aimed his weapon at him.

O'Donoghue said nothing, nor did Tadhg himself
say a word more. O'Donoghue thought ; and the result
of his thought was that he turned his horse out of the
stream and said to the men who were behind him :

'Did you hear what he said? He has pledged his word that if I cross the stream he will fire what's in that weapon of his through my heart; and he would undoubtedly do it, for he would not break his word. But I'll not kill myself for him,' said O'Donoghue; and he pursued the matter no further. He and his men returned home. The prisoner was taken to Ballyvourney; but I can't say what happened to him: I never heard that anything bad was done to him, and I imagine that if anything bad had been done to him I should have heard of it."

Do not cattle-raids and rescuings such as this remind one more of Nestor's night-raid on the cattle of the Eleans, described in the eleventh book of the *Iliad*, or of the great raid that gives its title to our own *Táin Bó Cualnge*, than of the settled civilization which was the ideal of the eighteenth-century Georgian squirearchy? And like the raids of which Homer speaks, these Irish raids could be productive of good poetry:

> *Buailidh, leagaidh, a's pleanncaidh*
> *Ba boga reamhra 'n tSasanaigh,*[1]

sang a poet of a night-expedition, led in 1780 by a cousin of the Liberator's father, to destroy the cattle of a tyrannous landlord who belonged to the Fuller family. The cousin, tradition says, though his real name was Domhnall (*Anglice* Daniel), had a nickname Tadhg na Stiall, which may be translated Tadhg the Slasher, given him by reason of his skill at wielding the blackthorn. He performed great feats on the night of the expedition:

> *An té chífeadh Tadhg na Stiall*
> *A' siúl trí Shliabh an Imiligh,*
> *A's nár lú 'ge cailleach 'na dhiaidh*
> *Ná Fuller mór liath agus gunna 'ge !*[2]

---

[1] Strike, fell, and smite the Sasanach's fat fleshy cows.

[2] What a sight to see Tadhg the Slasher walking through Sliabh an Imiligh, caring as little for big grey Fuller and his gun as though it were an old woman who was after him! [It is hard to believe that Tadhg na Stiall and Domhnall were really the same person; but whether they were one or two is of little importance for our present purpose.]

Oral tradition tells likewise of how he escaped conviction when arrested and tried at the Tralee assizes :

"As has so often happened, O'Connell was betrayed ; and he was arrested and tried at the Tralee assizes, where Fuller received compensation for his stock at the cost of the barony. The Grand Jury decided that the case against Daniel O'Connell was sufficiently substantiated to justify bringing him before a common jury for trial. Although he had witnesses to swear that he had gone to bed in his room that night, that the housekeeper had locked the doors, and that he was asleep in his bed when called next morning, their evidence did not convince the Grand Jury.

When the jury was being called, the accused person had the right to object to any juror for certain reasons. The first man named was a son-in-law of Fuller's. O'Connell's barrister told him to stand down. Daniel interrupted the barrister, saying : ' I have no objection to this gentleman's being one of the jury which is to try me. I know well that he is an honourable man who would never wrong me to gain another's favour, even though that other were his own father-in-law. Let him act on the jury.' The barrister withdrew his objection.

Fuller had a younger daughter, who was engaged to be married ; and she was in court, accompanied by the young man to whom she was engaged. He was the next person named. The young woman whispered to him : ' What a dreadful thing it would be were such a fine fellow condemned ! He proved he was a gentleman when he insisted on my sister's husband going on the jury. If he is condemned it will be a bad day for you so far as I am concerned ! '

Though there was plenty of sworn evidence against him, and though everyone was certain that he was guilty, Fuller's two sons-in-law saved him.

Count Maurice O'Connell, who was granted the title as a reward for brave service in the Austrian army, was a brother of that Daniel O'Connell. Daniel's witnesses had sworn truly that he had gone to bed in his room and had been there next morning, and that the housekeeper had locked the doors. He had made a hole through the roof of the house, through which he had gone out and come in again ! "[1]

Do not the insight into character and the ruse by which this Daniel obtained his acquittal strangely resemble the similar insight and similar ruses attributed to the later Daniel in stories concerning his career as an advocate ?

The Gaelic way of life, some aspects of which we have been considering, was still in a sense more grand, and certainly more picturesque and more poetic than the English or Anglo-Irish way. The very examples we have considered—and they could be multiplied—also, however, illustrate its comparatively primitive nature and its endemic lawlessness, inherited from past barbarism and perpetuated by contemporary oppression. Had the old patriarchal bond that united the Gaelic lord to his followers by ties of mutual interest still existed in the late eighteenth century, the Catholic gentry might still have unthinkingly continued to live the double life to which for some generations they had been accustomed, a life which was Gaelic in the home and on the farm, Anglo-Irish on the street and in the law-courts. But the patriarchal bond itself had been loosened.

About the year 1773 Samuel Johnson, in the Ostig section of his *Journey to the Western Islands of Scotland*, states that the Scottish chiefs, " being now deprived of their jurisdiction, have already lost much of their influence "; and he ventures to prophesy that " as they gradually degenerate from patriarchal rulers to rapacious landlords, they will divest themselves of the little that remains." The Liberator's uncle, Muiris an Chaipín (" Maurice of the Hunting Cap "), as pictured by popular tradition, would seem himself to have been an example of the partriarchal ruler fast on his way to becoming a rapacious landlord. *Sgian na coise cuime*, the symbol of his patriarchal authority, still in his day won instant obedience from tenants and followers. A revenue officer, for instance, who had interfered with the O'Connells'

---

[1] D. Ó Súilleabháin, *Seanchas na Deasmhumhan*, pp. 189-90.

smuggling, was immune from attack by Muiris's followers as long as he was accompanied by the bearer of the *sgian*, but when he dismissed the bearer he was immediately set upon and seriously injured. The story is told as follows by Mrs. Morgan John O'Connell :[1]

" One fine September morning, the 5th of that month, 1782, while Hunting Cap, his brother, and sundry cousins and nephews, with a throng of peasants, were happily engaged in landing a valuable cargo, Captain Butler swooped down on them with the King's men, and made a seizure of all their store. Hunting Cap submitted to the inevitable, and civilly invited the officer to break-fast. Hunting Cap's wife had a French silk gown in the cargo, and expressed a wish to ransom her finery.

' You shall have it free, madam, if it costs me my com-mission,' gallantly responded the officer, and he sent for the piece of silk for her.

Captain Butler determined to return to Waterville across country on foot, with a very small escort. Hunting Cap knew the peasants were furious at the capture, and dreaded mischief, so he besought the officer to let him send with him one of his nephews (the O'Sullivans of Couliagh), as otherwise he could not answer for the people. In Captain Butler's presence he handed the crooked knife to his nephew, bidding him escort the officer to the river-bank at Waterville.

Thus singularly guarded, the representative of law and order set out. In passing through the hamlet of Cahir-daniel they noticed lowering looks and hostile gestures, but a sight of the crooked knife caused the peasants to make way. Some distance beyond the village, Captain Butler begged young O'Sullivan to go back, and struck across the high mountain for his home. Whilst Captain Butler was crossing one shoulder of the mountain, a mob of angry peasants had skirted the other brow from Cahirdaniel. They fell on the officer, routed his men, and beat him to within an inch of his life."

[1] *The Last Colonel of the Irish Brigade*, I, pp. 304-5.

If in this Butler anecdote we see Muiris still possessing influence over his people after the manner of a patriarchal ruler, in other anecdotes he appears rather as the rapacious landlord :

"When his father died in 1770 (we are told[1]), Muiris succeeded to the property. In addition he was agent for Lord Carbery and various other landlords, to collect their rent for them in Íbh Ráthach.

The big landlords commonly insisted on having their rent paid them in gold. They would accept no other currency. Gold was scarce and hard for the poor tenants to procure. But the agents were able to provide against the scarcity in a way that was of advantage to themselves. And Muiris an Chaipín was as cunning and avaricious as any of them. He used to have a firkin of gold ready for the gale-days in a room beside the rent office. The man in charge of the gold used to give a golden guinea to the tenants for every twenty-six, or often twenty-seven or twenty-eight, silver shillings. That is how Muiris, and others like him, amassed their riches."

Now even in the days when the Gaelic ruler was in undoubted fact the defender of his people and the pivot on which depended all that was important in their lives, his rent-collecting may well have been resented by his subjects. But those rents were mainly in "victuals," and, as the sixteenth-century poet Spenser has told us, "of victuals they were wont to make small reckoning."[2] Victual and service rents were still in vogue in the early days of the eighteenth century :

"The O'Connells of Darrynane were prosperous people (writes Mrs. Morgan John O'Connell[3]), though their affluence consisted rather of flocks and herds and merchandise than of hard cash. The small mountain tenants mostly paid their rent in labour or in kind. Little

---

[1] By D. Ó Súilleabháin, in an article in *Béaloideas*, XV (1945), p. 10.
[2] *View of the State of Ireland* (see H. Morley, *Ireland under Elizabeth and James the First*, 1890, p. 71).
[3] *Last Colonel*, I, pp. 8–9.

money changed hands, unless on special occasions. Strapping ' boys,' sturdy girls, and hardy ' garrons ' (the little mountain horses) could give work instead of the rent."

In Muiris's youth servants were likewise paid in kind. When the change of times came (the same writer tells us),[1]

" ready money, which the poor people seldom saw before, came into use, and, instead of feeding great gangs of boys and girls, people began to pay workmen. Maurice O'Connell was too enlightened a man not to see the advantage of the new system, and he adopted it. Whenever he went away, however, his liberal old mother would summon in all hands to dinner. On one occasion, at a very busy time in late autumn, he returned (probably from November fairs), and found that all his paid workmen were having a very good dinner, the old lady looking on approvingly. He addressed her in Irish before them, so that the men might have no doubt as to his views :—

' I thought, mother, I had stopped that work.'

' The day was very cold,' rejoined the old lady, ' and they could not work if too cold.'

' I keep a steward to make them work.'

' The best steward,' rejoined the irrepressible old dame, ' is a full stomach.' "

Máire ní Duibh, the liberal old mother of that anecdote, was of the old world. Her son was of the new ; and, as the anecdote itself shows, the money economy of that new world was less favourable to the maintenance of patriarchal affection between lord and follower than the victual-and-service economy of the old. Clearly a breach was being gradually opened between the Catholic gentry and the peasantry to whom they had once been so closely united. The disarming of that gentry had rendered them useless as the military defenders of their followers. The abolishing of local hereditary jurisdiction had deprived them of one of their main civil functions. A change of economy was now loosening the bond of affection. And even their

[1] Ibid., II, pp. 114–5.

political ideals were beginning to differ. In 1778 the Liberator's uncle Daniel (later General in the French army and Colonel in the English) wrote as follows from Paris to his brother Maurice at Darrynane :

" Your publick papers have transmitted here the pleasing account of the new laws in favour of the Roman Catholicks. A revolution so unexpected and so long wished for must needs procure, in course of some years, an accession to the power and prosperity of the Kingdom of Ireland, and unite in one common sentiment of loyalty the hearts of that long-oppressed and long-unfortunate nation. One step more still remains to be made—I mean the liberty of spilling their blood in defence of their king and country. I doubt not 'twill soon be granted, tho' no motive cu'd ever induce me to bear arms against France, where I early found an asylum when refused one at home. I still wish the prosperity of the country, and at the same time that I pursue with inviolable fidelity that of my adopted king, nature, stronger than reason or principle, still attaches my heart to Ireland."[1]

The gentry's new political ideal of loyalty to the Hanoverian dynasty with " the liberty of spilling their blood in defence of their king and country " awoke no enthusiasm among the common people ; and when in 1795, after the Revolution, this exiled Irishman's hopes were realized, and a new Irish Brigade was recruited in Ireland for the English service, the officers of the old Brigade, Lecky tells us,[2] " found themselves strangers and aliens among their people, and were exposed to gross insults, as Wolfe Tone afterwards related, to the keen delight of his French friends." In Gaelic poetry, indeed, active dislike of the Hanoverian dynasty never ceased, and throughout the eighteenth and early nineteenth century the poets, when they did not sing of the return of a non-existent Prince[3] to defeat the Hanoverians, simply replaced the Prince's name by that of

[1] Mrs. M. J. O'Connell, *Last Colonel*, I, p. 207.
[2] Ibid., II, p. 200.
[3] *Filíocht Mháire Bhuidhe Ní Laoghaire* (ed. D. Ó Donnchú), p. 40.

Bonaparte, or by vague mention of the French or Spanish.[1]
To the reformed Catholic gentry, therefore, desperately
anxious to prove both their loyalty and their respectability,
Gaelic poetry and the Gaelic way of life offered little or no
attraction. Their abandonment of the Irish language
became more marked; and in the Liberator's day it was
treated by them as a purely peasant patois.

That O'Connell and men of his class individually suffered
any serious loss when, cutting themselves off from the
immature Gaelic tree, they grafted themselves on to the
mature Anglo-Irish tree, could hardly be argued. There
is genuine beauty in some of the Gaelic songs written in
praise of the Liberator by peasant poets, but they offered
no fodder assimilable by his wholly modern parliamentarian
mind. Indeed if he were to take their thought seriously he
could not but disapprove of it; for, being essentially in the
old tradition, it ran directly counter to his own thought.
When Diarmuid O'Mahony, for instance, in an Irish
Aisling, prophesied the attainment of Repeal in 1845, he
viewed it not as the gift of a Hanoverian government
following upon a period of peaceful agitation, but as the
conquest of English oppressors by foreign invaders, helped
by Irish pikes, whose wielders were protected by a warrior
O'Connell. Nor was O'Mahony's insistence on the
righteousness of James's cause exactly what O'Connell
would have wished, at the moment, to be stressed:

[1] Cf. P. Breathnach, *Ceól ár Sinsear*, pp. 62, 173; Idem, *Ar gCeól Féinig*,
p. 137; Idem, *Sídh-cheol*, p. 114; *Filíocht Mhdíre Bhuidhe Ní Laoghaire* (ed.
D. Ó Donnchú), pp. 37, 80; *Pádraig Phiarais Cúndún* (ed. R. Ó Foghludha),
p. 7; S. Laoide, *Duanaire na Midhe*, poem 6, p. 11. Occasionally, too, we find
similar sentiments expressed by officers in the foreign services. Richard
O'Connell, the Clare kinsman mentioned *supra*, p. 4, writes, for instance, in
1779 to Maurice Leyne : "Would to God, my dear Maurice, that we were
at the moment 200,000 strong in Ireland, and that I had the command of
our single company of Oak Park ! I would kick the Members and their
Volunteers and their Unions and their Societies to the Devil ! I would make
the rascally spawn of damned Cromwell curse the hour of his birth ! O,
Heaven ! can there be such brutes in human form ? But my dear country
swarms with them." (Mrs. M. J. O'Connell, *Last Colonel*, I, p. 223.) Don
Alexander O'Reilly, Count Commander of the Spanish Armies, Field-Marshal,
etc., who was born in Ireland in 1725 and died in Spain in 1794, is likewise
said (ibid. p. 303) to have had as his dream to lead a Spanish force against
England, and, in his native country, to overturn heresy and tyranny, and
burn to the ground his ancestral home, polluted by conforming kinsmen,
whom he would put to the sword.

Aisling chaoin do theagmhaigh linn
  I dtrácht na hoich' a's me chun sochaird,
Gur ghabhas tríd an gharbhchoill
  Gan neach am dhíon, ach éin a' siosmairt,
A' machtnamh síor ar cheasna Gaoidheal,
  Ag taxes, cíos, a's claont' á gcluichirt,
Ag cama-dhlíthe chlanna 'n fhill
  Ó thréig an rí ceart Séamus sinn-na.

'Éigse Mumhan, éistidh lium :
  Tá 'n gárda chúinn ar bhárr na tuinne ;
Beidh Repél rianta 'mliain a cúig ;
  Tá 'cimeád cúil dúinn Dónal Ó Conaill.[1]

That stanza and its chorus, with their rich series of vowel
assonance, make exquisite poetry. But O'Mahony, being
a Gael, formed a pattern whose strands have been gathered
not alone from many moments of a legendary and a real
past, but also from the even more vivid reality of the present,
will not place his *spéir-bhean* in the safe unreality of an
undefined antiquity, as Moore has placed his wholly artificial
Minstrel Boy. For the *spéir-bhean* who appeared to
O'Mahony, having been questioned by him in the way
all Irish poets question such an apparition, tells him she
is Ireland and prophesies a speedy pike-won victory over the
Calvinists :

Tá 'n Spáinneach flíteach buíonmhar tréan,
  Líont' 'o laochra gléast' i n-arm.
Ní gá dhóibh stríoca do ghaoith ná spéir,
  Go dtíd go Béarr' i n-iarthar mara.
Glan do phíce, a's bíodh sí ar faor ;
  Dinidh sgéal do líon gach baile :
Beidh camthaí líont' ar maoil gach slé
  'Díbirt thréada choimhthigh Chailbhin.

[1] A lovely vision appeared to me at night-time when I went to rest. I
seemed to pass through a wild wood, unprotected, hearing only the soft
sounds of birds. My thoughts were all of the trouble of Gaels, harassed by
taxes, rent, and wrongs, through the crooked laws of the tribes of treachery,
since the true king, James, abandoned us.
  Poets of Munster, hear me : the army is coming over the water ; Repeal
will be won in the year that ends in five ; Daniel O'Connell is our defender.
(See *Gadelica*, I, pp. 16–8.)

'Éigse Mumhan, éistidh lium :
    Tá 'n gárda chúinn ar bhárr na tuinne ;
    Beidh Repél rianta 'mbliain a cúig ;
        Tá 'cimeád cúil dúinn Dónal Ó Conaill.[1]

O'Connell hated pikes, and genuinely desired to see
Protestants occupy their proper place in a self-governing
Ireland.   That, in part at least, explains why, while accepting Moore's wholly unreal Melodies with enthusiasm,[2] he
was left unmoved by the much finer poetry of O'Mahony
and his fellows.   Moreover, Moore afforded O'Connell
real food for his intellectual life when, in another mood, he
wrote political poetry in the tradition of Pope, satirizing
Castlereagh and inculcating the principles of Fox and
Grattan.   Serious thought such as Moore's was naturally
not to be expected from the Gaelic peasantry of O'Connell's
day, nor indeed, with but few exceptions, were Gaelic
poets at any time inclined towards serious thought—pattern
and the expression of emotion being the aim they commonly
set themselves.

Yet if O'Connell and men of his class suffered little as
individuals when they cut themselves off from the immature
tree, the same can hardly be said of Ireland considered as
a whole.   The death of a culture which already enshrined
much beauty and might yet, under favourable circumstances, have grown to a really rich maturity, should certainly not have been permitted for the utilitarian reasons
advanced by O'Connell, and hardly even for the better
reason that it was immature and partly barbaric in quality :
Homer, the semi-barbaric forerunner of a fully civilized
Sophocles and Plato, did not delay their coming, but rather
was the cause of it.   Moreover, though considered as the
culture of an aristocracy Gaelicism may have been primitive
and immature, considered as a peasant culture it required

---

[1] The Spaniard, strong in fleets and armies, is surrounded by warriors
equipped with weapons.   His troops need fear neither wind nor sky till they
come to Beare in the west of the sea.   Clean your pike, and see that it is sharp ;
tell the news to all in every townland :   there will be full camps on every
mountain-top banishing Calvin's foreign flock.
    Poets of Munster, hear me :   the army is coming over the water ;   Repeal
will be won in the year that ends in five ;   Daniel O'Connell is our defender.
[2] W. J. O'N. Daunt, *Personal Recollections of Daniel O'Connell*, I, p. 150.

little change to make it wholly admirable. Nevertheless the lead set by the gentry was naturally followed in due course by the peasantry. That peasantry were famed for conversational eloquence ; and their poetic prayers, laments, love-songs, humorous verse, extempore stanzas, and patterned *aislingí,* gave to their everyday life a beauty that was unique in Europe. When they ceased to use the Irish language they therefore lost a rich treasure and received but little in exchange ; for the culture which the English language put at O'Connell's disposal is not a culture readily assimilable by peasant farmers and cottiers. Íbh Ráthach to-day has no Diarmuid na Bolgaighe, no Tomás Ruadh, no Murtaí Larry, to mention but three of the peasant poets who flourished there in O'Connell's time. A civilization which not alone produced a working carpenter who could praise his homestead as Murt praised his *Cnuicín Fraoigh,* or who could curse the crow that stole his potatoes as Murt cursed *Rúc an Droma Léith,* but also offered that poet neighbours who would learn his songs and sing them with full understanding of their excellence, is not a civilization to be heedlessly let decay.

> *Is ró-bhreá 'n t-am é,*
> *Ar theacht mí na Bealtain',*
> *A' féachaint anonn ar mo Chnuicín Fraoigh,*
> *A's grian gheal an tsamhraidh*
> *A' cur teas' insna geamhartha*
> *'S duilliúr glas na gcrann a' fás ann le gnaoi.*
> *Bíonn lach' ann ; bíonn bárdal ;*
> *Bíonn banabh ag an gcráin ann ;*
> *Bíonn searrach ag an láir ann, a's leanabh ag an mnaoi ;*
> *Bíonn bradán geal a' snámh ann,*
> *An breac ag éirí 'n-áirde,*
> *'S an té bheadh ar phonnc an bháis ann, d'éireódh sé 'rís.*[1]

[1] The coming of the month of May is a delightful time to be looking across at my Little Heather Hill, with the bright summer sun warming the blades of corn, and the green foliage of the trees growing there in beauty. The duck is there and the drake. The sow has its young there. The mare has her foal there, and the woman her child. The bright salmon swims there, the trout rises up, and the man about to die there would arise once again. (For the complete Irish text see S. Ó Súilleabháin, *Diarmuid na Bolgaighe agus a Chómhursain,* pp. 120–2.)

In the nineteenth century there was hardly a farmhouse or cottage in Kerry where that stanza of Murt's would not have been appreciated. To-day those who could appreciate it are rare even in Íbh Ráthach and have wholly disappeared from the greater part of Kerry.

To have asked O'Connell and men of his class to satisfy themselves with an immature Gaelicism when the mature culture of Anglo-Ireland was within their reach, would doubtless have been unreasonable. Might not bilingualism have offered a solution of the dilemma ? Bilingualism has its disadvantages. Daniel O'Connell's own bilingualism, and his soldier uncle's trilingualism, would seem, however, in themselves to be a proof that those disadvantages do not necessarily prevent high achievement. Where politics and nationality are concerned, practical men have to decide boldly and definitely. Such matters are, however, so complex that they evidently do not permit the calm certainty of a judgment based on full analysis. Historians, therefore, may be pardoned if they refrain from condemning Daniel O'Connell for his practical decision to do nothing to encourage the use of the Irish language. Nevertheless, they too are entitled to their preferences ; and, if they have learnt to know and love Gaelic Ireland, they will inevitably regret that one who was so great, so devoted, so brilliant, and on the whole so successful a fighter for his people's rights, decided so definitely against the desirability of marshalling his forces for a battle on the Gaelic front.

LOUVAIN, ST. OMER AND DOUAI

Thomas Wall

THE association of the Catholics of England and Ireland with centres of Catholic reaction in the Spanish Netherlands began in the second half of the sixteenth century and by the early seventeenth it had developed into a chain of Irish and English houses and colleges in Antwerp, Brussels, Douai, Ghent, Liège, Lille, Louvain, St. Omer and Tournai. The most important links in this chain were Louvain in Brabant and Douai in Flanders, not because these towns were of any great importance, but because they were seats of Pontifical universities.

Louvain had extended its hospitality to Irish students from the middle of the sixteenth century and in the seventeenth it was their headquarters in the Low Countries, with three well-organised Irish colleges, the Franciscan College of St. Antony, founded in 1606, the Pastoral College for the education of secular clergy, founded in 1623, and the Dominican College of the Holy Cross, established in 1624. Irish intellectual prestige in the university was more than respectable, especially in the seventeenth century when Ireland gave the university four rectors and some of its most outstanding protagonists in the theological controversies which then agitated Europe.

Douai was to English Catholics what Louvain was to the Irish. Its famous English College, founded in 1568, made the name of the town—in anglicized form, Douay or Doway—a household word in the penal days. The University of Douai, modelled on that of Louvain, was founded in 1559, and was from its inauguration a Counter-Reformation university. Its first chancellor, Richard Smith, was an Englishman and though it was originally staffed, for the most part, from Louvain, Oxford fellows and graduates held many of its most important posts. Through these it perpetuated many of the traditions of pre-Reformation Oxford and could claim to be the true Catholic Oxford exiled into Flanders.

It was their universities which gave Louvain and Douai an importance out of all proportion to their size in the religious conflict of the sixteenth and subsequent centuries, when they became the chief bases in the Low Countries from which the struggle for the faith in Ireland and England was directed and carried on. Far away and ineffective they must have seemed to the faint-hearted and despondent, and even the bravest may not always have found it easy to believe that the weak should confound the strong, that Douai and Louvain should perturb London and Dublin. For they were but two small towns, small enough, either of them, to be almost entirely dedicated to religion and learning and to take its whole character from its university. A collection of friaries, priories, libraries, convents, colleges, university halls and buildings; a huddle of steep red-tiled roofs, broken by dormer windows, in the shadow of an ancient spire or tower; leafy faubourgs and drowsy canals and a few bustling markets, where university professors in their gowns and members of the various religious orders in their habits were quite as much of a piece with the general scene and blended as harmoniously into the background of medieval church and town-hall and market-house as the country people in their picturesque costumes: there was not much in all this, as far as the eye could see, that suggested conflict or could be interpreted as a challenge and a menace to the Protestant ascendancies of Ireland and England. Yet when Bellarmine lectured in Louvain on the chief points of difference between Catholic and Protestant, Dublin was uneasy, and indeed all Europe gave ear; and it was in an attempt to answer the arguments of this great Jesuit controversialist that Dublin, after the example of other Protestant centres, provided a chair of controversy which Ussher filled with some distinction. And in Whitehall reports were received and carefully considered of the activities of Allen, Conry, Cusack and other founders of Irish and English Colleges who, deep in their academic and administrative work in Douai and Louvain, were pestered by the attentions of spies and, in Allen's case, of one would-be assassin.

These were the centres where Irish and English Catholics had so entrenched themselves after two centuries that it took the full violence of the French Revolution to dislodge them. It was only when the old accustomed positions became untenable, when the colleges and convents and halls were converted into barracks and military hospitals and factories, that they finally abandoned them and returned as fugitives to their own countries to found the colleges which the relaxation of the Penal Laws had just then made possible. The dispersal of the scholars in the Low Countries which was thus to issue in a revival of Catholic learning at home was not an unmitigated misfortune, though it was rude and unwelcome in the manner of its coming to those who were dispersed.

Daniel O'Connell was on the spot at this turning-point of history and was himself one of the fugitives who escaped from France just as the Revolution was reaching its greatest fury. It was appropriate that this young champion of the Catholic cause should have had an opportunity of observing this reversal of the past ; that he should have sojourned as a student, just before their evacuation, in those ancient sanctuaries of scholastic peace where so many of his countrymen as well as the recusants of England had found a congenial refuge in the centuries of persecution. His stay abroad was a brief one, six weeks in Louvain, ten months in St. Omer, and five months in Douai, all within the uneasy interval between the outbreak of the Revolution and the Reign of Terror, but brief as it was, it was not without a deep influence on his life and thought.

As he and his brother Maurice were setting out for France in the autumn of 1791, many had already fled from that country and others were daily leaving it to swell the armies of *émigrés* over its borders. Their uncle, Colonel Daniel O'Connell, still held his commission in the French army and was eager still to advise and protect Louis XVI ; a shrewd and cautious man, when the Colonel did flee, a little later, his flight was so planned as not to compromise his future career. This uncle was educational agent to his family and all their connections in Kerry ; he had taken

out many boys to place them in the army or in colleges to
study for the priesthood or for the medical profession. He
had been interested in his brother Morgan's sons as early
as 16th April, 1783 : " Pray, how old are Morgan's sons ?
Are they stout and promising ? "[1] he had enquired of his
brother Maurice of Darrynane, known as " Hunting Cap."

And when the boys, Daniel and Maurice, were old enough
to go abroad, this wealthy and childless uncle, Maurice
O'Connell of Darrynane, had sought advice of the Colonel
as to the best place to send them ; and the latter had replied
on 16th June, 1789, that in his opinion the college of
St. Omer's was the most suitable place. Another cousin,
he wrote, " Maurice of Tarmons, proposes, I believe, to
spend next summer in Ireland, and you can charge him
with the care of the two boys as far as St. Omers, where
I shall previously make it my business to ensure their
admittance."[2]

But the situation had so seriously deteriorated by the
first month of 1790 that the Colonel wrote advising his
brother not to send the boys abroad " until tranquility be
more solidly established than it is." The troubles of France,
he anticipated, would soon extend into the neighbouring
countries and the situation, in the Netherlands especially,
then under Austrian rule, was very critical.[3] In a letter
of 2nd September, 1790, he confirmed this opinion. He
deplored the wretched condition " the finest country in
Europe " was reduced to and warned his brother, " I think
you must lay aside all thoughts of sending our young
nephews over. I know no place either in France or the
Low Countries where you can safely send 'em."[4]

So the boys remained in Father Harrington's school at
Reddington, near Cove, until August, 1791, when Dan was
sixteen years old, a year older than his brother, Maurice.
What decided their uncle to send them abroad just then,
against Colonel O'Connell's advice, we have no means of
ascertaining. But both boys would soon be beyond the

[1] Mrs. Morgan John O'Connell, *The Last Colonel of the Irish Brigade*, ii, p.10.
[2] Ibid., ii, p. 80.
[3] Ibid., ii, p. 84.
[4] Ibid., ii, p. 90.

usual age—from thirteen to sixteen years—for admission to
college, so that there could be no delay if they were to go
at all. And that their destination was the English College,
Liège, suggests that "Hunting Cap," in his remote Kerry
home, may have entertained a hope that in the impending
wars the neutrality of Liège, under its Prince-Bishop, would
be respected, a hope which in the event was not fulfilled.
So to Liège the boys were sent, travelling by brig to Dover,
by the packet from Dover to Ostend, and by diligence thence
to Liège.

All his biographers relate, on the authority of John
O'Connell whose biography of his father was published in
the latter's lifetime, that young Dan's first experience of
the English coast was a ducking in the surf at Dover as he
disembarked;[1] and they tell also, following O'Connell's
own recollection communicated to O'Neill Daunt, that one
of his first experiences on the Continent was to be taken as
an Englishman with no sympathy for the revolutionary
ideals of France. A Frenchman, travelling with him in the
diligence, badgered him with abuse of England and losing
all patience with the youngster's complacency, exclaimed,
" Do you hear ? do you understand what I am saying, sir ? "
" Yes, I hear you ; I comprehend you perfectly." " Yet
you do not seem angry ? " " Not in the least." " How
can you so tamely bear the censures I pronounce against
your country ? " " Sir, England is not my country. Censure her as much as you please, you cannot offend me. I
am an Irishman and my countrymen have as little reason
to love England as yours have—perhaps less."

The college at Liège to which the boys were going had
an interesting history. Late in the sixteenth century a
famous English Jesuit, Robert Persons, had founded a
college at St. Omer in the province of Artois for the education
of English Catholic boys. There it had prospered until
1762, when the Society of Jesus was suppressed in France,
and in that year the staff of the college succeeded, by one
of the most dramatic adventures in the history of any school,
in transplanting their whole college, without loss of a single

---

[1] *The Life and Speeches of Daniel O'Connell, M.P.*, i, p. 6.

boy, from St. Omer, in France, to Bruges, in the Austrian
Netherlands. Each day, until all the boys had gone, some
went out as for a walk and by wagon and canal boat reached
Bruges without arousing any suspicions in the French
authorities. The French, who would have liked to keep
the boys, were thus left with an empty building that
yielded them no revenue. The Jesuits were not long in
Bruges, however, when the general suppression of the
Society was promulgated and the Austrian authorities
moved against its members there. It happened that the
English Jesuits had a house in the Principality of Liège,
whose Prince-Bishop, Mgr. Welbruck, was sympathetic to
the Society, and though he had formally to announce the
suppression, he did not disturb the community of the
English house ; and it was here that the priests and students
from the college of Bruges re-assembled to carry on their
customary studies and activities until they came to Stonyhurst in 1794.

That the arrangements for their going abroad were hasty
and that " Hunting Cap " had not the benefit of the Colonel's
advice in the matter, became apparent when the O'Connells
reached Liège. It was only there, at the end of their long
journey, that it was discovered that Dan was beyond the
prescribed age for entrance to the college. That the authorities of the college did not stretch a point in so extreme a
case may be accounted for by their own insecure position
at the time. They may have been unwilling to accept
responsibility for the two forlorn travellers when their own
future was in jeopardy, for it must have been obvious to
them that they should soon be in the way of contending
armies, with no assured refuge whither they might flee.
So with letters of introduction to the Franciscans and
Dominicans the boys set out for the town towards which,
if they had no other fixed destination, all wandering Irish
scholars in the Low Countries gravitated, Louvain.

They were in the unfortunate position of having to consult
their uncle in Darrynane about every move they made and
even about the subjects they should or should not study ;
their uncle Daniel was nearer, and him they consulted also,

but even he had to defer to the judgment of Uncle Maurice who was paying for their education and exercised complete control over them. Letters travelled slowly in those days, so that the boys had to mark time for some six weeks in Louvain before they heard from Darrynane. It was a happy delay that gave them leisure to explore the old university town. With no town in Europe was Ireland so intimately connected as with Louvain, no town of its size that had so many Irish associations, or to which Ireland owes so much. Its university had received hundreds of Irish boys as poor students, providing them with board and education, and when they had graduated there it had not denied them the reward of their ability and industry— industry and ability proved by the severest tests of any university in Europe. Four Irishmen had been elevated to the highest dignity the university had to offer, that of Rector Magnificus, and one of these, Thomas Stapleton of Fethard, was elected Rector no less than nine times. The O'Connells probably saw the handsome monument to this great man in the church of St. Pierre, and other memorials of Irish interest, in their wanderings around the city.

At the time the two O'Connells were in Louvain, Ireland was represented on the university staff by two Waterford men, John Power, who later became bishop of his native diocese, and Francis Ahearne (O'Hearn) whom the boys must have often met, for he was attached as professor of rhetoric to the College in which they stayed. Dr. Ahearne seems to have cut quite a figure in the life of Louvain. He is said to have boasted in the university library that he had trodden more square feet of Europe than any man living or dead and that he knew more languages than any one in Louvain. With a knapsack on his back and a staff in his hand he had, during his vacations, trudged Europe from end to end, penetrating into strange and perilous places, and having many curious adventures. He was a pioneer in the use of the Flemish language as a literary medium, for which service the Belgians have honoured his memory by a monument in Brussels and by publishing an account

of his life in Flemish.　So elegant was his style in the use
of many tongues (including his native Irish) that it was
said in his praise that the mantle of Lipsius had descended
upon him—and that, in Louvain, where the memories of
Erasmus and Lipsius are equally cherished, was no small
compliment.

The O'Connells were made to feel quite at home in the
university city.　They visited the Irish Franciscans and
the Irish Dominicans, for Maurice told his uncle that the
Dominicans and Franciscans were very civil to them.　They
probably visited the Pastoral College also, but they did not
stay in one of the Irish houses, which were exclusively for
clerics ; they were lodged in the Collège de la Sainte
Trinité in the middle of the town, near the Old Market.
This was a preparatory school for young gentlemen and
what was alleged to have been an autograph of Daniel
O'Connell, written with a bodkin on one of its doors, used
be displayed to Irish visitors.　Besides Francis Ahearne,
another Irishman, Thomas Flynn of Lismore, taught in
this college while the O'Connells were there.　Their time
in Louvain was not entirely wasted.　" We attended the
University schools whilst at Louvain," wrote young Maurice
in a letter of 17th January, 1792, to his uncle at Darrynane,
" and had recourse to the library of the Dominicans."　The
university was just then enjoying a respite from its quarrel
with Joseph II of Austria, against whom it had to contend
strenuously for its autonomy ; it had not yet become
involved in the graver troubles of the French Revolution.

On the 19th of October, 1791, the letter from Darrynane
arrived in Louvain and was acknowledged by Maurice
O'Connell on the 29th of the same month.　The boys were
told to go to St. Omer.　They immediately set out for
Ostend, accompanied by a Mr. Curtin, and having made
financial arrangements with the agent on whom they had
credit there, they proceeded to St. Omer.　The expense of
the journey from Louvain to Ostend was about two guineas
each, Maurice informed his uncle, who demanded a strict
account of all expenditure ; from Ostend to St. Omer by
way of Jurens cost them two pounds, ten shillings each,

St. Omer is a small town in Artois, no bigger than
Clonmel or Carlow, with broad streets and squares, but
with little animation.   In the religious conflict of the
sixteenth century its position had strategic importance.   It
was at that time in the dominions of Phillip II and was
also within twenty-four miles of Calais, convenient to the
English coast.   And when the Jesuit, Robert Persons, was
looking about for the site of a college which would do for
the English Catholic laity what Douai was already doing
for the clergy, he perceived the suitability of St. Omer,
and there the English College was founded in 1592-3.
It was this college which made the name of St. Omer—
anglicized as St. Omers or St. Omer's—a familiar one in
the annals of the English Catholics, in the story of the
English martyrs and in the reports of English intelligence
officers.

The building which the O'Connells entered in 1791 was
not the original foundation but one that had been erected
after a fire in 1725, and it was no longer in possession of
the Jesuits.   After the suppression of the Society in
France in 1762, the secular clergy of the English college
at Douai had taken over the college at St. Omer,
reluctantly and with the intention of restoring it some day
to the Jesuits.   They transferred their preparatory school
from Douai to St. Omer, and Alban Butler, author of the
well-known *Lives of the Saints*, became its first Rector.   In
one of the stories told of this saintly man we get a glimpse
not only of the academic leisureliness of the streets of
St. Omer but also of its pastoral surroundings where the flat
land, won with great pains from the marshes, was intensively
and jealously cultivated by the industrious peasants.   Alban
Butler was a bibliophile who read at all hours and in all
places, in the streets, in company, at his meals, in his walks,
in his carriage and even on horseback.   " I have met him,"
one who knew him in St. Omer told his nephew, Charles
Butler, who was one of the first Catholics before O'Connell
to distinguish himself in the legal profession and who
incidentally never manifested any friendship for the latter,
" with a book under each arm and a third in his hands,

and have been told that, travelling one day on horseback,
he fell a reading, giving the horse his full liberty. The
creature used to eat a few ears of corn that grew on the
roadside. The owner came in haste, swearing he would
be indemnified. Mr. Butler, who knew nothing of the
damage done, no sooner perceived it, than, blushing, he said
to the countryman with his usual mildness, that his demand
was just " and giving the man a louis d'or, he ambled away,
still reading.[1]

Alban Butler was succeeded as president in 1787 by
Dr. Gregory Staplyton whom the great bishop, John Milner,
described as " a gentleman of ancient family, of unimpeachable orthodoxy and morality." He was president when the
O'Connells arrived in St. Omer and his deep discernment of
character is manifest in the report of the boys which he sent
to their uncle, a report which, in the light of their future
careers, must be considered one of the most remarkable ever
written. It was enclosed with a letter written to Darrynane
by young Maurice on 17th January, 1792. The boys had
then been in St. Omer only three months, but in this period
the watchful president was able to observe their progress
and appraise their respective worth. The bluntness of
" Hunting Cap's " request for a candid report and his suggestion that presidents were not much given to telling the whole
truth in such documents may have affronted this " gentleman of ancient family " somewhat ; and the preamble of
Dr. Staplyton's report, keeping the stern but fond and
anxious uncle in suspense until its close, may have been a
dignified and gentle rebuke for his brusquerie.

" You desire to have my candid opinion respecting
your nephews and you very properly remark that no
habit can be worse than that of the instructors of youth
who seek to gratify the parents of those under their care
by ascribing to them talents and qualities which they
do not really possess. You add that, being only the uncle
of these young men, you can afford to hear the real truth
respecting their abilities and deficiencies. It is not my

[1] Charles Butler, *Account of the Life and Writings of the Rev. Alban Butler*
1800, pp. 4-47.

habit to disguise the precise truth in reply to such inquiries as yours; you shall therefore have my opinion
with perfect candour.

I begin with the younger, Maurice. His manner and
demeanour are quite satisfactory. He is gentlemanly in
his conduct and much loved by his fellow-students. He
is not deficient in abilities, but he is idle and fond of amuse-
ment. I do not think he will answer for any laborious
profession, but I will answer for it, he will never be guilty
of anything discreditable—at least, such is my firm belief.

With respect to the elder, Daniel, I have but one
sentence to write about him, and that is, that I never
was so much mistaken in my life as I shall be unless he
be destined to make a remarkable figure in society."

One can easily appreciate the feelings of gratified relief
and joy with which the concluding part of this report was
perused in Darrynane and communicated to the boys'
parents in Carhen. And their own letters from St. Omer,
especially Dan's, were similarly gratifying in showing consistent progress in the schools. Their uncle may have been
a shrewd and tight-fisted man, but he was also a man of
method and foresight. Every letter he received he dated
and endorsed in his own neat hand, sometimes making an
abstract of it, and placed it carefully away in that handsome
brass-mounted escritoire of his in Darrynane. He thus
accumulated—a rare achievement in the penal times—a
great hoard of old papers, with many historic postmarks,
for the delight of those who love to rummage through such
documents, enabling them not only to reconstruct the life
of Paris and France before the Revolution as seen through
the eyes of Irish officers, but also to obtain such glimpses
of the famous colleges of St. Omer and Douai in their last
days as his nephews' letters afford.[1]

[1] These papers with others which belonged to Maurice O'Connell's successors in Darrynane are now preserved in University College, Dublin. Many
of the letters have been printed in *Correspondence of Daniel O'Connell the Liberator*,
by W. J. Fitzpatrick, London, 1888, 2 vols. They have also been extensively
used in Mrs. Morgan John O'Connell's *The Last Colonel of the Irish Brigade*,
London, 1892, 2 vols. Some of them were also printed in the serial, "The
O'Connell Papers" in *The Irish Monthly*, 1882. I have used the original
papers in writing this account of O'Connell's schooldays abroad, a phase of
his life which has been somewhat neglected by his biographers.

The boys wrote six letters, three each, from St. Omer to Darrynane during their nine months' stay in the college. It cannot be said that these letters are very intimate or interesting; there are no accounts in them of their games and recreations, of their masters and friends; no echoes of the old town of St. Omer escape into them, no consciousness of the historic past of their college, of its martyrs and other famous men; no impressions of the people of Artois whom they saw in their walks, no vignettes of the scenery and landscape of that country which must have seemed tame and delicate and melancholy as compared with Kerry and Darrynane, with its moist and relaxing air so different from the bracing air of the Kerry mountains. Perhaps the formal relations between the uncle and his nephews did not invite intimate disclosures and communications of this kind; they were always on their best behaviour with him and observed all the conventionalities of model epistles, especially in the ending which seldom varies : " Present our love and duty to our dear Grandmother, Father and Mother and all other friends."

The double censorship which the letters had to undergo may also help to explain their uncommunicative restraint. They were submitted open to the superiors of the college, and in Paris they underwent a political scrutiny. " It is said," wrote Dan in a letter of 30th June, 1792, " that all the letters which leave this kingdom are first sent to Paris, where they are opened. If this is the case, it may in some measure account for the great length of time our letters take before you receive them." This prying into private correspondence began as a source of amusing excerpts for Louis XIV, and proved too valuable a source of information for the police to be discontinued.

If they were not very generous in describing the homely details of their life in St. Omer, the boys compensated their uncle by the minute accounts they gave of their studies and the curriculum in the college. For they had to satisfy Uncle Maurice that they were making progress and that his money was being wisely spent on their education.

" In this College," wrote Dan on 3rd February, 1792,
" are taught the Latin and Greek authors, French,
English and Geography, besides lessons given during
recreation hours is music, dancing, fencing and drawing.
I have not yet enquired about rhetoric but will do it
(please God) as soon as I receive an answer from Uncle.
We have composed for the second time since I came here.
I got second in Latin, Greek and English, and eleventh
in French ; before the places are read out there is a scene
or two of a play acted on a small stage which is in the
college by one of the first four schools (each in its turn) ;
these they call Orations, and of them there are eight in
the year. Of consequence we compose eight times ; there
is a whole play acted in the month of August."

After Easter he was promoted to a higher class or school
in which the oratorical bias was even more pronounced.
He now read Mignot's harangues, Cicero and Caesar—the
Caesar was given him for translation into Greek—
Demosthenes, Homer, and Xenophon's Anabasis. In French
he read Dagaso's speeches. This emphasis on oratory, on
declamation and theatrical display, was not peculiar to the
college in St. Omer ; though English and Irish Catholics
were conscious that they had to fight their cause with
words, not with arms, and this may have been added
stimulus for them to cultivate eloquence. Rigidly excluded
from public life as they were, they had yet to be as skilful
as possible in the arena of argument and disputation. But
in the general content of its curriculum, St. Omer was in
line with other European colleges and in accord with
European tradition since the Renaissance.

The discovery, early in the fifteenth century, of complete
texts of Cicero's *De Oratore* and Quintilian's *Institutio
Oratoria* had a profound influence on educational theory
and practice in Europe ; it had given education a method
as well as an aim. Old Cato's definition of an Orator
became a maxim of educators : *vir bonus dicendi peritus*, the
honest man skilled in the art of speaking, not the glib man
nor the loquacious man, nor the irresponsible demagogue,
but the good and grave and learned man, the man of

affairs who had something to say and knew how to say it
effectively, the preacher, the teacher and above all the
tribune or public representative who could sway by eloquent
words courts and senates and assemblies and crowds, and
influence them unto justice.

It was fundamental in this idea of the orator that he must
be a good man, *non posse oratorem esse nisi virum bonum*, and
that he must have the common good of his people at heart.
The educators whom Quintilian influenced had little
sympathy for the recluse who withdrew from the common
concerns and duties of life to retire into some cloister of his
own mind, or to burn the midnight oil over purely speculative study or disruptive theories. The orator must be a
man of learning, but of learning that is capable of ready
and effective expression; knowledge must be available
for public service, ready, like weapons in an armoury, for
prompt use in dispute or declamation. Man was a member
of society, and the aim of education was to make him, in
the words Dr. Staplyton used of young O'Connell, "a
remarkable figure in society," a good and patriotic citizen,
a wise and eloquent and accomplished public man. All
the exercises of the school were adapted to this end and the
school itself was conceived of as a vestibule to the theatre of
life, a gymnasium or palaestra where (as Cicero had said)
"those who are preparing for what is to be done in the
forum, as in the field of battle, may alike previously learn
and try their power, by practising in sport."

This idea of education, common to European schools,
prevailed in St. Omer. The boys lived in community as
much as possible, they were not encouraged to mope or
to develop aloof individualistic tendencies. Even during
a recess from study, when the boys went once a fortnight
for a day to a country house, situated, as Dan told his uncle,
in a beautiful valley about a league from the town, there
was no nook to which a shy youngster could retire, and
Dan makes this an excuse for a delay in answering his uncle's
letter—" I had no place to retire to from whence I might
write to you." Emulation was another factor in their
education which kept the boys together and conscious of

DANIEL O'CONNELL.
From an early Lithographic print

[By courtesy of the National Gallery of Ireland]

one another ; once every month they competed for places
in the various subjects. The dramatic displays and orations
were also the result of concerted activity amongst the boys
themselves, under the guidance of masters. They composed
once a month, and even the composition had to be declaimed
to the assembled school, so that it generally had a rhetorical
ring about it.

One specimen of Dan's English composition survives from
his days in St. Omer ; at least one alleged to be such is
printed in the *Memoirs, Private and Political, of Daniel
O'Connell,* compiled by Robert Huish, and published in
1836, well within O'Connell's lifetime. Its subject is the
different modes of education in England and France. The
pre-eminence of France in matters of art and culture has
often been acknowledged ; Paris, " queen amongst cities,
moon among stars " has been acclaimed by her admirers
the intellectual capital of Europe, and Daniel O'Connell,
when he was in St. Omer, seems to have been one of her
most enthusiastic admirers. " What is she now ? " he
asks in the peroration of his essay,

" Is she not in most essential points the mistress of
Europe ? Do not the youths of all countries go to pay
homage to this queen amongst the nations, whilst her
own subjects keeps their state at home ? Are not her
laws of fashion and dress everywhere obeyed ? Is not
her language the currency almost of the world ? Her
rapid progress in arms, in commerce, in polity, is too
notorious to need being mentioned."

And this pre-eminence of France he traces, not to that
island of Paris where Philosophy had her royal and ancient
seat in the shade of Notre Dame, but to Cardinal Richelieu
who " knew that men, like land, were to be improved only
by culture." Richelieu " established several academies,
his successors added to them, and improved upon his design,
so that there are in France numbers of seminaries where
youth may have every assistance, both in theory and
practice, towards making themselves masters in any profession or art to which their genius or choice may direct

them, whether in civil or military life, in arts or sciences."
Out of these nurseries France is supplied with statesmen,
ambassadors, negotiators, officers, excellent writers and
artists of all kinds, and, he adds, " what is most wonderful
of all, admirable orators, and the most excellent composi-
tions in eloquence that the moderns can boast of."

The lesson that a little field of not very kind land, if
cherished and tilled and cultivated, will yield a goodly
harvest, was easily learned in St. Omer. Colonel Daniel
O'Connell had supervised a detachment of 300 soldiers in
the canalization of this country in 1769, and by gradual
draining what was once a marsh became a garden. It was
divided into small plots, intersected by canals, along which
the country people travelled in long narrow boats. And the
idea that average ability may, by attention, be enlarged
and go a good way remained with O'Connell after he had
left St. Omer. It was when he was studying in London that
he wrote thus of his ambition to his uncle :

> " Though nature may have given me subordinate
> talents, I never will be satisfied with a subordinate situa-
> tion in my profession. No man is able, I am aware, to
> supply the total deficiency of ability, but everybody is
> capable of improving and enlarging a stock however
> small and, in its beginning, contemptible. It is this
> reflection that affords me consolation."

Greek and Latin, with English and French—the boys
were obliged to speak French—were the core of the curriculum in St. Omer ; arithmetic and geography were subsidiary subjects ; music, dancing, fencing, drawing and
mathematics were optional and an extra fee was charged
for tuition in these. Dancing and fencing were still considered to be necessary accomplishments of a gentleman, and
exercise in them was valued for the grace and dignity of
carriage which they helped to give. Music was appreciated
as a recreation and a diversion from the cares of life, and
stringed instruments were preferred because to play with
one's hands was deemed more graceful and becoming
than to distort one's face with puffing and blowing at

wind-instruments. In these accessories as well as in the
cultivation of oratory St. Omer's was in accord with
European educational tradition since the Renaissance.

Maurice and Daniel practised fencing and seem to have
got some fun out of it. A fee for their fencing master as well
as a sum for broken foils is one of the items on their bill
from St. Omer. But Maurice dropped as many of the
optional subjects as he could and made good use of the
respite from learning others which the long delay of a reply
from Darrynane gave him. Dan learned dancing and
drawing for the full time he was in St. Omer, but it was
only when he went to Douai that he bought a fiddle and
added music to his accomplishments.

It is not suggested that to a training along those lines in
St. Omer we owe the eloquence of O'Connell, but it did
at least help to take him out of himself, to cure him of the
shyness which afflicted him in Harrington's school, and to
curb his passion for books and study to which, like many
another shy youngster, he was addicted. O'Connell himself
told O'Neill Daunt, with some little pride, that he was the
only boy who was never beaten in Harrington's school, but
the well-informed James Roche, reviewing this statement
in the *Cork Magazine* (September, 1848, p. 643), qualifies
it thus :

" I have been assured that, if not beaten by the master,
he was by the scholars, for his unsociability, apparent
shyness, and preference of study or secluded reflection to
play. Nor yet was he, I have been equally assured by his
schoolfellows, particularly distinguished amongst them for
superior capacity, at that early period, though shortly
afterwards, during his foreign tuition, he gave unerring
promise of future eminence ; as he also became one of
the most joyous, pleasant companions in social intercourse, when at the bar-mess or in society."

When the O'Connells were at school and for some time
afterwards, a course of philosophy was regarded as the
culmination of the study of the humanities and preliminary
to professional training or even to a life of leisure. In such

colleges as Stonyhurst this course, as a substitute for
the Arts course in a university, was only discontinued
when Catholics began to enter the universities. At St. Omer,
Daniel informed his uncle in a letter of 16th April, 1792,
philosophy was not publicly taught; besides, St. Omer
being only a preparatory college, it did not provide a
sufficiently advanced course in mathematics and rhetoric.
So their uncle, who apparently knew little of the seasons of
the academic year and was inclined to hustle his nephews,
ordered them to Douai; though Dan, in a letter of 30th
June, 1792, had not reported very favourably of Douai,
saying, for one thing, that French was almost totally
neglected there. Their uncle's letter arrived on Wednesday,
15th August, and the following Monday the boys moved
to Douai.

It was the wrong time of the year, as they soon discovered,
to have changed school. The classes in philosophy and
rhetoric had begun in Douai at Whitsun, after the feast
of Pentecost, and they had to proceed with much leeway
to make up privately. Besides, they moved at short notice,
without sufficient time to acquaint themselves with the
conditions at Douai, which was a more austere place than
St. Omer. Douai was a seminary as well as being a college,
and the boys were certainly not pampered there. "We
are obliged," wrote Dan on 14th September, 1792, "to
pay for the washing ourselves. At St. Omer everything
was done for the boys, here the boys are obliged to do
everything themselves." Though he adds, somewhat surprisingly, "This college is much better in every respect
than the other." It may have been that he had outgrown
St. Omer, entering there rather late, so that he felt more
comfortable amongst his real contemporaries in Douai.

A vignette of the English College at Douai appears on
the title-page of some old editions of the *Memoirs of Missionary
Priests* by Bishop Challoner, himself a devoted son of that
college and a pious and faithful chronicler of the many
martyrs and missionary priests who had studied there in
the days of persecution. Originally established in a hired
house in 1568 by William Allen, afterwards Cardinal, the

college which is illustrated in Challoner, and which the O'Connells entered, was an eighteenth-century building, somewhat gaunt and sombre but spacious, its vertical lines relieved by verdant trees in the foreground. It was built near a cemetery in the Rue des Morts, opposite the old parish church of St. Jacques, and so letters to O'Connell in Douai were addressed to " Monsieur O'Connell, Au Grand Collège des Anglais, Rue des Morts, à Douay, En Flandre." The anglicized form of the name, Douay or Doway, still familiar in association with the English version of the Bible, was always used by English and Irish Catholics.

The two boys started before breakfast on their journey from St. Omer to Douai and arrived late in the evening, to find that in Douai students were required to furnish their own rooms. With nothing but the beds, they spent the first night in some distress. Dan was taken, as he himself says, " with some slight fits of the ague " and was confined to the infirmary ; so to Maurice fell the task of writing to Darrynane, which he did on 4th September, requesting their uncle to send immediately twelve or thirteen pounds, and to mention what he wished them to learn, music, etc. Maurice's letter, as always, was brief ; the course of rhetoric had begun, he said, and therefore " we have no time to spare, but will in our vacation, which begins shortly." He had just seen the President, Rev. John Daniel, who would also write to Darrynane shortly.

Dan wrote on 14th September, and having told of their plight on the first night, related how an Irish student, a Mr. Duggan, from near Newmarket in Co. Cork, came to their rescue on the following morning. The procurator also was kind ; he advanced them a guinea and a half, with which they bought most of the little things for their rooms, mirrors, candlesticks, basins, etc. They had to buy buckles also, at four shillings each, a piece of expenditure that was excused by the fact that the St. Omer's buckles were small iron ones. Mr. Duggan had pressed another half-guinea upon them to buy knives and forks, etc., for the refectory. With further credit advanced by the procurator, Mr. Joseph Beaumont or Baymont, they were enabled to buy tables,

four chairs, a desk, a cupboard and a dressing-table for
washing and powdering (their hair), etc. This was rather
a substantial outlay—and the pension at Douai was twenty-
five guineas a year—but Dan, greatly daring, goes on to
tell his uncle that they get small portions at dinner and
that most of the lads (those who are on bourses excepted)
get what were called " seconds " and cost an extra three
or four pounds a year. "We would be much obliged to
you for leave to get them, but this as you please. I hope,
my dear uncle, that you will not think me troublesome in
saying so much on those heads; you may be convinced
that it is only a desire of satisfying you and of letting
you know in what way your money is spent that makes
me do so."

But there was soon a more serious cause of worry than
their " seconds " at dinner or their being late for the course
in philosophy. France had declared war on Austria in
April, 1792, and the war opened with a disgraceful panic
of the French troops at Tournai when they fled to Lille
and there brutally assassinated their General, Theobald
Dillon, an Irishman and a gallant officer, whom they
suspected of being sympathetic to the aristocrats. In August
the King of France was imprisoned in the Tower of the
Temple ; in the same month, Colonel Daniel O'Connell,
in a letter to his nephew Maurice at Douai, told of his
escape out of France and of his journey up the Rhine to
join the *émigré* armies. Dumouriez, a friend of Colonel
O'Connell, who had in vain pressed the latter to accept
a high command in the Revolutionary armies, won the
battle of Jemappes, thirty-six miles from Douai, and the
thunder of the cannon was audible in the English College.
The massacres of September, 1792, were still fresh in the
public mind and when a waggoner of Dumouriez's army
scared the two O'Connells and a group of sturdy boys from
the English College, out for a walk, by simply roaring at
them " Voilà les jeunes Jésuites, les Capucins, les Récolets "
their fright—they ran all the way back to the college—can
only be explained by the general feeling of terror that
prevailed.

The Superiors of the English College were aware of the dangers that threatened them. Early in 1793 some of the more valuable plate of the college and some of its most treasured relics, including the red biretta of St. Charles Borromeo, had been buried for safety. Those of the boys who wished to go home, and had authority from their parents to travel, were allowed to do so. The O'Connells, of course, had to consult Darrynane before they could do anything. There is amongst the O'Connell papers one letter from young Maurice which is more crumpled and frayed than the rest and shows signs of haste in its composition. It is dated from Douai, 4th January, 1793, and is probably the last letter sent from there to Uncle Maurice. Dan and himself, Maurice said, were in danger of being isolated in Douai, exposed to the insults of the Revolutionaries and without any means of communicating with Darrynane. Many of the boys had already gone and the number in the college was dwindling daily. " From above 206 who were here before the revolution there are not now 90, and these decreasing every day. Duggan and some others go next week. I hope we shall not be forced to accompany them. In case we should, we will go to London, write immediately, and having been supplied with money by the procurator or Mr. Kirwan, will wait until we hear from you." In all his apprehensions and distress he does not forget the conventional greetings, " Dan joins me in duty to my father, mother and sisters, wishing you and them all the happiness and compliments of the season."

Uncle Maurice had, of course, been hearing of the troubles in France through other channels. One source of information was his Cork butter merchant, Charles Casey, who acted as his paymaster to Father Harrington while the boys were in the latter's school and who continued to act as paymaster to the Presidents at St. Omer and Douai, through a London merchant, Mr. John Kirwan. In a letter of 23rd July, 1792, Mr. Casey, having assured Mr. O'Connell that he had stood by while the butter was being inspected and that he himself was as good a judge of butter as any inspector, etc., went on to remark casually that he had sent directions to his friend in London about the President of Douai. In a postscript he added a piece of news which he had just heard "All was quiet in Paris at 3 O'Clock on the 14th inst., there was a report by Dublin that the King was murdered that evening. I don't believe it." With such reassuring information it is to be hoped that Uncle Maurice was not unduly worried about his nephews in Douai.

Before a reply to their letter of 4th January could have reached them, the boys, on their own initiative or on the advice of Father Daniel, left Douai on 21st January, the day the King was guillotined in Paris. Not without enduring sundry insults and menaces, they reached Calais and embarked for England. As soon as the packet was under way they plucked from their hats and flung into the sea the tricolor cockades which they had been obliged to wear for safety in France. They were not sorry to have done with revolution and revolutionaries.

Their soldier-uncle, Daniel, had reached London before them, and on their arrival he immediately concerned himself with making arrangements for their continuing their education in London. They had abandoned their furniture and other belongings, including Dan's violin, in Douai, so their three months in the English College cost their uncle more than a hundred pounds, part of which, in confiscated goods, was a contribution to the French Republic. And in London, where things were excessively dear on account of the war, they had to replenish their wardrobe with suits of clothes, shirts, hats, neckcloths, shoes, stockings, etc., and they seem to have done so on what would now be considered a lavish scale, so that, said Dan, writing to Darrynane for money, " a large sum of money is soon expended."

In London also, studying law, Dan drew up a programme which he expounded to his Uncle Maurice in a letter of 12th December, 1795. " I have now two objects to pursue— the one, the attainment of knowledge ; the other, the acquisition of those qualities which constitute the polite gentleman. I am convinced that the former, besides the immediate pleasure it yields, is calculated to raise me to

honours, rank and fortune ; and I know that the latter
serves as a general passport : and as for the motives of
ambition which you suggest, I assure you that no man
can possess more of it than I do."

He seems to have devoted as much care and attention
to the second object as he did to the first. He who had once
been shy and given to poring over books was now determined to make a remarkable figure in society. He did not
need to be told that—the words are Newman's—" the
polished manners and high-bred behaviour which are so
difficult of attainment, and so strictly personal when
attained, which are so much admired in society, from
society are obtained." He changed his lodgings to Chis-
wick, to a house where there were " people of rank and
knowledge of the world ; so their conversation and manners
are perfectly well adapted to rub off the rust of scholastic
education." He was preparing himself, as he said, " to
appear with great éclat on the grand theatre of the world."

In this he was but carrying out an idea of education
which his uncle, the Colonel, a polished man of the world,
had outlined in 1789 when he wrote to Darrynane suggesting
that St. Omer's was the most suitable college for the boys.
He had impressed upon " Hunting Cap " that a college education was not sufficient for young gentlemen, they must also
resort to polite company. A college education, he wrote,
" has the sole advantage of pushing youth to the study of
Belles Lettres, by giving them a knowledge of the Greek
and Latin tongues, a tincture of Mathematics, Logic and
Philosophy," but if " Hunting Cap's " object was " to give
our nephews a polite literary education, so as to qualify
them to appear in the world with some advantage, that
purpose can be fulfilled only by resorting to good company
and at no small expense." The recipe was certainly very
effective in O'Connell's case. It was in London that he
emerged from his chrysalis, a mature young gentleman,
dining with the Days, visiting the theatre where he listened
with a critical ear to Charles Kemble, another past pupil
of Douai, who had already made for himself a considerable
reputation as an actor.

The colleges in which he had studied abroad had been confiscated soon after he had left the Continent. St. Omer had been converted into a military hospital and the college at Douai was leased to a spinning factory. Those who had remained behind in both houses were imprisoned in Doullens. On their release they returned to England and branched out to found the two great colleges, Ushaw in the north and Old Hall in the south. Daniel O'Connell told his uncle that the plate of Douai had, with his own violin and furniture, been confiscated, but this was only partly true, for the more valuable plate of the English college had been buried, and when it was recovered by excavation in 1863, it was divided between St. Cuthbert's College, Ushaw, and St. Edmund's College, Old Hall, joint heirs to the glories of *Les Grands Anglais*.

In Ireland there is no college that can claim so direct a descent from any one of the colleges that came to an end abroad with the Revolution. There was an Irish College in Douai which endured for two centuries and never lost its identity, though there had been a scheme to amalgamate it and the Scots College with the far more famous English College into what was to have been called the British College. Not only is there no college in Ireland that can claim succession from this Irish College, but one wonders if there is anywhere in Ireland a chalice, a missal, a piece of plate, a book or any other link with the institution founded by Christopher Cusack in the Rue de Bonnes, under the ancient belfry of Douai ; so completely was it, with other Irish houses, overwhelmed by the tide of revolution.

As it happened the Irish bishops were not caught unawares by the collapse of their colleges overseas. Availing themselves of the concessions of the Relief Act of 1782, mean and grudging and insolent as these concessions were, they had begun to establish colleges at home. The building of the great college of St. Patrick in Carlow was begun in 1782, and in the same year Bishop Troy, in Kilkenny, acquired the mansion known as Burrell's Hall for use as a college. In Kilkenny the development of the infant college was considerably endangered by the anti-Catholic vigilance of

Thomas Lewis O'Beirne, a one-time student of St. Omer who had become a Protestant and had been appointed Protestant Bishop of Ossory; he had all the bitterness of a pervert, with much of the eloquence for which the college in St. Omer was famous—a voice of exquisite modulation whose effect was heightened by a " pale and penetrating face, with long flowing snow-white locks." In Carlow also there was some difficulty in obtaining a licence to teach from the Protestant authorities. But both colleges were conscious that the winter of the penal laws was past and that the spring had come. Their optimism was expressed in their mottoes, that of Carlow being *Rescissa Vegetior Assurgit*, and that of Kilkenny, *Hiems Transiit*.

The genial face of the Liberator had not yet appeared to gladden their spring and his voice was not yet heard in the land, that voice of which a countryman was to say that it could be heard " a mile off, and it sounded as if it was coming through honey." How often had some refugee Irish student approaching one of the towns of the Low Countries heard for the first time the carillons from its belfry, a sound so jubilant over that flat country that it may have seemed to him, coming from a country where church bells were silent, as if the town had released a flight of doves to salute and welcome him. With something of the same feeling must many have heard the great voice of O'Connell for the first time, coming out of the silence of their penal times with its message of hope for a down-trodden people :

"And as I thought, rose the sonorous swell,
  As from some church-tower swings the silvery bell,
  Aloft and clear from airy tide to tide,
  It glided easy as a bird may glide."

Perhaps the most objective accounts of the studies abroad of Daniel and Maurice O'Connell are the bills their uncle had to pay for them; and, as these have not been printed before, I append two of them, the bill for their last months in St. Omer and their only bill from Douai :

ST. OMER :

	£	s.	d.
To board from 23 June 1792 till 20 Aug. 1792 .	7	14	6½
To fencing from 1st April 1792 till 15 Aug. 1792	1	13	9
To broken foils .		5	4
Master Daniel for dancing from 15 March till 15 Aug 1792		13	9
Master Maurice to do. from 15 March till 15 June		8	3
Master Daniel to drawing from 1st April 1792 till 15 Aug 1792	1	0	3
To extra pocket money	2	1	2½
To postage of letters . . .		5	7
To clothes on departure . . .	1	14	0
To coach and other expenses . . .	2	4	8
	£18	1	4

DOUAI :

MASTER DANIEL O'CONNELL :

	£	s.	d.
To board from entrance Aug 20 1792 till departure 21 Jan 1793	11	0	2
To entrance money		15	0
To postage, pocket money ordinary and extraordinary .	2	14	7
To furniture, etc., for his chamber . .	4	2	1
To extra wardrobe £0 10s. 8d. ; extra kitchen £0 13s. 11d.	1	4	7
To Violin Master and Violin . . .	1	1	7
To infirmary £2 8s. 2d. ; cash for books 10/- .	2	18	2
To equipment at departure £4 7s. 0d. ; cash for journey £4 15s. 5d. . . .	9	2	5
To share of coach to Calais . . .		10	10
To paid by Mr. Varley in London to and for them both .	34	17	6
	£69	5	10

MASTER MAURICE O'CONNELL :

	£	s.	d.
To board as above	11	0	2
To entrance money £0 15s. 0d. ; pocket money, ordinary and extraordinary, and postage £3 1s. 9d.	3	16	9
To furniture for his chamber £3 7s 2d. ; extra wardrobe, £0 10s. 8d.	3	17	10
To extra kitchen £0 10s. 2d. ; infirmary, £0 17s. 5d. .	1	7	7
To cost of books £1 0s. 3d. ; item for an extraordinary hat £0 10s. 0d.	1	10	3
To fencing master £0 8s. 3d. ; equipment at departure, £4 2s. 2d.	4	10	5
To cash for journey & coach to Calais . .	5	6	3
To fire for both during the winter . .		10	0

Douai, March 3rd, 1793.   Total of both accounts . £105 5 1

REVOLUTION AND COUNTER-REVOLUTION

Kennedy F. Roche

" There was sedition in his very walk."

In the mid-eighteenth century, we have it on the highest legal authority, " the law did not presume a single papist to exist " in Ireland. The eyes of the law must then have met with little offence. Not so those of the King's Protestant subjects, who could distinguish a Catholic by his very gait, shambling, shuffling ; by his cowering, apologetic air. Sufferance was the badge of that ruined race, which shrank even from pity, lest attention should be drawn to its existence. The law, though blind, had ears.

But the urgings of Protestant friends were gradually to fan a spark of courage ; as the years went by and nothing worse happened, it came to be felt that no great harm could come of expressing submission and loyalty. Although it meant using the voice, this was at last done. The breathless time of waiting passed, and a flood of great joy succeeded : the submission and loyalty were accepted by the Viceroy, who expressed his thanks. Now that so much could be done with impunity, the more daring Catholics bethought themselves of petitioning for the right to petition. They were assured that no objection could be made to petitioning, and so, at last, they screwed their courage to the sticking-point and petitioned for a removal of some of their grievances. So stood the Catholics of Ireland before the stress of the American War brought an improvement in the eyesight of the law. It came to perceive them dimly in 1778 and allowed them to lease " unprofitable bogs." Reverses to the allied arms brought an immense increase in the law's vision by 1793 : the bulk of the penal laws was repealed, all restrictions on Catholics' right to hold property were swept away, the professions thrown open and the elective franchise was given to them. In this year indeed the Catholics became plainly visible.

It was not long afterwards that the great Agitator, who was to remove the last deficiency in the law's eyesight, and to daze and stupify its highest officers by his violent insolence in their own very courts, entered upon the Irish scene. He trailed his coat all his life, he defied and abused, he roused and rallied the subject masses, he swept up seven millions and made a nation of it. And, so solidly did he hammer it, that his work could never be undone. From the first, there was revolution in him : a moral revolution. He revolutionised both the Irish mind and the Irish scene. He was the well-spring of the psychological change ; in his own person he was the model of the new Irishman. As he strode the streets of Dublin on his way to or from the Four Courts or the Catholic Association Rooms, head erect, umbrella slung over his shoulder in pike or musket fashion, his bearing attracted the attention of all passers. Counsellor O'Connell had the buoyancy of a man who enjoys aggression. " There was sedition in his very walk."

The people of Ireland were not unacquainted with the concept of revolution, but this revolution which commenced in the first decade of the nineteenth century was something new. For one thing, it seemed embodied in this one man. And this man was far from simple. He had, it is true, much of the intellectual furniture which we associate with the French Revolution and the United Irishmen ; but he was a southern Irish Catholic landlord, or rather chieftain ; his appeal could succeed only with the great Catholic mass of south and east and west, to the exclusion of the traditionally Radical north ; and of this hitherto silent and almost inert mass, he seemed the personification : characteristically southern and characteristically Catholic, he put his stamp on the new revolution and he seemed to call to the deeps of the Irish Catholic nature and to stir it as none but one of their flesh and blood, and a leader of genius at that, could do. Romantic nationalism did not arrive in Ireland until his reign was nearly over ; O'Connell himself had much of the utilitarian in him, but his kinship with the bulk of the nation not only created a fellow-feeling between leader and followers which made the new movement really formidable, but showed to the southern Irish that they were as capable of making a figure in the world as any other nation. Pride of race, once developed, makes external restraint intolerable ; it dispenses with utilitarian apologetic ; " better self-government than good government " is its final word. The period of O'Connell's public career marks the early stage of that transition from the eighteenth-century rationalist " patriotism " to the state of mind known to us as " national self-consciousness," which knows no satisfaction save in complete autonomy. Had a Joseph Chamberlain been given the administration of Ireland in 1801, he would have brilliantly succeeded ; eighty years afterwards he was far too late. This revolution in sentiment was not effected without its price : the greater part of the gentry fell out by the way, and the intransigent north-easterners met the challenge of their neighbours by drawing further apart and developing a counter-nationalism of their own.

Finally, the new revolution, while O'Connell remained at its head, had a characteristic that made it unique : it was bloodless. Had it been other, its authors might not have happened upon many devices, pacific in themselves, but which, allied to physical force, were found in later times to be most powerful levers in the overturning of the administrative machine of the occupying power and its subsequent dislodgment with incalculable economy in blood. The importance to small nations of these adjuncts to physical force is inestimable ; administrative sabotage has, since O'Connell's day, been developed into an exact science and has added to the armoury of the militarily weak a weapon of the deadliest efficacy.

What was the nature, as to doctrine and technique, of the revolutionary movement which issued in the tragic outbreak of 1798, on the eve of O'Connell's entry into public life ?

The Society of United Irishmen was the offspring of the Volunteer body of '82 ; its spiritual ancestry runs back through that line of humane Protestants to Swift and Molyneux, who raised their voices against the malversation and cruelty which they saw all about them, masquerading as administration. The parent body, originally recruited though it was to protect the Irish shores from invasion and to keep order within during the emergency of the American War, proved to be the vehicle of a great organised Protestant demand for an end to the oppression of Catholic and Dissenter and for the inauguration of a more liberal regime, under which all Irishmen should work together for the good of a common country. By its latent force, it obtained from Westminster the recognition of the legislative independence of the Irish Parliament. A more lasting effect than this, however, followed from its recruitment of Catholics into its ranks.

The American revolt was a tremendous inspiration to the discontented in all western Europe and its import could not be lost on the liberal-minded Protestants of Great Britain and Ireland. Here was an armed rising by members of their own race in the name of those very principles upon which they had been brought up, the principles of Locke and Sidney and the old Whigs whose names they had been taught from earliest youth to revere ; the principles of the Social Compact, of the liberty of the subject, equality before the law and government by consent. " We hold these truths to be self-evident : That all men are created equal, that they are all endowed by their Creator with certain inalienable rights; that among these are life, liberty and the pursuit of happiness. That to secure these rights, governments are instituted amongst men, deriving their just powers from the consent of the governed ; that whenever any form of government becomes destructive of these ends, it is the right of the people to alter or to abolish it, and to institute a new government, laying its foundations on such principles, and organising its powers in such form, as to them shall seem most likely to effect their safety and happiness." The significance of the American uprising, the first of the revolutions, was not, and could not be, fully appreciated for many a day after its triumphant conclusion, but it was recognised immediately by sympathetic beholders everywhere as more than transient. The entry of the new Republic among the sovereign states of the earth and the efficiency of its institutions showed the experiment to be a success ; no longer could it be contended that government on lines other than illiberal or autocratic is impossible.

It was not, however, from America alone that the United Irishmen drew their inspiration.

France was to be the scene of the next great experiment, conducted on a basis different in essentials from the American, and far less pleasing in both its conduct and its outcome than the first.

The doctrines of the French Revolution have been the subject-matter of more volumes than a lifetime's industry by a team of research workers could now enable them to enumerate. For a whole generation before the fatal month of May in 1789, when King Louis' advisers unwittingly opened the flood-gates, political theorists had been propounding new principles, weaving vast schemes for the perfect government of man, constructing utopias of exquisite gossamer, whilst all the time the leaders of polite literature were busily sapping all the foundations on which ordered society rests. The earlier political writers, such as Montesquieu, inculcated the principles of a sober and pedestrian Whiggery; they admired the " balanced constitution " of Great Britain and established a certain anglophilism which was not, however, destined in most quarters to survive the American War. But even without the revival of the old distrust of England, the diluted republicanism of 1688 would never have naturalised itself in France; French logic picked it to pieces, French intellect could never have made peace with its compromises and its fictions; a muddled Whiggery would have sat ill on the genius of France, which has in it something of that luciferian quality that keeps a people in perpetual unrest.

The mental pabulum designed to satisfy in some measure this French appetite for novelty, consistency and completeness was forthcoming in continuous supply throughout the half-century that preceded the great outbreak: in the writings of the materialists, Helvetius and d'Holbach, to whom the re-ordering of society was a simple exercise in applied mechanics; in the naïve academic socialism of Morrelly and Mably, who peopled imaginary republics with citizens devoid of human failing; in the romance of Jean-Jacques Rousseau, the apostle of Deism, who looks at once back to the individualism of the past and forward to the totalitarianism of the future. In the welter of speculation, it is possible to distinguish two main schools : the materialist and the intuitionist.

The former was frankly atheist and epicurean in the philosophic sense of the term. It saw all creation as the " Great Machine" and man as a mechanism whose behaviour is rigidly determined by two principles : attraction to pleasure and aversion to pain. Man being entirely the product of external circumstances, the possibilities of improvement are limitless ; regulate the circumstances and you regulate the men ; set the circumstances into an improving trend and you set mankind on the road to perfection. The materialists never solved the problem of regulating the regulator, but the notion of a controlling providence or a Natural Necessity or Harmony which makes all human activity work out for the best in the long run was imported. This notion, minimising as it does the need for authority, came to constitute the basis of materialist Liberalism ; it appealed very strongly to the English Radicals, who took it up and developed it into the foundation for the *laissez faire* politics and economics elaborated by Jeremy Bentham and the Mills. But this unanimous confidence is not evident among the French Physiocrats. Helvetius' *Mind* can read equally well as an apologia for Enlightened Despotism and for a libertarian polity. In this very equivocality of the materialist and agnostic ethic lies the key to the history of the French Revolution and to that of all the revolutionary movements that have followed it, down to our own days. Much, indeed, was left to depend on confidence in the underlying harmony.

The intuitionist school, with which the name of Rousseau is inseparably associated, impliedly accepted the same experientialist or sensationist psychology as the basis for speculation. But it was not atheist : it posited the existence of a Supreme Being. This Being might be, according to the temperament of the believer, either a remote First Cause, a Mover of Movers, who allows men to conduct their own

affairs in their own way, or He might be a good God who
reveals Himself to us in the wondrous order and regularity
of the universe, in the beauty of the earth; a lenient, indulgent
God who whispers consolation to us when we are unhappy.
The remote God has no dealings with us, but the good God
of Rousseau speaks direct to the soul of each man; He
makes no supernatural revelation of Himself, He has appointed no teaching authority on earth : " My own mind
is my own Church," as Thomas Paine puts it. Reason is
the candle He supplies us with to light our way through
the labyrinth of life ; reason, powerfully aided by, sometimes
supplanted by, " sensibility." Such is the simple religion
of Deism : the creed of the Savoyard Vicar. For the
natural amorality of man, the intuitionist school substitutes
the Natural Goodness of man : man is born good, but he
is corrupted by the world, by the evil institutions, the
tyrannical conventions of the mal-organised society he finds
around him ; nevertheless, underneath the layers of corruption which the world splashes upon him, man remains
good. Given the chance, he will be thoroughly and consistently good. The fault lies entirely outside himself : in
the institutions of society. The moral is obvious : " Clear
the ground and build all anew from the foundations."

By different routes, then, the two schools reach the same
practical conclusion. Nor are the routes as widely apart
as they may seem. Materialist and intuitionist have one
fundamental article of disbelief in common : they both
deny the existence of objective moral law. To the former,
" morality is a calculation of consequences " ; to the latter,
a yielding to a *penchant*. The transcendent is eliminated
and man is made the Final End.

The segregation of thought into " schools " leaves out of
consideration the masses of the less serious who pick up
conceptions as the fancy takes them or whom the disputa-
tions of the day drive into an attitude of general scepticism.
Of these, Voltaire may well be called the type : a cynical
half-deist, half-materialist, for whom God was the great
Policeman, Whom it would be necessary to invent if He
did not exist. Voltaire had one great aim in life : the

discrediting of Catholicity. The mode was deadly : by identifying it with cruelty and obscurantism ; by keeping afresh the memory of bygone occurrences without an attempt to set them in historical perspective and with the worst possible complexion upon them ; by going further, and inventing atrocities. " Zapata, not having got any answer, proceeded to preach God simply. He proclaimed to men the Father of men, who rewards, punishes and pardons. . . . He was gentle, kind and modest and he was roasted at Valladolid in the year of grace 1631." " Fanaticism " was the bane of humanity ; the remedy was the subjection of all religious authority, Protestant as well as Catholic, to the civil power. The success of the Voltairean method was attested to by a vast growth of religious indifferentism and the strengthening of that faith in the omnicompetent, neutral State, which has since become the chief characteristic of the anti-clerical tradition.

Throughout this entire period, no serious effort was made to reform the government of France. The institutions of centralised despotism, perfected by Louis XIV, were permitted to continue unimpaired, but in the control of incompetent functionaries, as blind to the signs of the times as an owl to the mid-day sun. Deprived of an outlet, the immense talent of France was left to its own devices, to dream and scheme, to theorise and speculate, to dissipate itself in utopia-building, unchecked by the wisdom which experience and responsibility bring ; all this vast wealth of intelligence, which a liberal polity would have drawn into political and administrative activity, was permitted to waste and misemploy itself, until the fumes of the great ferment finally blew the imprisoning walls of the Old Regime asunder.

When the Third Estate succeeded in its demand that the Orders sit together, the first fissure was made in the structure of the old monarchy ; when the resultant body proceeded to call itself the National Assembly, the breach was complete and France found herself with a government of litterateurs. Now at last the flood of theory was loose; now the logic of the Enlightenment was to sweep away all the

anachronisms, chop away the anomalies, round off the
irregularities of the old France, and clip and trim her into
a symmetrical pattern, pleasing to the eye. The political
honeymoon, enlivened by the fall of the Bastille on 14th
July, lasted all that summer. The famous night of 4th
August saw the patriotic orgy of the surrender of privileges :
nobles renouncing their feudal rights, clergy their tithes,
magistrates and municipal councillors the charters and
ancient liberties of their districts ; all these things were laid
upon the altar of *la Patrie* and the work of the long line of
French kings was completed in the name of Liberty, Equality,
Fraternity. To the enthusiasts of the time, it seemed that
the springtime of the world had come ; history was at an
end and mankind was about to enter the Golden Age.

A fortnight later, to crown the Revolution and provide
the immutable, fundamental law of the new era, came the
publication of the Declaration of the Rights of Man. A
document of seventeen articles, the acceptance of its doctrines
was proposed to the Assembly by Lafayette, the hero of the
American War, and it bears the mark of the American
Declaration of Independence, except for the less humble tone
of the Preamble and the substitution of the term, " Supreme
Being," for the word, " God." The Declaration proper sets
out all the principles of secularist liberal-democracy : the
sovereignty of the Nation, equality before the law, the inviola-
bility of " the rights to liberty, property, security and
resistance to oppression." The Nation being sovereign, no
man or body of men can exercise legitimate authority,
unless it emanates expressly from the Nation. All men
being born free and equal in rights, all must be treated on
this basis by the law ; but the legitimacy of social distinction, founded on common utility, is recognised. Article
Four defines liberty as consisting " in being able to do
whatever does not injure another " : hence, " the exercise
of the natural rights of each man has no limits except those
which assure to the other members of society the enjoyment
of these same rights," and " these limits can be determined
only by the law." The law, which is " the expression of the
General Will," has the right to forbid " only actions which

are injurious to society." In the making of the law " all citizens have the right to take part, personally or by their representatives." Article Ten calls for immunity for every man from trouble on the ground of his opinions, "even his religious opinions," " provided that their manifestation does not disturb the public order established by the law." Article Eleven asserts the right to the free communication of thought and opinion, with " the liability of answering for the abuse of this liberty in the cases determined by the law." The penultimate Article Sixteen declares that "Any society in which the guarantee of rights is not assured, or the delimitation of the powers not determined, has not got any Constitution." These, in brief, are the principles of 1789. Their appeal to the ill-governed and the discontented in every land can well be imagined.

But the difference between statement and implementation was soon to be illustrated, for the only issue of the famous Declaration within the next fifteen years was three practically still-born Constitutions, followed by an offspring, totally unlooked-for in 1789, but undeniably vigorous, the Napoleonic Empire. From first to last, the course of Liberalism in France has been storm-tossed and uncertain ; buffeted and belaboured from Left and Right, submerged for the greater part of the century after the Revolution, jeopardised by its own extravagant pretensions, French Liberalism has never satisfactorily demonstrated its viability. " Truth," said Bismarck, " is the first casualty in war " ; he might with equal accuracy have attributed the same fate to liberty. But the failure of French Liberalism cannot be accounted for by external enmity alone. It carried within itself the seed of its own destruction. Lacking confidence in the Natural Harmony, it fell back on a guarantor of Artificial Harmony : it sought the guarantee of liberty in the omnipotent secular State, its deadliest enemy. In the name of liberty and equality, Liberalism tore down the barriers that hedged the individual from the power of the central administration : the local liberties and charters, the powers of subordinate bodies. In the name of national sovereignty, it set itself to destroy the greatest of all protections, the power of the Church. Half a century of anti-Christian polemic produced its results very soon after the outbreak of the Revolution, and the French Church, debilitated by its long and close association with the State and hindered from making those periodic adjustments to the needs of the times which an unfettered body would make, found itself in an uncomfortable and unenviable position.

The suppression of the clergy as an Order in the State (27th June, 1789) was the first blow; the secularisation of Church property (2nd November and 19th December, 1789) was the second; suppression of the religious orders (13th February, 1790), the third; and finally, on 12th July, 1790, came the Civil Constitution of the Clergy. Suppression and confiscation were outrages that might be suffered, as all violations of right have to be suffered when redress is refused; but the Civil Constitution of the Clergy, striking as it did at fundamental principles of doctrine and ecclesiastical organisation, and demanding the severance of the French Church from Rome, brought about a complete and instant breach between Catholicism and the Revolution. Carried away by their twin passions for the elective principle and for uniformity, and by their desire to vindicate all the pretensions of the self-sufficient Nation-State, the framers of the Civil Constitution proposed that all offices in the French Church be filled by election: the bishop, by the electors of the Department, the curé by the administrative assembly of the District; no elector, be he Protestant, Jew or atheist, to be debarred from voting; the bishop-elect was to be instituted by the metropolitan and, on institution, was to take an oath of fidelity to " the Nation, the Law, and the King "; the new bishop was forbidden to apply for confirmation to the Pope. Such are the lengths to which the absurd logic of the doctrinaire can lead.

The price paid for this piece of tyrannous folly was the instant alienation of the mass of practising Catholics everywhere, and the removal of that influence which would, in time, have served to Christianise the Revolution, or at least prevent the revolutionary logic from developing. Thus

was precipitated that active persecution of the Church
which led to internal civil war and enabled the reactionary
powers of Europe to point to French irreligion as a warning
to their subjects ; thus was created the gulf between clerical
and anti-clerical which has split France from top to bottom
and been her prime weakness ever since.

From that month of May in 1789, when the States
General came together at Versailles, the eyes of all foreign
governments and of the urban population of all western
Europe were fixed on France. At first, the great event was
hailed with approval by the overwhelming majority.
Edmund Burke, whose shrewd mind saw very early the
defects of certain of the new principles and the perils which
attend an attempt to impose freedom from above on a
people bred in an authoritarian tradition, was the first
statesman to sound the note of warning. The confiscation
of Church property caused uneasiness even in Protestant
countries. The Civil Constitution of the Clergy heightened
uneasiness. Finally came the declarations of war and the
execution of the King, which ranged the public everywhere
on the one side or on the other, for or against the Revolution. In all tolerably well-governed countries, active
sympathy with the French was, in general, confined to
intellectuals educated in the Voltairean tradition. In
England, they found some friendship in the middle classes and
among the tradesmen of such large centres as London and
Birmingham and in the growing industrial towns of the
north, where Radical Clubs or Corresponding Societies
sprang up. The rural population took its politics from
the squires.

In Ireland, it was inevitable that the overthrow of an
ancient autocracy should have made a deep impression
and that the Declaration of the Rights of Man should have
excited enthusiasm and hope : a people suffering atrocious
misgovernment is not apt to observe doctrinal difficulties
in a document which appears to promise deliverance, and
it has never been easy to convince simple men of the truth
of the adage concerning the relative merits of known and unknown devils. Among the Catholic peasants of the south

and west, agrarian conspiracy and outrage were by no means unknown ; the secret society and its ugly proceedings were the too frequent response of infuriated, ignorant men to injustices practised upon them.   Ribbon-men, Whiteboys, Rockites, Defenders, Peep-o'-Day Boys and the innumerable local and nameless conspiracies which misery and degradation breed were building up what promised to become a horrible tradition, sufficient to render a people unfit for self-government long after the disappearance of its causes. That the tradition of vendetta was prevented from taking a wider and more lasting grip on the Irish people is due solely to the uncompromising condemnation of these moonlighting confederations by the Catholic clergy in its own dark hour of persecution, long before it had any allies.   The part that this *jacquerie* could play in a revolutionary movement can readily be understood, and there is evidence that its exploitation was at least considered.   But it is a significant fact that the works of Thomas Paine and the other revolutionary pamphleteers of the time, although broadcast in their original English and translated into the Scottish Gaelic for distribution in the Highlands, were never translated into Irish.   As soon, indeed, as the anti-clericalism of the French Assembly became evident, the prospect of winning the southern Irish peasantry to the cause of the Revolution disappeared.   For this disappearance Wolfe Tone and many other prominent United Irishmen were later to speak disparagingly of the Catholic clergy. It is true that when the Insurrection actually broke out in the summer of 1798, the Radical north, which was the cradle and centre of the revolutionary movement, remained almost calm, whilst the fiercest fighting took place in the Catholic south-east, especially in Wexford ; but this revolt was the outcome, not of revolutionary sentiment, but of the unbearable atrocities of the soldiery, and its object was the simple and pathetically vague one, " to free our native land."

In the Presbyterian north and in Dublin, conditions were far different.   The Dissenters of the north had provided in their emigrant relatives sturdy and enthusiastic soldiers for Washington in the War of Independence. They had made no secret of their desire for a British defeat and they openly rejoiced when it came. Their sympathy with the Revolution was just as openly expressed; the Civil Constitution of the Clergy was no cause of dismay to them; the execution of a King was not shocking. After the outbreak of war in 1793, the toast of " France " continued to be given in Ulster. Scarcely two years before the war, the Society of United Irishmen was founded in Belfast, its objects being parliamentary reform, emancipation of the Catholics and Dissenters and the promotion of unity among Irishmen. As an open society, with these moderate and constitutional objectives, it drew flocks of recruits in the north and east of Ireland and burgeoned out in branches in most of the urban centres of those parts. Organised liberalism had at last arrived in Ireland; for a while, it looked as if the Plantation of Ulster had proved a failure. Westminster and the Castle were profoundly disturbed. " I cannot help feeling," wrote the Secretary of State to the Viceroy, " a very great anxiety that such measures may be taken as may effectually counteract the union between Catholics and Dissenters." In the summer of 1795 the first of the Orange Lodges was founded and the tide began slowly to turn. In 1798 the north remained quiet. Within ten years the danger of unity had passed for ever.

The fortunes of the United Irishmen were bound up with those of the man who has become accepted as their spokesman. Theobald Wolfe Tone, a nominal Protestant, made no secret of his enthusiasm for the ideals of Liberty, Equality and Fraternity, for the Rights of Man, the principles of national sovereignty and representative democratic government. Ireland's deplorable condition arose, believed Tone, from the fact that she had no national government; her fatal weakness, the circumstance that fastened misgovernment on her, lay in dissension amongst Irishmen, in those " intestinal broils " which the Castle took care to perpetuate. " Divide and Rule " being the motto of the people's enemies, the course to be followed by its friends was clear : unite and conciliate. With this object in view,

Tone never ceased to advocate the emancipation of the Catholics and Dissenters. On the departure of Richard Burke, he accepted the secretaryship of the Catholic Association, and his inspiration is evident in that bold gesture of calling a National Convention of Catholic delegates in Dublin in 1792. The advances which the United Irishmen were at this time making and the resolute handling of the Catholic case by Tone contributed in very great measure to hasten Pitt's conviction that a further Relief Act was a pressing necessity. This came in 1793, when all the remaining disabilities of the Catholics, except exclusion from Parliament, the inner bar and a few of the highest civil and military offices, were removed and the franchise was given to the Forty Shilling Freeholders. By this time, Tone had become a public figure. With the progress of the French Revolution, his political ideas kept pace. At the outset of his career, he was satisfied with the ideal of a national government; the form of this government he considered a matter of secondary importance. Within a year or two, however, he arrived at two conclusions of moment : that the prime necessity of Irish well-being was the complete breaking of the connection with England and that the only conceivable form of a good government for Ireland was the republican one. Early in 1794, he was in communication with the Committee of Public Safety ; the betrayal of the emissary, Jackson, compromised him and he fled to America, whence he went to Paris early in 1796. The story of the two naval expeditions, in the autumn of 1796 and in that of 1798 which culminated in his capture at Lough Swilly, is well known. Taken in arms against the Crown and wearing the uniform of France, in whose army he had been given a commission, he knew what awaited him. " In a cause like this," he told the courtmartial, " success is everything. Success in the eyes of the vulgar fixes its merits. Washington succeeded and Kosciusko failed."

The discovery of communication with the French sent the United Irishmen underground. As a secret society, they elaborated their organisation ; at its head, they had their secret Directory, who promoted the plans for a rising in conjunction with the French invasion which Tone had gone to arrange. Arms were procured and stored in depots, plans made to secure disaffection in the Crown forces, recruits were enlisted, drilling was practised and the strategy of the campaign was worked out in detail. But the promised French help did not come. Two years passed by, and the inevitable results of inactivity began to show themselves ; the counter-activity of the Castle riddled the Society with spies, poured troops into the country and fanned the spark of orangeism into a flame. The Catholic hierarchy, too, did not welcome the prospect either of an invasion by the French, who were now openly and militantly anti-clerical, or of a challenge by inexperienced Irishmen to that military might which they well knew to be awaiting the opportunity to show what armed licentiousness could do. Long deferred, the Rising came in the early summer of 1798; but without French help, without the formidable organisation it was once to have had, without adequate arms, deserted by the doughty warriors of the north, who now had found more congenial occupation, practically confined to the southern and eastern counties, it partook of a character not contemplated a few years before. The months of May and June, 1798, saw scenes in the counties of Carlow, Wicklow and Wexford which rivalled in frightfulness anything depicted by the historian of battle and massacre. " Within these twelve months," wrote Sir Ralph Abercromby, " every crime, every cruelty, that could be committed by Cossacks and Calmucks has been transacted here." He wrote before the outbreak of the Rising and with reference to the indiscipline of the troops throughout all Ireland. In Wexford, where the fight assumed the nature of a religious war, the carnage was particularly hideous. " May every virtuous revolutionist," warned O'Connell in later years, " remember the horrors of Wexford." The revolt was stamped out in blood and flames and, when the fighting ceased, the countryside was given over to the military and militia to take their pleasure. So ended the project of the United Irishmen and such were the circumstances that ushered in the Union.

The year 1775, which heard the first rumblings of this era of revolutions, witnessed the birth of Daniel O'Connell at Carhen House, near Caherciveen, in the County of Kerry, far away, indeed, from the salons and the taverns and the council-chambers in which the ideas of a new age were being shaped. The O'Connells of Iveragh, clinging to the rocky coast of the secluded corner of Kerry to which they had been driven, looked back through the centuries, to an ancestor who had fought at the Boyne for King James, to another who had died by the roadside on his way " to Hell or to Connaught," to another who had served Queen Elizabeth, to others who had held the commissions of medieval kings and who rose and fell in the manner of the turbulent nobles of old, back to the dim Gaelic past when the chieftains had no one to fight save their own kind. The normal career in such a family would be the Army or the Church. The O'Connells had given members to each. Daniel himself was once intended for one or the other. But their army was the French Army and their Church the Catholic Church. The O'Connells were a survival from the older Ireland and, in relation to them, the established institutions of their time were alien. The times were sadly out of joint for such as they; the balance was fearfully precarious.

On the one hand, the highest honours of the Court of France were open ; they were in fact attained by Daniel's uncle, John, Count O'Connell, through the easy establishment of his pedigree " as a gentleman by birth and descent from the year 1400 down to the present day." On the other, there had long been the danger that " the Sassenach would scale the mountains " and drive them from house and home. By the year of Daniel's birth, however, the worst times had passed and his seventh year saw the removal of a great insecurity, the refusal to Catholics of the right to long leases. In 1793, the old Catholic families were made at last safe by being placed in full equality with Protestants in respect of the acquiring and holding of all forms of property : the estates to which they had managed to cling without legal recognition of their ownership were made secure. Henceforth, the division in the Catholic movement was to become accentuated, the plebeian element becoming increasingly aggressive and uncompromising in its demand for complete emancipation and developing, under the influence of the French Revolution, a democratic liberal ideal, whilst the aristocratic party, trusting to Grattan and Plunket as their parliamentary champions and to the exertion of influence on the Cabinet and Court for the removal of their remaining disabilities, took their stand on the side of established authority. To the Catholic gentry of Ireland, the Revolution was abhorrent on religious and political grounds : it was atheistical and anarchical, levelling and regicidal. The prospect of a French invasion was an object of especial horror to them. When the ships of Wolfe Tone's first expedition sailed into Bantry Bay, Maurice O'Connell of Darrynane, now Deputy Governor of the County, was narrowly outpaced by Simon White in the transmission of the news to the garrison at Cork. Lord Kenmare was equally zealous at this juncture, and Lord Fingall led his own troop of cavalry against the insurgents at Tara Hill a year and a half later.

If Daniel's antecedents were not the kind that produce revolutionaries, neither were his early experiences. Sent with his brother, Maurice, to the school of St. Omer at Liège at the end of 1790, on the reluctant advice of Count O'Connell, who feared for the future, transferred thence in January of 1791 to St. Omer in France across the frontier and thence, in August, 1792, to Douay, Daniel was to find himself eventually in the war zone itself. Before the boys had left St. Omer, their uncle, the Count, was no longer able to assist them. An intimate adviser of the King and Queen, he had pressed for the posting of troops in Paris to restrain the revolutionary mobs in July, 1789, but his advice, supported by the Queen, was rejected by the unfortunate King. Concerned in several arrangements to secure the escape of the Royal Family from Paris, he found himself threatened with arrest and fled from France to join the *émigré* army across the Rhine in July, 1792, scarcely a month before the storming of the Tuileries and the downfall of the monarchy. In ever-increasing danger, young

Daniel and Maurice continued their studies.   In the late autumn of 1792, the revolutionary armies of Dumouriez swept into the Austrian Netherlands and the boys found themselves engulfed.   The French troops were extremely anti-clerical.   On one afternoon, when out walking, Daniel and some of his friends were pointed out by a waggoner who commenced to yell at them : " Jesuits !   Capuchins !   Recollets ! "   The boys fled back to the college as fast as they could.   By the end of the year, it became evident that the students could no longer remain.   On 21st January, 1793, the day of the King's execution, the O'Connells left Douay for Calais.   The danger of the journey was great ; mobs surrounded their carriage and shouted : " Young priests ! " and " Little aristocrats ! "   Soldiers battered the vehicle with their musket-butts.   For safety, the boys had followed the universal custom of wearing the tricolour cockade.   When they heard at Calais of the King's death, they took the cockades down and flung them into the sea even before the boat started.

When he arrived in England, it is not surprising that Daniel should have confessed himself " half a Tory."   Had he gone back to Kerry, it is probable that he would have been confirmed in the conservative views of a refugee from the Revolution.   But his society and his views were soon to change.   Entered as a student at Lincoln's Inn in January, 1794, he passed out of the circle of the exiled Royalists in London and from under the immediate custody and charge of his uncle, the Count, who had resided there since the defeat of the allied armies late in 1792.   Henceforth, young Daniel found himself at large in the world ; he had now the freedom of the student, his own lodgings, his own programme of studies and social activities.

One of the major events of the year 1794 in London was the trial for high treason of Hardy, the secretary of the London Corresponding Society.   This the young law student attended and he assures us that it resulted in " fully and finally converting him to popular opinions and principles and confirming his natural detestation of tyranny and his desire of resisting it."   In this same year, he joined the

Honourable Society of Cogers (i.e., Thinkers), a debating club which met at the White Bear in Bride Lane and whose objects were : " the promotion of the Liberty of the Subject and the Freedom of the Press, the maintenance of loyalty to the Laws, the rights and claims of Humanity and the practice of public and private virtue." Among its members, at different times in its history, were the famous Jack Wilkes, John Philpot Curran, Lord Denman, Lord Russell of Killowen and Charles Stewart Parnell. In these early years, Daniel must have been as fond of talking as he ever was later, for we find that the attention of his uncle was soon attracted to his activities. The Count was shocked and dismayed. " He spoke of my folly in being a democrat, of my absurdity in displaying my political opinions." He would have been more grievously shocked, had he known what his nephew was reading.

An impression once existed that O'Connell " read nothing but law-books." Whence it can have been derived, it is quite impossible to say, since every one of his public speeches reveals a knowledge of politics, economics and history, whilst his published correspondence and the recollections of his biographers display him as an extensively and widely read man, varied in his interests and of impelling intellectual curiosity. But the persistence of such an impression, obviously baseless though it was, may have been encouraged by something in the man's own character. O'Connell was not the intellectual type. He was a man of action, of powerful impulse and overwhelming emotions, of superhuman energy, of shrewdness and adroitness scarcely surpassed ; his genius was that of the leader, not the scholar. He became " the inspired peasant," the " Member for All-Ireland " ; the " incarnation of a people," said Balzac, who linked his name with that of Napoleon ; " the greatest popular leader the world has ever seen," said Gladstone. In his time, he set up a State within the State.

For more than twenty years, the Irish masses were as clay in his hands ; they obeyed his least injunction, they sought his pleasure in everything, they felt with him, they prayed for him, and none dared speak against him. And for the same twenty years, the Press of Europe watched him, friend and enemy speculating on his next move and wondering often where it would all end. On his part, he repaid all this watchfulness, all this devotion and this hate, with unending activity, political and professional, on behalf of the Irish democracy which he was raising up. Few men can have crammed so much into the span of a life as O'Connell did. In the end, the keen brain was to exhaust itself and the powerful body was to sink under the strain. To examine the doctrine of a man of action can never be easy, nor can the results of the attempt ever be fully satisfying, for his exposition of it is necessarily fragmentary and incomplete. He proceeds by means of rough-and-ready slogans and popularisations. The fragments have to be sought in brief sentences that lie embedded in masses of ephemera, as nuggets lie in clay. Elements have to be inferred from those chance aphorisms, exhortations, witticisms and asides in public speech or intimate conversation which the faithful reporter or biographer may have happened to record. Frequently, indeed, the inference may have action alone, unaccompanied by utterance, to sustain it. To analyse the ideas of a thinker is, by comparison, a simple and straightforward exercise : one goes to his " Works." But Daniel O'Connell left no *œuvres complètes*. We look in vain through all his utterance for sustained doctrinal exposition. He did not even trouble to preserve the letters he received. That a great portion of his own voluminous correspondence has been saved and collected is due to no effort on his part, but without it and without the Journal which he kept intermittently for a few years in early life and intended for no other eyes, it would be difficult to expatiate on his religious and political ideas and impossible to speculate upon their evolution.

How closely did O'Connell approach to the doctrines of the French Revolution ? What was the result of the impact of his Catholicism on them ? And, in technique, how much did he borrow and how much reject from it ?

That his doctrinal contacts with the Revolution were not few nor very loose between the years 1795 to 1797, is evident

in the Journal. His reading at this time appears to have
been very varied, but it included a considerable quantity of
the revolutionary theology and politics. Amongst the
former, we find Thomas Paine's *Age of Reason*, an elaborate
apologetic of Deism, combined with a sustained attack on
Christianity and the dogmatic principle, which the author
of *The Rights of Man* had recently given the world ; Voltaire's
Questions, which he wrote under the nom de plume of
Domenico Zapata ; and the *Recueil Nécessaire*, an anthology
of passages from the writings of well-known Freethinkers.
That this reading did not result in a permanent loss of his
religion, it is superfluous to state, but that it produced a
temporary shaking of faith is undeniable. There are some
passages in the Journal clearly irreconcilable with Christianity and indicative of a mind far from happy. Speaking
of the *Age of Reason*, he says : " It has put the foundation
of the religious question of the Christians in a point of view
in which a judgment is easily formed on its solidity. I now
have no doubts on this head. I may certainly be mistaken.
But I am not wilfully mistaken, if the expression has any
meaning. My mistakes I refer to the mercy of that Being
Who is wise by excellence. To the God of nature do I
turn my heart ; to the meditation of His works I turn my
thoughts. In Him do I find my soul saturated. He will
not, justice tells me, punish for a darkness, if such it be, that
cannot be removed ; He will not punish for the unbiassed
conviction of a soul. To affirm the contrary would, in my
apprehension, be to calumniate." Concerning death, he
writes : " But, the mind, the mind ! Through what variety
of untried being is that to roam ? What changes is it to
suffer ? Does it perish as a dependent on the corporeal
system ? . . . Our best surmises are founded on an analogy.
Now, what analogy can there be between any part of corporal existence and the state of the mind when separated
from the body, supposing separation actually takes place ? "
Miss Hunter, one of his fellow-boarders, remarked of him
that " in fifty years, he would doubt whether he was a man
or a cabbage stump, so much was he inclined to scepticism."
The tormenting problem of religious strife was one of his

chief causes of worry : " Christianity has had her millions of victims. The great Moore fell beneath her axe. The innocent babes have bedewed her altars with their blood. As for the system of the Jews, murder and rapine were its first principles. Could not men be moral without such assistants ? We are not permitted to inquire. The hue and cry is raised against the man who dares to investigate the claims of those *principles*, as they are called, which have caused the devastation of empires. Why should truth be so disagreeable to the human ear ? Is it that her light would dazzle ? No. Persecution springs from self-love. Those who do not pay the tribute of coincidence to our decisions become our most hated foes. We would tear them ; we would devour them. Of all the animals that infest this wretched planet of ours that species of monkey called man is certainly the most absurd and unaccountable."

Among the primarily political works which he read during this period, that which produced the most lasting effect was the *Political Justice* of William Godwin, the future father-in-law of Shelley. A synthesis of eighteenth-century thought, the book pushes to its logical extreme, with unenglish relentlessness, the premises of the sensationist psychology. By means of reason, which Godwin sees as a compulsive faculty, mankind is destined to attain perfection, moral and intellectual, to overcome all obstacles, social, political and, finally, physical, and to become eventually as gods, enjoying mastery over the passions and over the external world, in an earthly paradise from which the necessity for government and all external restraint has been banished :

> " Sceptreless, free, uncircumscribed, but man,
>   Equal, unclassed, tribeless, nationless . . ."

The method was syllogistic and the end celestial. The comprehensive radicalism of the book, which was published in 1792 at the price of two guineas, led to a discussion in the Cabinet as to the advisability of its suppression, but it is said that Pitt decided his colleagues against interference on the ground that " a book at two guineas is unlikely to cause a revolution " ! It remains remarkable to this day for the

range of institutions which it condemns : Church establishments, aristocracy, monarchy, privilege, property, contract,
social conventions : everything, in fact, which the Revolution attacked, and much more besides. But it broke completely with the Revolution in respect of one particular : the
use of physical force. Human reason, says Godwin, is capable
of infinite progress, but it must be allowed to do its work
unhindered. Any attempt to hasten the attainment of
desired objects by a physical assault on the obstacles is
more likely to result in a set-back than an advance : the
particular obstacle may be removed, but the victory may
prove to be a pyrrhic one ; the departure from the orthodox
path may of itself raise new and unforeseen difficulties.
" Revolutions suspend the wholesome advancement of
science and confound the process of nature and reason."
The central proposition of Godwin relative to politics is
that "All government is founded in opinion." Bad governments exist because public opinion is not enlightened enough
to change or get rid of them. Change the opinion, and you
change the government. " Make men wise, and you make
them free." Godwin's system enjoyed a wide vogue in his
own day. It provided the inspiration of the *Prometheus
Unbound* and much else of his son-in-law's poetry. It was
adopted by Kropotkin and the Russian quietists and it
helped, together with Quakerism, to launch the modern
doctrinaire Pacifism on its career.

" I have finished Godwin," wrote O'Connell on 30th
January, 1796. " His work cannot be too highly praised.
All mankind are indebted to the author. The cause of
despotism never met a more formidable adversary. He goes
to the root of every evil that now plagues man and degrades
him almost beneath the savage beast. He shows the source
whence all the misfortunes of mankind flow. That source
he demonstrates to be political government." He also read
the now forgotten *Vindication of the Rights of Women* of Mary
Woolstonecraft, who later became Godwin's wife. As to the
portion of power in the government of nations that ought
to be confided to the female sex, he had an open mind :
" However, Godwin has in some measure made up my

mind on the subject by proving that government to be the best which laid fewest restraints on private judgment. Surely the judgment of the one sex ought to be as unshackled as that of the other." He does not, however, mention reading Paine's *Rights of Man*, which was then the text-book of all English sympathisers with the Revolution.

Apart from these works of a primarily political kind, we find the *Confessions* of Rousseau ; the novel, *Caleb Williams : or Things as They Are*, by Godwin ; and *The Jockey Club*, an exposure of the vices of people of rank and fashion. On the last work, he comments : " Vice reigns triumphant in the English Court at this day. Vice and error are the rulers of the practice of the English government. The English are become besotted and slavish. The spirit of liberty shrinks to protect property from the attacks of French innovators. The corrupt higher orders tremble for their vicious enjoyments." A few days later, he adds : " I love liberty as conducive to increase the portion of human happiness. A great deal of the misery of man can clearly be derived from the form of government under which he lives. Oppression harasses his faculties. Privilege confined by *accident* insults his understanding. His industry is consumed to support the follies and vices of men who help him not. When it is exclaimed, 'the splendour of government must be maintained,' it should mildly and firmly be replied, ' No, but the happiness of the people should be established.' In fact, the only rational motive of forming a government is the good of the forming parties." Colquhoun's *Police of London*—not a political work, but a description by a magistrate of the state of the criminal population of the metropolis —drew the comment : " The sacred claims of *meum* and *tuum* are not strongly imprinted in our breasts even by the state of society in which we now live. Distinction of property is a great evil ; the spirit of self is a great evil ; the love of superiority is a great evil. Man is a complication of evils. It is a very doubtful question whether the disposition of man can ever be so much improved as to admit of real liberty. I believe it is capable ; and this belief is founded on the knowledge of what has already been done."

This is the O'Connell we find in Dublin in the troubled year of 1797 : the impressionable law-student of twenty-two years, widely read, not only in the radical literature of the time, but in a diversity of subjects, from history to chemistry, as well as in the law. It cannot but strike one that this breadth of reading seems to have included none of the counter-revolutionary literature, which at this time was beginning to flow from the printing-presses. There is no record, for instance, of his having thought it worth while to glance at the *Reflections on the Revolution in France* of his great compatriot.

The eve of the Insurrection finds him dividing his time between his omnivorous reading at the Dublin Library in Eustace Street (" was the Library to remain open till one o'clock, I am sure I should frequently be there at that hour ") and the society of his young friends. He was, he tells us, himself a United Irishman at this period and his friend, Richard Newton Bennett, was " an adjunct to the Directory of the United Irishmen." He seems, too, to have been as irrepressible as ever, for his landlord warned him of the danger of airing his views so openly. " It would be a devilish unpleasant thing to get *caged*," he muses. But " Nonsense ! " he reassures himself, " *Liberality* can never become dangerous." His constant visits to the Dublin Library at this time and early in 1798 drew upon him an attention he could well have done without : that of the notorious Francis Higgins, the " Sham Squire," who reported him to Under-Secretary Cooke as " one of the most abominable and bloodthirsty Republicans I ever heard," who had been waited upon with a letter by " James Tandy, the son of Napper Tandy, an agent of the United Irishmen in France." There was, needless to say, no more truth in these charges than in the accompanying statement that O'Connell held a Colonel's commission from France. The horror of bloodshed is an emotion that possessed O'Connell all the days of his life, while his republicanism, if it ever developed at all, would not have gone beyond the academic variety. Indeed, all the signs we can discover in the Journal reveal young Daniel to have been nothing more at this time than a rather loquacious camp-follower of the United Irishmen. Thinking in later years of his good fortune in having attended only " as a spectator " a meeting of the Reformers at which John Sheares was present, he told O'Neill Daunt that " I felt warmly, and a young Catholic student stepping prominently forth in opposition to the Government would have been in all probability hanged."

He learned much " by being a looker-on at this time," the chief lesson being " to have no secrets in politics." He saw " the perpetual peril of treachery," and the spectacle of revolutionary preparations at close quarters filled him more and more with misgivings on the subject of these violent proceedings. ". . . Let me tremble whilst I ask myself how much of myself entered into my desire or dread of a revolution," he commands himself on 25th March, 1797. A month earlier, he had written cautiously of the anticipated effects of the French Revolution on the French character : " The Athenians loved liberty. Here, the altered situation of the French has or may produce [*sic*] a resemblance." The arrival of the French at Bantry Bay near the Christmas of 1796 disturbed him considerably : " I know not what conjecture to make with respect to the future. I love, from my heart I love, liberty. . . . But I know that the victories of the French would be attended with bad consequences. The Irish people are not yet sufficiently enlightened to be able to bear the sun of freedom. Freedom would soon dwindle into licentiousness. They would rob, they would murder. The altar of liberty totters when it is cemented only with blood, when it is supported only with carcases." Again, early in March, he jots down : "A revolution would not produce the happiness of the Irish nation." The " middle-course " came more and more to commend itself : " We talked some pure, because moderate, democracy. Hail, Liberty ! How cheering is thy name ! . . . Strange it might appear that thou shouldst be hateful to any. But thou art calumniated, as thou art disgraced by thy nominal advocates. The interested, those who grow fat on the miseries of mankind, the tyrant and the demagogue condemn thee. The one raises his

voice aloud and is heard in the public places to declaim
against thee ; the other more effectually damns thee by his
support."

In February, 1797, he joined the Lawyers' Corps of
Artillery, of which many of his United Irishmen fellow-
students were members, and on two or three occasions
exposed himself to considerable risk by his refusal to perpetuate or permit acts of inhumanity against civilians. He
was spared the worst of this terrible period, however. The
Castle having taken no action on the Sham Squire's report,
he was called to the Bar on 19th May, 1798, the day on
which Lord Edward was seized, and four days before the
stoppage of the mail coaches was to give the signal for
insurrection. In June, he left Dublin, which was then
becoming unbearably uncomfortable for a young man in
his circumstances, for the peace of Carhen, where he
intended to take an extended holiday. It was nearly his
last holiday, for he caught a dangerous fever in August,
and the final episodes of '98, the victories and defeat of the
French invaders in Mayo and the sea-fight in Lough Swilly,
were long over before the young lawyer emerged once more
into the haunts of men.

As in project, so in retrospect, O'Connell disapproved
of the Rising. " I dined to-day with Bennett," he says on
2nd January, 1799, " We talked much of the late unhappy
rebellion. A great deal of innocent blood was shed on the
occasion. Good God ! What a brute man becomes when
ignorant and oppressed ! Oh, Liberty, what horrors are
perpetrated in thy name ! " He was often to recount, too,
the instances of savage cruelty practised by the military
and he stressed the provocation of Lord Kingscourt and
" Tom the Devil " to the peaceable peasantry of Wexford.
Reflection confirmed the impressions he had formed in the
months before the outbreak, that the whole scheme was
rash, ill-organised and unlikely to succeed, that too many
of the leaders were of the factious type who gambled for
self-aggrandisement with the lives and happiness of the
innocent masses whom they professed to champion. But
the bitterest reflection of all was that it facilitated the

Union ; in his *Memoir on Ireland*, he expresses the conviction that the outbreak was actively fomented by the British government to provide the excuse for the extinction of the Irish Parliament. All around him, in those gloomy months with which the century drew to a close, he saw the aftermath of defeat and the omens of further degradation. He saw the Irish people as the only sufferers and he attained to one determination : that, never again, so far as in his power lay its prevention, should such a thing be permitted to happen.

Almost exactly a year before he heard the maddening bells of St. Patrick's ring out the end of the Irish Legislature, Daniel O'Connell entered the field of public life. " It was the Union that first stirred me up to come forward in politics." As he addressed that meeting of his fellow-Catholics at the Royal Exchange on 30th January, 1800, he was cheered to the echo by his audience. That first speech, as he was afterwards to remark, contained all the principles of his subsequent public life. By this, his twenty-fifth year, he had discarded the unorthodox elements of the revolutionary creed, but, retaining what was reconcilable with the Church's teaching, he had hammered out a synthesis of his own : the Catholic liberal creed towards which his countrymen had long been groping, which was seized on with avidity by those of his co-religionists in Europe who sought a way out of the impasse created by revolutionary anti-clericalism and traditional cisalpinism. His revulsion from revolutionary politics is clearly traceable in the Journal, but we have never been told how he made his way back to complete religious orthodoxy ; indeed, were it not for the coming to light of the Journal, we should never have known that he was even tempted to wander from it, for all the records of his public life and private conduct show him as a Catholic of inflexible principle. Knowing of his experience, however, we can see that it played no inconsiderable part in the formation of his doctrine of civil tolerance and in the development of that constitutional inability of his to indulge in any religious bigotry. Seldom has the transformation of a man from bewildered perplexity to confident certainty been so swift. From 1800 onwards,

O'Connell was no longer the pupil; he was henceforward the mentor.

What were the principles upon which he henceforth acted, and which enabled him to call himself " always a Radical " and yet be acknowledged as a Catholic of unassailable orthodoxy? Superficially, they appear identical with those of contemporary Radicalism : with his reformist allies, he demanded freedom of conscience and of speech, he stood for government by consent of the governed, for civil and political equality. He struggled on behalf of the Dissenter and the Jew, as well as for his fellow-Catholics. He fought, not only for the repeal of the Act of Union and the right of Irishmen to be governed by a body of their own choice, but for the same right of Englishmen. He supported the campaign against negro slavery, pleaded the cause of the Indian peasants and of the neglected and ill-treated people of every land, colonial and European. In Parliament and outside, he flung his full weight into the agitation for electoral reform and extension of the suffrage. He believed intensely in the virtues of private enterprise and set himself against Socialism from the first. The changes he sought were purely political ; throughout the long Repeal campaign, he was always careful to emphasise that the existing social system had nothing to fear from the restoration of the Irish Parliament.

But no amount of superficial agreement could conceal the basic difference between the political creed of O'Connell and that of his agnostic reformist or revolutionary contemporaries. He fixed his liberalism securely in objective law, in the immutable and eternal law of justice which God has given to man as the concomitant of his rational nature, whilst they sought anchorage in the quagmire of felicific calculi, in the fallacies of behaviourism, in unfounded plausibilities and assumptions. Christian liberalism sees man *sub specie aeternitatis ;* the Revolution has no answer to the *whence,* the *whither* and the *why.* " By their fruits ye shall know them." O'Connell's rigidity of principle often angered his critics. His refusal to take the by-paths of expediency exasperated the impatient. At the end of his

days, when his mental powers were sinking, he did indeed
on occasion show signs that this hatred of compromise had
become an obsession. Towards individuals, especially in
the heat of conflict, he was only too often unfair and insulting : one cannot forget his treatment of Vesey Fitzgerald,
which was far from atoned for by the casual apology which
he made when the election was over. But, with this solitary
exception of mob-oratory at elections, his career is devoid
of resort to facile short-cuts. At his very first public appearance, before his fellow-Catholics at the Royal Exchange,
he preferred the re-enactment of the penal code, " in all
its pristine horrors," to the surrender of his country's
identity. He saw the Test Act as an oppression, he supported to the full the demand for its repeal and he rejoiced
in the removal of this last grievance of the northern Dissenters against Britain : a southern Irish Cavour might
have viewed the Test Act in a different light. He rejected
a substantial subscription to the Repeal funds from a southern
American state, on the ground that " it was tainted with
the sweat of slavery." " If the Repeal of the Union depended upon my change of opinion or the suppression of my
sentiments with respect to the slavery of the negro, I would
neither change the one nor suppress the other." He refused
the request of the Czar for an autograph signature, but gave
one with pleasure to the King of Bavaria. He rejected offers
of the highest judicial offices in the land and probably the
peerage itself. He had, admitted Melbourne, " no price."
On the great issue of university education, he was
immovable : " Let there be Presbyterianism for the
Presbyterians, Protestantism for the Protestants and Catholicism for the Catholics," but education without religious
teaching he would not tolerate. The prize of university
education for the Irish middle classes was a glittering one,
and many patriotic Irishmen saw great possibilities in the
intermingling of the Catholic and Protestant youth of
Ireland, but O'Connell saw the project as one founded on
the principle of religious indifference. This principle, if
such it may be called, is the fundamental cause of O'Connell's
quarrel with secularist or anthropocentric Liberalism.

It has long been a cause of surprise to many non-Catholics, and to a not inconsiderable number of Catholics, too, that a liberal-democratic system of politics could profess itself to be in accord with the doctrine of the Church. How, it was asked by those outside her fold, could this ancient body, for centuries the ally of kings, so authoritarian in her organisation and her discipline, so intolerant of all divagation from her teachings, so opposed to political and social change, so illiberal in her principles, find any place in the world of Liberalism and Democracy? How could her followers, with her approval, throw themselves into the new movements and demand freedom of religion, of speech, of the press, universal suffrage, representative government and the liberation of nations? And how, asked many good Catholics, could the Church countenance the propagation of heresies, how compromise with anarchic individualism, how consent to her disestablishment, and, abandoning the dynasties that had sheltered and protected her, agree to commit herself to the whims of unstable Democracy?

The error of both groups lies in the fact that these questions spring from misapprehension and have no relevancy whatever to the matter. To expound adequately the attitude of the Church to the principles and practices of Liberalism and Democracy would call for the writing of volumes and would take us far away from O'Connell, but no discussion of his Catholic liberalism is possible without an indication of orthodox principles. The literature on the subject is indeed voluminous; it extends back to the medieval schoolmen, down through the theologians of the Counter-reformation, and opens into a flood during the nineteenth century, when the clarification of principles relative to politics became a matter of urgent necessity.

First, in relation to Democracy: the legitimacy of the democratic form of government, or of any other form, monarchic, aristocratic or mixed, has never been questioned. The Church is concerned, not with the forms of governments, but with their behaviour. Even at the height of the anti-French reaction in 1797, Cardinal Chiaramonti, the future Pope Pius VII, who was later to be imprisoned by Napoleon, counselled the acceptance of the cisalpine Republic, declaring that there was no opposition between democratic government and the Catholic Church. Twenty years earlier, the great majority of American Catholics had supported Washington in the War of Independence. But the Church will not admit the revolutionary theory of the sovereignty of the people. While there is nothing to preclude a community from electing or nominating its government, when competent to do so, the popular election does not *confer* authority, for authority comes from God. The election or nomination merely fixes by whom the authority is to be exercised ; it does not confer rights on the government, but designates the Ruler.

Secondly, in relation to the complicated questions of rights and liberties, the Church distinguishes carefully between fundamental principle and the dictates of prudence in concrete, historic circumstances. This is the distinction of the *thesis* and the *hypothesis* ; that which may not be approved in principle may be tolerated as the best attainable in given conditions. The principle of Natural Right was no discovery of the revolutionaries ; it is an essential inherent in Christianity. In an anthropocentric system, the very term, Natural Right, is meaningless : " nonsense on stilts," said Bentham. Only in the framework of Christianity can the significance of the term, and the significance of its qualificative, " inalienable," be appreciated. In the Christian teaching, the individual is the only being which has real existence : society, the group, the nation, the State, all exist for the individual, to aid him towards his Final End, which is God. He, therefore, has an indefeasible right to all those things that are necessary to the attainment of this End. The dignity of man demands that he be hedged around with safeguards and guarantees against harm. Man, because of his origin and End, has one great primary duty : to save his immortal soul. From this duty arises that complexity of duties that confront him throughout life, all directed to the accomplishment of that first of duties, and capable of being summed up as the duty to know God, to avoid ignorance, to do no wrong to others, and to promote the good of society. The obverse of duty is right, and the consequence of right is freedom. Man has a natural right to perform a natural duty and to the means to its performance, and the indispensable means is freedom to that performance. Freedom is the means and justice the end. Freedom, then, is limited by the requirements of natural duty. In all the Christian scheme of things, there is not an inch of room for the arbitrary. No choice, no decision, no act, can be classed as neither good nor bad : the laws of Eternal Justice reach down into all the minutiae of life.

Not even, therefore, in affairs apparently the most trifling is man free to do whatever he likes, to follow the prompting of whim. Freedom exists, not for the gratification of appetite, but for the maintenance of the Law. This is what the Revolution forgot. Leaving out of account the origin, the nature and the End of man, it could not be expected to have any accurate conception of his duties. It failed to connect right with responsibility to any degree approaching adequacy. In its preoccupation with the Rights of Man, it forgot the duties of man, and, as it had no yard-stick to measure the extent of these rights, it produced claims for the most extravagant liberties. " But what worse death is there of the soul than liberty of error ? " Unqualified freedom in anything : in thought, word, printing, in political or in economic activity, in public or in private life : all the unconscionable freedoms of agnostic Liberalism stand irreconcilable with truth and justice. It does not follow from this, however, that certain liberties which are condemned in principle may not be tolerated in practice. Prudence demands that certain evils be tolerated to avert greater : God Himself permits evil to exist. Thus, whilst the modern liberties of speech and of the press are theoretically indefensible, the circumstances of the modern world indicate that it is necessary to tolerate them. " Out of evil, good cometh." The modern press, with all its shortcomings, has proved a bulwark of ordered liberty, an insuperable obstacle to the success of ambitious demagogues. Tolerance in these matters of speech and printing may not,

it goes without saying, be extended indefinitely ; this proposition is recognised, indeed, in the Declaration of the
Rights of Man itself and in the legal system of every country.

This distinction of *thesis* and *hypothesis* is also observed by
the Church in her relations with the rulers of states. The
principle is : that all Christians *ought* to be Catholics, that
all Christian governments *should* make the Catholic religion
the established religion of the State, that the State should
protect the Church and recognise her laws, in return for
which protection and recognition the Church would
partner the State, recognising its independence and supremacy in its own sphere, working together with it for the
good of society and supporting it by preaching that its
authority comes from God and that obedience to its laws
is a matter of conscience. In practice, the relations of the
Church with certain governments are established in the
terms set out in Concordats, whilst with others, such as
those of Great Britain and the United States, she is content
to avail herself of the legal rights possessed by all citizens
and groups and take her place in the State without any
formal relations with the administration. In general, it
may be said that the Church is prepared to make such
concessions to the spirit of the age as may be made without
surrender of principle and that she does this to facilitate
her access to the minds of men.

The question of religious toleration had worried O'Connell
excessively in his student days and we cannot imagine his
anguish being soothed by the writings of Voltaire. " *Hodie
venenum in ecclesiam infunditur*," wrote the puritan Milton
of the day Constantine made his Donation. There can be
no doubt that the centuries-old partnership of civil and
ecclesiastical power brought many results unprofitable
to true religion. " Evil communications corrupt good
manners." It is impossible to the modern mind to see
through the eyes of the men of old, to whom loyalty and
orthodoxy were one, and heresy and treason synonymous,
by whom the very idea of a separation of Church from State
would have been utterly incomprehensible, had they heard
of it. In justice, too, to both the medieval Church and the

civil authority, the nature of many of the heretical outbreaks
of the time ought to be recalled ; too often have the social
and political implications and consequences of these movements been ignored or forgotten, and the medieval heretic
seen as Voltaire saw his Zapata—a gentle nonconformist
whose only wish was to be let alone, a John Stuart Mill
born before his time; too seldom does the modern historian
see such bodies as the Albigenses for what they were—highly
dangerous anarchists whose wild and indecent exploits
would have been tolerated in no society—or realise that the
Church again and again tried to stay the hand of the
secular power and counselled the tempering of justice with
mercy.   But, while all this is true we can still see clearly
enough that the State took full advantage of the partnership ; that it established in many regions a stranglehold on
the Church which prevented reform and left her in a
weakened and anaemic condition and, that, when the
whirlwind came, it left her to pay the penalty for its sins.

The religious wars which followed the Reformation
demanded the devising of some *modus vivendi* between
Catholic and Protestant, and the first attempt is represented by the formula, *cuius regio eius religio*, of the Peace
of Augsburg ; but the crude injustice of this arrangement
became more and more evident as Catholic and Protestant
groups settled down and regional politics became less
immediately associated with religion.   The Church has
always drawn a distinction between heresy and invincible
ignorance of doctrine : to apply the term, " heretic," to
a non-Catholic who adheres to his own beliefs in good faith
is, according to her teaching, the grossest of uncharities.
Forcible conversion is a contradiction in terms, for " Man
cannot believe otherwise than of his own free will."   The
condemnation of freedom of worship is, thus, a *thesis*, for
" the ideal is unity in true worship " ; its permissibility in
certain circumstances is an *hypothesis*.   Hence, condemnation of the principle of freedom of worship is not aimed at
" civil tolerance " of non-Catholic cults.   As witness to
this fact, Pope Pius IX reminded his critics that " The
Jews and Protestants enjoy liberty and peace here with me.

The Jews have their Synagogue in the Ghetto and the
Protestants their Temple at the Porta Del Popolo." And
O'Connell himself recalled with pride that the Act of the
Maryland Council which established religious freedom in
the Colony in 1672 was drawn up by a Jesuit.

There is an infinitude of difference, then, between the
revolutionary principle of freedom of worship and the
Christian principle of religious tolerance. The former is
the principle of neutrality, based on scepticism or indifference. The latter is called for by the requirements of civil
peace, but its basis is the love of our fellowman. " Our
efforts," wrote O'Connell, " are consistent with humanity,
sound order and religion : our maxim is that true liberty
can have no solid or permanent basis save religion ; whilst
we have conscience free, we assist the ameliorating influences
of our common Christianity, and devote our exertions in
favour of human freedom to the protection and guidance
of Christian charity, for we know ' the greatest of all is
charity.' " The distinction between his political creed and
that of contemporary agnostic radicalism is evident, too,
from his complaint of the supporters of the Bequests Bill :
"A fatal liberalism is but too prevalent, and these pseudo-
Liberals are extremely anxious to have an opportunity of
assailing the party of the sincere and practical Catholics as
being supporters of narrow and bigoted doctrines." In
the course of one of his public speeches, he summed up his
liberalism in that homely fashion so characteristic of him :
" Let us differ no longer with a man because of his religion.
If he be wrong, that is his own affair, not mine. For my
part, I can never fall out with my neighbour for his religion,
for I find I have quite enough to do to mind my own—
heaven help me !—and indeed, I think if we would generally
come to the resolution of paying to our own religion one
half the attention we now direct to that of other people,
we would be all better and happier far. . . ." O'Connell
saw that religion and the civil authority move on different
planes ; the one cannot legislate for the other. Catholic,
Protestant and Dissenter ought to unite on the civil plane,
where the only denomination known is that of " Irishman."

The Protestant minority belongs no less than the Catholic masses to the people of Ireland and its civic rights deserve equal respect. On the religious plane, they are doctrinally distinct, but bound by the bond of charity : " The doctrine of Catholics is this—we pray for everybody—we pray with none but Catholics." To the end of his days, he held out the Emancipation victory as a great civil and political advance for the Catholics, " secured without the sacrifice of an atom of principle." During his term of office as Lord Mayor of Dublin, it was his pride that no one could deduce his religion from his administrative acts.

The principles of his liberalism unfolded themselves fully in the course of the first great struggle of his life, the agitation against the proposals for the Veto and the payment of the Catholic clergy. His demands may be reduced to one : "A free Church in a free State." He sought for the Catholic Church in Ireland unconditional Emancipation, but no privileges. " I want nothing for the Catholics which I am not ready to assert for others. Let there be fair play and justice for all." He insisted throughout on the independence of the civil power, as the well-known declaration that he would as soon receive his politics " from Constantinople as from Rome " makes clear. Of the earlier Bill which embodied the provision of the Veto and the proposals for the payment of the clergy, he declared : " It was on the ground of its danger to civil liberty that I objected to the late Bill. It would have the effect, if passed into law, of placing in the hands of the Ministers a new and extensive source of patronage, and, for that reason, I would rather the Catholics should remain for ever without emancipation than that they should receive it upon such terms." This desire and aim to steer between erastianism on the one hand, and the excesses of ultramontanism on the other, he very succinctly stated in the outspoken Address to Pope Pius VII : " We seek to obtain from our Government nothing more than the restoration of temporal rights ; and must most humbly, but most firmly, protest against the interference of your Holiness, or any other foreign prelate, State or potentate, in the control of our temporal conduct or in the arrangement of our political concerns. . . . We have confined ourselves in this memorial to the recapitulation of objections, founded upon spiritual considerations ; because as, on the one hand, we refuse to submit our religious concerns to the control of our temporal chief, so, on the other hand, we cannot admit any right on the part of the Holy See to investigate our political principles, or to direct our political conduct, it being our earnest desire and fixed determination to conform at all times and under all circumstances to the injunctions of that sacred ordinance which teaches us to distinguish between spiritual and temporal authority, giving unto Caesar those things which belong to Caesar and unto God those things which belong to God."

In pursuit of this principle of avoiding confusion of allegiances, O'Connell had two great objects in view : to secure the advance of Christian democracy and to disarm the Revolution.

He has often been criticised for introducing unnecessary heat into the Veto controversy, for precipitating a dissension between the Catholic gentry and the democrats and, thereby, creating that division widened later by the mode of his conduct of the Repeal agitation, between the people and the upper classes, which drove the latter into Unionism and reaction and eventually lost them their place in the life of Ireland. That Emancipation, accompanied by the Veto or by the payment of the clergy, or by both, would have come in time, is certainly true. The Veto was not inconsistent with the discipline of the Church : it was conceded to the Head of State in all Concordats between the Holy See and Protestant powers. Nor was payment of the clergy by the State, Catholic or Protestant, a procedure to be reprobated in all circumstances. O'Connell's method, it is charged, had the abruptness of the revolutionary : he forced issues and created dissension, instead of trusting to the peaceful evolution which would in time bring the satisfaction of general desires and weld the elements of the nation into homogeneity.

That the sacrifice of the contributions which aristocracy can make to the life of a nation is a heavy one, cannot be

denied : its heaviness has become painfully obvious in the
Ireland of to-day. But, heavy as it is, there are heavier.
The fundamental weakness of the conservative case against
O'Connell lies in its assumption of the inevitability of a
beneficent evolutionary process in Irish affairs. In a
reasonably well-governed country, reliance upon evolution
is the true principle : the statesman will not endanger
present good by going ahead too fast. But the Ireland of
the early nineteenth century was not the best of fields for
an evolutionary experiment : " a starving population, an
absentee aristocracy, an alien church. . . ." All the
conditions that breed lawlessness and sedition were rife.
On the Continent and in England itself, the spirit of revolutionary democracy was making rapid strides. Hitherto,
the independent Catholic clergy had preserved the Irish
people from its inroads ; but what might not the result be
if these clergy lost their immense prestige in the eyes of
their Irish flocks ? Would a State-paid and Castle-approved
hierarchy be equally successful ? Would the future of the
Church be assured ? This danger of the alienation of the
people from their clergy and its terrible possibilities were
the spur to O'Connell's resistance to " conditional " emancipation. He knew well, as anyone who knows Ireland even
to-day knows, that the loss of the Catholic faith would
probably bring in its train the disruption and disintegration
of the Irish nation ; for the Irish, unlike those consolidated
nations with a history of independence and internal tranquillity behind them, had had no opportunity to develop
traditions and conventions not closely connected with
religious belief; the cement of society, the whole code of
Irish behaviour, was supplied directly by the Catholic
faith alone. If it went, the Irish would be at the mercy of
every wind that blows. The civil disturbance that would
ensue might well mean national extermination. There
would be little point in deploring the loss of an aristocratic contribution to the national life, if there were no
national life to contribute to. The alienation of the Irish
gentry may well have been the effect of O'Connell's two
great agitations, but it certainly was the contrary of his

intent, as his constant reassurances and appeals to them and the number of them in his Repeal Association very clearly show. His life-long aim, which he never tired of proclaiming, was the unity of all Irishmen and the security of all classes : the realisation of those very conditions which enable wealth and station, as well as industry and worth, to enrich the life of a country.

In matters of detail, O'Connell, like all human beings, occasionally erred. On the Veto question, he was sometimes a little hysterical in his speech and less than fair to honourable opponents. But, on the broad principle, it is the measure of his greatness as a statesman that he saw what his conservative contemporaries failed to see : the terrible imminence everywhere of the revolutionary threat to religion and order and the most effective means of containing and defeating it. He would have forestalled the Revolution by measures of wise reform, he would divert the energies expended in criminal local conspiracies into useful activity, he would discipline the masses and educate them in citizenship by admitting them to a wider share in political power, he would draw the fangs of the Revolution by rescuing the Church from all suspicion of association with reaction. His policy was revolutionary and counter-revolutionary.

The agitation against the Veto must be viewed against its background in the France of the time. O'Connell, although he never visited France from the time of his hurried departure in 1793 to the year of his death, took a keen interest in French affairs and watched closely and with deepening anxiety the progress which anti-clericalism continued to make during the periods of the Empire and the Restoration. Paradoxical as it may seem to the superficial view, the Church was in certain respects safer under the voltairean Empire than it later was under the protection of the House of Bourbon. The greater part of Napoleon's reign saw him at odds with the Pope. The story of the period is one of patient endeavour by the aged Pope, Pius VII, to secure the safeguard against Napoleon of the essentials of Church discipline in France, and of Napoleon's determination to make the French Church an adjunct to his throne and to make the Pope his vassal in Europe. At last, in 1809, when all attempts at conciliation had failed, the Pope excommunicated him. Within a month, Napoleon arrested the Pope and had him removed from Rome. From July, 1809, to May, 1814, when Napoleon's Empire was crashing down before the advance of the allied armies, the Pope remained a prisoner. Encroachments on the discipline of the Church had frequently been made by sovereigns of France before Napoleon's time, but what the French Royalists would have aquiesced in from the Bourbons, they would not take with good grace from the upstart Bonaparte. By the year 1814, at which time the anti-Veto agitation was at its height in Ireland, Catholics everywhere were exasperated by the tyrannous proceedings of Napoleon. The whole issue of State interference with the discipline of the Church, which had long lain dormant under the Old Regime, was becoming revived and was soon to come to a head.

The restoration of the House of Bourbon brought relief, but the question of establishing relations between the Crown and the Holy See was soon seen to be fraught with new difficulties, as the King's ministers endeavoured to placate anti-clerical opinion. These ministerial efforts in turn gave offence to the majority of Royalists and France found herself with two parties, the one anti-royalist and anti-religious, the other professing its devotion to " Throne and Altar." The danger to religion in such an atmosphere needs no pointing out. On the one side, hate of religion and hate of the Bourbons fanned each other into a frenzy of blasphemous obscenity. On the other, orthodoxy of faith seemed to entail blind devotion to the dynasty. " It was impossible," says M. de Grandmaison, " that good Christians should be other than Royalist." This trend filled the watchful O'Connell with the very deepest dismay. " Infidelity," he wrote, " which is more persecuting in its nature than the most intolerant of the unhappy sects that have rent the seamless garment of Christ—infidelity, which has deluged France with the blood of the Catholic Clergy, was losing ground by degrees since the Concordat obtained

by Napoleon ; but the progress of Christian truth and of
genuine piety was much impeded since the return of the
Bourbons by the unhallowed commixture of zeal for religion
with servile attachment to the Bourbons. ' *La religion et
le Roi* ' were put in juxtaposition, and the latter *seemed* as
much an object of worship as the former, but only *seemed*,
for the Catholic Clergy of France have been basely and
atrociously calumniated by many, and, I am sorry to say,
by none more than by Brougham, when he called them
bigoted and besotted. They were not, and are not, either
the one or the other. The charge is false and, indeed, in
every respect, unbecoming. No, the Catholic Clergy of
France are learned, pious, exemplary, and most charitable
and zealous. But they were placed in a false position."

Nobody, he admits, could blame the French Catholics for
their horror of revolutionary politics : they had experienced
republican " liberty " ; but the object to which this horror
had impelled their affections was unworthy of them. " The
Bourbons were a foolish race of despots, and every crime
they committed was attributed to religion. Religion being
thus enlisted as an ally of the Bourbons, shared in the hatred
which the acts of the Bourbons engendered. Almost all
the patriots were anti-religionists, if not infidels. All the
courtiers pretended to devotion, or, at least, the far greater
part of them, and it was suspected that many affected more
piety than they felt. Religion was thus placed in a false
position. Catholicity in France was situate somewhat as
Protestantism has been, and, to a certain extent, still is,
in Ireland. It was considered to be the enemy of the
people and of liberty." Years after the writing of this
passage, it may be remarked before the subject is left, the
career of the July Monarchy had made him relent a little
towards the elder branch of the royal house : " My opinion
is," said he in 1844, " that Europe will never be perfectly
safe until that branch of the Bourbon family be restored—
restored under liberal institutions."

Such was the French background to the anti-Veto
struggle. In Belgium, or, as it had formerly been called,
the Austrian Netherlands, the clouds were also gathering.

The peacemakers of Vienna had joined this predominantly Catholic territory to the Protestant Kingdom of Holland. Difference of religion caused friction between the two peoples from the first, the most serious cause of trouble being the Dutch king's despotic behaviour in the matter of the nomination of bishops and his failure to perform his obligations under the Concordat between the Netherlands and the Holy See. O'Connell's admiration was aroused, not only by the manly resistance of the Belgian Catholics to this interference with their Church, but by the general liberality of their politics. " It is a curious thing to see how completely I am borne out in my often repeated assertion, that sincere Catholics are, after all, if not the only, certainly the most persevering friends of rational liberty," he wrote to Francis Walsh in September, 1830. " The Belgian deputies were Catholics, the Dutch deputies were Protestants. The Catholics uniformly voted for laws tending to freedom and opposed everything that partook of slavery. The Protestants did directly the reverse." At the time of his writing, the Belgian revolution—one of the few he ever approved—had taken place and Belgium had become an independent State. When she came to seek a monarch, it is instructive that O'Connell's name was one of those proposed for the office, and that he received some votes.

There was considerable interaction among the three struggles which went on, in Ireland, in Belgium and in France, between those years from 1815 to 1830, but the impetus came from Ireland. By the latter year, O'Connell's speeches were being reported in translation in all the Catholic countries of Europe, and even outside these countries and all over the North American continent, the mobilisation of the Irish was watched with intentness. To England's old enemies, the French, it was a cause of exultation. Its magnitude, its discipline, the forcefulness of its leader, indicated that here at last was a really formidable threat to the hereditary oppressor of the Irish and the hereditary foe of France. Irish visitors to Paris were lionised and besieged with inquiries on the state of the country ; Moore's *Melodies* were translated into French ; works on Irish history, novels of Irish life, were sought and eagerly read ; the old friendship between the two countries was constantly recalled. Everywhere was sympathy for " the poor Irish " and anger at their cruel tormentor. Racial affinities were discussed and it was felt in the Liberal salons of Paris that France, as the great Celtic Power, should interest herself in the fortunes of this small kindred people engaged in a fight for its survival against the Teutonic enemy. Soon, a flow of French visitors began to arrive in Ireland to study conditions on the spot. In 1826, at the height of the Emancipation campaign, the Liberal parliamentarian, Duvergier de Hauranne, accompanied by the Duc de Montebello and two young friends, made an extensive tour of the country, visiting many of the aristocratic houses, meeting O'Connell and his lieutenants, attending public meetings of the Catholic Association and making notes of everything that impressed them. The reports which they brought back induced many more to come. In 1834, the celtophile Michelet felt impelled to come and see the ancient land for himself. These Liberals were struck by the strangeness of the Irish scene. Duvergier found the Irish clergy " poor, tolerant, liberal and pacifist," representative of " the veritable Catholicism in its primitive purity " ; he saw that " Catholicism is national in Ireland." It seemed a strange reversal of the conditions in France. The interest of such Liberals as Duvergier in Ireland was primarily political. They found it difficult to associate Catholicism with " the spirit of liberty " ; they found O'Connell " no veritable Liberal," he seemed " to have a *penchant* for the ancient monarchy," " he loves the Catholic clergy too much." But, despite these drawbacks, his movement seemed to be revolutionary : the emancipation of the Catholics would be a means to complete liberty, the first step towards a Liberal Revolution, violent or pacific.

But the news from Ireland attracted keen attention also in a quarter far removed from the politically-minded Liberals. Ministerial interference in religious affairs gave rise among the Royalist Catholics to an ultramontane party, pledged to protest without cease against all restrictions on the organisational activity of the Church. In time, the realisation grew that anti-clericalism was not the only enemy : the Church needed to be saved from her friends as well as from her declared foes. She was being compromised by her association with the Crown and impeded in the fulfilment of her mission by the stranglehold of the State. Where were these unhappy Catholics, acutely conscious of the sad position of the Church, to look for inspiration ? In Ireland, they found a situation very like their own in some of its salient features ; there they saw a policy and a strategy to follow. Foremost in energy and in eloquence, the recognised spokesman of the Ultramontanes, was the unfortunate Abbé de Lamennais ; at first a Royalist who looked to the authoritarian State to protect religion and curb the impiety of the revolutionists, he thundered for years in the *Conservateur* and the *Drapeau Blanc* against all yielding to the irreligious spirit of the Left ; but he gradually came to see that the old Gallican spirit was alive in the counsels of the administration. The remedy for the situation seemed indicated in Ireland. The cause of Catholic liberalism drew another remarkable recruit from a point directly the opposite to that of Lamennais' original position : Père Lacordaire found his way from republican Liberalism into the Church and was for long ill at ease in his new surroundings and sorely pressed by the problem of reconciling the ancient, uncompromising faith with the needs of the new society. From midway between these two points came Charles, Vicomte de Montalembert, an anglophile monarchist who favoured a moderate constitutionalism. The interest of these men in Ireland was primarily religious : the struggle for Emancipation was seen in a supranational context, as the first step, not in a local, political revolution, but in the freeing of the Universal Church from the shackles of the secular power throughout the world. To them, martyred Ireland was the figure of persecuted Christianity, her gallant fight an episode in the perennial combat with the Prince of this World. She was the Holy Island, emerald gem of the sea, " living fragment of the Middle Ages."

When Montalembert in 1830 came, as on a pilgrimage to his spiritual homeland, he was delighted beyond all measure by the fresh and living faith which he saw around him everywhere. To him, Ireland was no place of contradictions; comprehension of faith in charity, no bewildering anomaly. Here was a free and popular Church which sought only an unprivileged place in a free State; here was a poor and democratic clergy without temporal ambition, without jealousy, but rewarded by their flock with a devotion which many a Prince-Bishop might envy. Here, indeed, was the cradle of the Catholic renaissance. Montalembert never forgot these impressions. Years afterwards, on a raw and gloomy day in the spring of 1847, when he led a little gathering of friends to greet the dying O'Connell in his Paris hotel, he reminded him : " We are your children, or, rather, your pupils. You are our master, our model, our glorious preceptor. It is for this reason that we come to bring you the tender and respectful homage which we owe to the man, who, in our time, has done most for the dignity and liberty of the human race, and especially for the political education of the peoples of the West. You are not the man of one nation only : you are the man of all Christendom. Your glory is not only Irish : it is Catholic. Everywhere that Catholics revive the practice of the civic virtues and devote themselves to the conquest of their legitimate rights, it is, under God, your work. Everywhere that religion tries to emancipate itself from the yoke that many generations of sophists and legists have forged for it, it is, under God, to you it owes success." " Never weaken," murmured O'Connell, " . . . Go forward ! Courage ! "

While in Ireland, Montalembert had visited O'Connell at Darrynane, and before he had left the country he received news that his friends had launched their new movement with the establishment of the *Avenir* newspaper, bearing the device, " God and Liberty." The Revolution of the previous July had expelled Charles X and overthrown the clerical party. The anti-clericals were intoxicated with joy : legitimism and religion had gone together ;

the hated Christianity was doomed ; deprived of its govern-
mental protection, it must wilt and wither away ; the future
belonged to Humanity. The suddenness of the collapse
of the Old Regime left the Catholics stunned, the horrid
sacrileges with which the Paris mob celebrated the triumph
terrified them, the irreligious exultation of their enemies
left them dumb. What were they to do ? Suffer in silence
and wait for Henry V ? This was the thought of many,
but it was far from the thoughts of Lamennais and his
friends. Now is the time, they cried, for Catholics to take
the offensive, to meet Liberalism on its own chosen field,
to show their opponents and the world once for all that
Christian doctrine is " essentially liberal, because it is all
charity." The Church, which had turned from the rulers
of the Lower Empire to the barbarian chiefs and made them
into Christian monarchs, could turn from their feeble and
ungenerous descendants to the new Democracy : " She
will baptise this savage heroine, she will make a Christian
of her, as she has already made Christians of the barbarians."
To the dismayed clergy, Lamennais called : " You tremble
before Liberalism : Catholicise it, and society will be
reborn." To the gloating Liberals, he cried : " You seek
the Church in the dust of an upturned throne : *Christus
surrexit, non est hic.*" He might have become the O'Connell
of France. To all governments, he appealed : " Let men
protect religion less and tolerate it more." Give the Church
her freedom, and she will be well able to look after herself,
was the burden of his preaching. The new party flung
itself at once into politics, its declared objects being the
separation of Church from State, freedom of speech, freedom of the press and liberty of education. It established the
Agence Générale Pour la Défense de la Liberté Religieuse, on the
model of O'Connell's Catholic Association, pledged to support the return of deputies favourable to the Catholic claims,
to combat anti-clerical legislation and to present the Catholic
case to parliament and the electors. By the Left, it was
assailed with concentrated fury ; on the Right, it was
regarded as the undertaking of madmen, and the orthodoxy
of many of its tenets impugned. The extravagance of its

claims in respect of freedom of the press brought censure eventually from Rome, and its advocacy of the separation of Church from State was rebuked as imprudent. The unhappy Lamennais, at first submissive, finally rebelled and left the Church. Montalembert, Lacordaire and all their other friends submitted to censure, but never abandoned the cause of moderate liberalism. Theirs was the effort which gave the initial impetus to the popular, democratic Catholic movements which are, in the ruined Europe of to-day, the backbone of the political defence of western civilisation against the oriental despotism which has appropriated the Revolution.

The place of Daniel O'Connell in the history of his own country is that of the first Irishman who was not " bested in the game." Emancipation was a complete victory. Repeal, in the year of his death, was an apparent failure. " 1843," he had told the world, " will be the Repeal Year." But four years later he was to stand before the House of Commons and to tell them : " Ireland is in your hands ; if you do not save her, she cannot save herself." Yet, the failure, tragic and total as it seemed, was only apparent. 1843 was, in fact, the year that doomed the Union. It placed us " on the high ground." What was the leverage ?

The obstacles which O'Connell found in his country's path on that first day of January, 1801, drove many a public-spirited Irishman into private life. Every known means had been tried to improve the political condition of Ireland. The armed force of the United Irishmen had not only failed, but had sunk the country into inexpressible misery. The eloquence of Grattan, Plunket and Bushe had been vain in the defence of the last vestige of even theoretical independence. The arms and the money of a powerful Empire seemed invincible ; the resources of patriotism, bankrupt.

The obstacles were diverse and only too well known : the implacable might of Britain, the impregnable power of illiberal landlords, the apathy and indiscipline of the Irish. Frontal assault on the former two was clearly unthinkable, and the Irish people as they then were seemed a handicap, rather than a help, to a popular leader. Quite clearly, the well-tried methods were unsuitable and inadequate. The situation called for a new technique, for a revolution in revolutionary strategy. This was precisely what the ingenious brain of O'Connell supplied. It was his discovery that positions which are unassailable in front can sometimes be turned that made him the Liberator. He evolved the technique of what has since become universally known as " passive resistance " ; he perfected the art of beating the enemy on the enemy's own ground and with the enemy's own legalistic weapons ; in a colloquial phrase, he was able to put the opponent in an " impossible position." He learned to play politics as a game of chess.

But before he could even start this practice, he had to improve the efficiency of his own instrument, the Irish people. The work of improvement engaged the entire time of his public life. The political education of the Irish had to begin almost at the elements ; it had to make up, in the space of a lifetime, the leeway of centuries ; it had to be an intensive cram, hard indeed on the pupil, but infinitely harder on the master : it eventually sapped his mental strength and wore him out, but its success constitutes one of the very greatest feats in history.

The Irish masses had, since 1793, very ample legal rights, but they did not see them ; the opportunities which legal rights confer were existent, but infinitely remote under actual conditions. It was O'Connell's first task to convince them of their rights and to bring the opportunities within reach. The first requisite to the success of this was peace and order. The blind helot-instinct to strike at the immediate oppressor, real or apparent, to return evil for evil without investigation of cause or thought of consequence is the first of obstacles in the path of a people towards nationhood. For the greater part of his life, O'Connell found it the only internal danger. The co-ordinated violence, which we call rebellion, directed against the central power accounted ultimately responsible for manifold evil, came also under his ban. " He who commits a crime gives strength to the enemy," became the watchword of the

Repeal Association. O'Connell had learned in 1798 " to
have no secrets in politics " ; he knew the opportunities
which conspiracy offered to the informer and the *agent
provocateur*. Not only should the people, he demanded,
reject the recruiters of secret societies, but they should seize
them and hand them over to the police—and enjoy frequently the embarrassment of the latter ! " Your oppressors desire nothing so much as to see you in arms—to hear
you utter seditious cries against the Government, in order
that they might have new pretexts to oppress you still
more." " Obey," he told them, " obey even the semblance
of authority." Illegal acts of the executive should be dealt
with after their occurrence by invoking the law against the
abuser of authority, not by resistance on the spot. In
physical force, he always saw the ruin of Irish hopes. " One
living Repealer is worth a churchyard-ful of dead ones."
But his abhorrence of force is not to be attributed solely to
the tactical requirements of a local situation. It had a wider
context, woven by a Christian conscience out of his observation of revolutionary trends in the outside world and by the
train of reflection to which Godwin had given the impetus.

Those condemnations of physical violence have been a
source of unending controversy ever since the unhappy day
in July, 1846, when the Young Irelanders, having refused
to accept the Pledge against resort to force " under all
circumstances," walked out of Conciliation Hall. The
bitterness to which the unfortunate mismanagement of this
particular affair gave rise has created much confusion on
the subject of O'Connell's pacifism. That he ever disapproved absolutely of the employment of force is a contention that cannot be sustained. In April, 1820, he sent
his son, Morgan, to join in the South American War of
Independence, informing Bolívar that " . . . Hitherto, I
have been able to bestow only good wishes upon that noble
cause. But now, I have a son able to wield a sword in its
defence, and I send him, illustrious Sir, to admire and
profit by your example . . . to contribute his humble but
zealous exertions for the success of the arms of the youthful
but already renowned Republic of Columbia," and assuring

him of his fervent prayer " that you, illustrious Sir, will imitate the virtues of Washington—may, like him, live to see the enemies of your country confounded and defeated, and to enjoy the heartfelt gratification of beholding your country perfectly free. . . ." Over four years later, he made the speech for which he was arrested : " Oppression drives the wise man mad ; it has not yet had that effect upon the Irish people ; it has never driven them to the extremity of desperate resistance, and Heaven forbid it should ; but, if such an event come to pass, may another Bolívar and the example of Greece animate their efforts."

In 1830, he approved of the Belgian revolution and, at first, of the French. As time wore on, however, the closeness of association between revolution and irreligion, on the European continent, and between it and political instability on the South American, came to assume in his mind the appearance of inseparability, and he never again, after the disillusion of 1830, expressed admiration of the use of arms. Henceforth, he took his stand upon an extremely conservative position in relation to the morality of revolt : he justified the use of force only in the last extremity of self-defence : " Resistance is not right until legal authority is done away with, and the iron and red hand of power is raised against the people." Throughout the entire Repeal campaign, this was the gist of his pronouncements : " Let them attack us ; we will resist ; but we shall resist only if we are attacked." At the same time, he never ceased to warn the government of the consequences of a refusal to grant a legislature to Ireland. There would be no rebellion so long as he lived, but it was not in the nature of things that the present state of affairs should last indefinitely ; sooner or later, when his guidance had been removed by the hand of death, the terrible day would come when Irish patience would snap : " But he is no statesman who does not recollect the might that slumbers in a peasant's arm ; and when you multiply that might by vulgar arithmetic to the extent of 6,000,000 or 7,000,000, is the man a statesman or a driveller who expects that might will always slumber amid grievances continued and oppression endured too long ? " His

Monster Meetings were " the safety-valves " of Irish indignation, he told *The Times ;* far from arousing the war-like passions of the Irish, he was providing a harmless outlet for them in the peaceful simulacrum of military manoeuvre : the musterings, the marchings and the parades. At the same time, he was disciplining them, canalising their energies into national effort and educating them to think nationally. To the charge that his language was often violent and inflammatory, he retorted : "A French author says—I do not quote him as an authority, for no man hates French infidelity and French republican opinions more than I do ; but a French author says that ' you cannot make a revolution with rose water.' He would make it with blood—I would make it with public opinion and I would put a little Irish spirit into it." Were he an unprincipled seeker of power, he could easily have made an alliance with the Chartists of England, which would have shaken the State to its foundations, if it did not overthrow it ; but he rejected again and again the overtures of the Chartists, " those men of fire and faggot," and warned the Irish in England to have nothing to do with them.

It was one of O'Connell's claims that Chartism would have obtained a firm foothold in Ireland, had he not been there to combat it. The time might even come, he warned, when his services would be needed to defend the Crown against revolt in England itself ; and he would be ready to do so and able to do so, for he had developed such skill in countering violence " that he had no doubt that even in England he would effect such an organisation as would save the country from any revolutionary movement." Offers of assistance from the revolutionaries of France and from Irish elements in America, he invariably refused, but he never failed to call the attention of the government to the fact of these offers. The choice between revolution, accompanied perhaps by exhibitions of hostility on the part of Britain's foreign rivals, on the one hand, and peace, on the other, lay, not with him, but with the legislature : if the intolerable Union outlived him, bloodshed and eventual separation of the two countries would be the inevitable

consequence. The result of such an upheaval would be
tragic for all concerned : for the Irish people themselves
and for the common people of Britain, no less than for their
rulers : " Every outbreak of that kind necessarily increases
tyranny, changing what may be hard to bear into a despotism
not long endured." Even at the height of his triumphs in
1843, this fear that he had created an instrument which
would slip out of the control of its maker began to trouble
him ; it came over him occasionally, " like the incubus of
a sickly dream," that some small outburst might start a
fearful avalanche of revolt. He had himself occasionally
used military phraseology to decorate his speeches, but in
the *Nation* newspaper he was soon to find it employed in a
less figurative sense. The " Morality of War " and the
" Duties of the Soldier " were being discussed openly in the
nationalist press ; the numbers of Irishmen in the Crown
forces reckoned ; " Something " was coming ; and, among
the people, the question was circulating : " When will the
Counsellor call us out ? " The very real terror which he
came to feel, not for his personal safety, but for the fate of
the vast national movement he had built up, explains fully
his dissociation from the *Nation* and his rough treatment of
the Young Irelanders. Indeed, towards the end of his life,
it tended to become an obsession. The only blood he would
permit to be shed for Irish independence was his own ; he
would never send another to his death in any cause. He
saw his faithful Irish people, not as an abstraction—for he
never thought in abstractions—but as men and women, and
he remembered that many, too, brought their children to
his mass-meetings. " This Proclamation must be obeyed."
It is idle to think of the revolutionary Myth that might have
been created by the massacre of Clontarf, for it was not in
the nature of the man to allow it.

In discarding all thought of physical force, the new
movement would make itself irresistible. Exact compliance
with unjust law entails external submission, but no deference.
It would leave the executive powerless to interfere. " Moral
means, reasoning, peaceable combination, the electricity of
public opinion "—these were the weapons that would

conquer. If the people of Ireland, Catholic, Protestant and Presbyterian, would unite together as one man, their demands could not be refused ; they would become necessarily free. Conversion was the one need. Hence the reliance which O'Connell placed, from the beginning of his career to the end, on publicity; hence the monster-meetings, the newspaper-allies, the reading-rooms, the clubs—all the elaborate paraphernalia of advertisement. Even at his own trial for conspiracy in 1844, he could not forbear from thinking of the courtroom as a good platform for the broadcasting of his ideas. " It is delightful to me," he laughed, " to have an opportunity of stating these facts in a place from which I know they will be extensively circulated." "Agitate ! Agitate ! " Inform and enlighten, disarm hostility and create confidence : this was the mission he set himself and this was the policy he enjoined on each and every one of his millions of followers.

But the power of the word, great as was his faith in it, would not of itself, he knew, bring down the Walls of Jericho.

The immediate obstacle to successful agitation was the Convention Act of 1792. It was apparently an insuperable one, for it clearly and definitely made all elected political bodies, outside Parliament and the administration, illegal. In barring delegation, it not only deprived agitation of a permanent organ, but denied it the opportunity to demonstrate its strength in terms of the numbers of its supporters. The Catholics had fallen back on the principle of "Aggregate Meetings," assemblies of notabilities gathered professedly as individuals, and not as delegates. O'Connell seized upon this principle and developed it beyond recognition. He drove his famous " coach-and-six " through the Convention Act, not once, but on every occasion that offered throughout his entire life. Not only did he reconstitute the Catholic Committee on a permanent basis, but he proceeded to plan the organisation of the whole country in county and district branches, to be representative in fact, although not formally elected. In 1811, the Catholic Board, recently established on an elective basis, was proclaimed, and the aggregate principle was once again resorted to. In 1815, the new Catholic Board suffered the same fate. In 1823, O'Connell founded the Catholic Association and immediately put his plan for the nation-wide organisation of the Catholics into operation. If he had done nothing more than take this step, his name would still have won a place in history, for he would have gone down as the founder of the first fully-fledged democratic political party known to the world. Hitherto, the Catholic organisation had been a loose aggregation of the country gentry and the wealthier merchants of the large towns. Now, the entire Catholic population was called in, enrolled in parish branches, officered by the priests, regimented in effect behind O'Connell. It was divided into two elements : the members, paying an annual subscription of one guinea, and the associates (that is, the entire adult section of the seven million Catholics of Ireland), paying one penny each per month. Its foundation was the decisive step in O'Connell's career. With three-quarters of the population marshalled in iron discipline behind him and the inexhaustible war-chest at his disposal, nothing but the actual exercise of physical force against him could put him down ; and this force could not be used so long as he kept within the bare letter of the law. This " litigious and dissatisfied obedience " he never ceased to give, and the government of Ireland found itself henceforth in a situation it had never occupied before, in all the six centuries of Anglo-Irish relations : forced to watch the growth of a nation-wide movement of liberation, in the open daylight, before its own very eyes, and powerless to intervene without producing an effect the opposite to that desired. Banning O'Connell's associations proved worse than useless : each Proclamation brought a change of name to the prohibited body, a new flow of recruits and a fillip to popular enthusiasm. When the Catholic Association was proclaimed in 1825, the New Catholic Association immediately took its place and the tempo of agitation quickened further. This was the Jugger-naut that rolled over the Beresfords in 1826, into Monaghan and Louth directly afterwards, and finally crashed into

Clare in that momentous July of 1828. By popular combination and the power of the war-chest, the greatest turning-manoeuvre in Irish history was achieved : the sanction of eviction which lay behind the landlord's injunction to his tenant-voter was fatally impaired. That vast peaceful army, bivouacked around the town of Ennis on those summer nights, opened " a prospect tremendous indeed."

This immense organisation, with its hierarchy of Repeal Wardens and Inspectors in the place of the priests, was at his disposal once again in the long campaign against the Union. As before, his ingenuity was to hold the Convention Act at bay, but on this occasion, he led the Castle into a ludicrous contest. In October, 1830, his "Anti-Union Association " was proclaimed before it was fully established. It was promptly succeeded by " The Irish Volunteers for the Repeal of the Union." This was immediately proclaimed. He then established " Repeal Breakfasts " at Holmes' Hotel, Dublin, each one called ostensibly for the benefit of some private charity. " If the Government think fit to proclaim down political breakfasts," said he, " then we will resort to a political lunch. If the luncheon be equally dangerous to the peace of the great duke, we shall have political dinners. If political dinners be proclaimed down, we must, like certain sanctified dames, resort to ' tea-and-tracts,' leaving us still to fall back upon the right to meet at suppers, until suppers also be proclaimed down." The provisions of the law could not be extended to cover breakfasts, so a legal agency was brought into existence to carry on agitation in the intervals between the proclamation of one association and the establishment of another. The " Breakfast " appealed strongly to continental Radicals : " Reform Breakfasts " precipitated the downfall of the July Monarchy in February, 1848. In January, 1831, came "A General Association for Ireland to Prevent Illegal Meetings." It was banned on the following day. O'Connell then constituted himself " The Repeal Association," as one man could not be dispersed by any proclamation ! His assistants he styled "A Body of Persons in the habit of meeting weekly at breakfast at a place called Holmes' Hotel."

It was banned. The "Anti-Union Association " was resur-
rected. It was banned. Next day, came "An Association
of Irish Volunteers for the Repeal of the Union." The ban
followed. Then came "An Association of Subscribers to the
Parliamentary Intelligence Office." It again was proclaimed, but came up again as "A Party Meeting for Dinner
at Hayes' Tavern." As it was now evident to the exasperated
Castle that O'Connell was prepared to exhaust all the com-
binations of which the contents of the dictionary are capable,
a comprehensive Proclamation was issued against the meeting of any party, club, society, association or body, calling
itself by any name whatsoever. O'Connell continued alone
and turned every function he attended into a public meeting.
" Things are now come to that pass," declared the Lord
Lieutenant, " that the question is whether he or I shall
govern Ireland."

When the agitation was fully resumed in April, 1840, the
government declined to begin again this game of blindman's
buff with O'Connell, and the " National Association of
Ireland," renamed the " Loyal National Repeal Association " in 1841, was allowed to go its way. Members of all
classes of society, peasants, merchants, landlords, peers,
priests and bishops, flocked into it and paid their subscriptions. By the beginning of 1843, all plans were ready for
the great, final agitation, which was to rise to fever heat
during the summer and autumn of that year, before the
blow fell on the October morning with the proclamation
of the Monster Meeting projected for Clontarf. Never
before in the history of any European country had peaceful
assemblages of such dimensions been brought together for
a political purpose : at Mullingar, 150,000 ; at Mallow,
400,000 ; at Tara, 800,000, or a million, according to
The Times ; at Lismore, 400,000 ; at Mullaghmast, 400,000.
Never were such displays of oratory known. Bulwer Lytton
sought to communicate his experience :

> " Then did I learn to seize the sudden clue
> To the grand troublous life antique—to view,
> Under the rock-stand of Demosthenes,
> Mutable Athens heave her noisy seas."

It was the very peak of O'Connell's success. The long years of training had produced their results among the Irish. Not even an accident disturbed the perfect order of the tremendous gatherings. He had his own police, " O'Connell's Police," their designation inscribed on their hatbands, to direct and marshal the assembled thousands and to watch for the slightest indication of danger to the peace, but none ever arose. Throughout the country, too, in this year of 1843, the statistics of crime reached the lowest level yet known. Self-government was now a moral fact.

But the police force was not the only adjunct of administration developed during this period. The dismissal by the Lord Chancellor of the magistrates who had attended Repeal meetings gave O'Connell the idea of establishing his own courts of justice. He set up Arbitration Courts all over the country, presided over by the dismissed magistrates, and having a jurisdiction roughly equivalent to those of petty sessions and quarter sessions combined, and to these the people began to bring their disputes. He had plans for an extension of the principle to matters cognisable by the High Courts of Judicature and boasted that he would in time empty the halls of the Four Courts. The nature of these new courts, together with the fact that they did not administer oaths, entailed no breach of law, in O'Connell's opinion ; but, on the question of their legality, no decision stands.

The need of the people for training in the practice of representative government impelled O'Connell into the Radical agitation for Municipal Reform which culminated in the English Municipal Corporations Act of 1835, followed by a similar measure for Ireland in 1840. Democratisation of the municipal franchise altered the character of the representation immediately : henceforth, the local elective bodies became, as he intended them to become, " the normal schools of agitation " and the local parliaments of the people. At the end of 1841, he was elected Lord Mayor of Dublin, the first Catholic to occupy the position since the Revolution of 1688, and, in February, 1843, the

Corporation approved by a majority of twenty-six his motion to petition for Repeal. A few days later, the Corporation of Cork adopted the resolution.

To crown this work of giving Ireland, in the words of Gavan Duffy, " the form as well as the bulk of a nation," came the " Plan for the Renewed Action of the Irish Parliament." This entailed, in effect, the establishment of a shadow parliament in Dublin, consisting of three hundred members, representative of all the boroughs and counties of Ireland. The " Council of Three Hundred " would be " selected " by the householders of these districts ; they would assemble in Dublin " by accident " and could " dissolve themselves the next day, if the law requires it " ; they would establish a treasury for the Irish Fund, and there was no reason why they should not be accepted " as a Conciliation Board "—" not sitting as deputies, but merely happening to have the confidence of localities," " and we fancy," said the *Nation*, " their advice will pass for law with the people." Their chief function would be the discussion of the " Plan for the Renewed Action " of the legislature which would follow Repeal, and they might be kept in being to discuss with the British Cabinet the details of arrangements for the transfer of powers, as soon as the latter decided to accede to the Irish demand.

Throughout the " Repeal Year," O'Connell never attended Parliament. He had put a motion for Repeal before the House of Commons in 1834, and received the support of one English member. After this disastrous repulse, he never again submitted the question to debate in the House. By 1843, he was convinced that success depended on " ourselves alone." Outside assistance in any shape ought not, he had learned, to be depended upon. But, although he neglected Parliament at this stage, and remained in Ireland to concentrate on the work of organisation and agitation at home, he was not prepared to adopt that policy which has since become familiar to us by the name of Abstention. In 1845, he indeed toyed with it, but eventually rejected it through misgivings on its legality.

The technique which O'Connell brought to perfection in this stirring year of 1843 was the chief agent of his world-wide fame. He had been consulted by English Radicals outside Parliament, desirous to discover how far they might with safety imitate his methods of constitutional agitation. His great meetings were copied by the supporters of the Reform Bill and later on by the Chartists ; they produced in Spain the revolution that expelled the Duke of Victory ; agitation became the vogue in France, in Hungary, in Vienna, over most of Germany and in Italy ; few regions of western Europe escaped the contagion of excitement which was to boil over in 1848, the " Year of Revolutions." O'Connell's progress fascinated. Such gigantic unrest in Ireland could not, to the mind of Europe and America, but be the prelude to a national revolt. It is one of the major paradoxes in the world's history that a man who was so averse, conscientiously and temperamentally, to Revolution, should have, in effect, stimulated so much revolutionary excitement at home and abroad.

What made O'Connell's technique so remarkable is not so much originality of conception in its elements, as his use of these elements and the skill with which he co-ordinated them. Indeed, the only really new element of strategy employed was the Arbitration Court, and this he owed to the accident of the Lord Chancellor's dismissal of the magistrates. It is easy to trace the original of the Council of Three Hundred back through Wolfe Tone's Catholic Convention of 1792 and the French National Assembly of 1789 to the Colonial Congress of Philadelphia. The Monster Meeting is but a development of the old English institution of assembly for the purpose of petitioning. The capture of the corporations represents nothing more than an extension of the principles of political strategy from the parliamentary arena to that of local government. The idea of a popular police was readily suggested by the National Guard. The newspaper alliance was nothing new. The Reading-rooms suggest indebtedness to the Jacobin Clubs, as does the general rigidity of the organisation, with its wardens, its district inspectors and county inspectors, and the concentration of control in the central committee in Dublin. Nor can the principle of the party-fund have been completely new, although O'Connell's mode of collecting it and his extensive use of the proceeds on publicity were unprecedented. He made his own of every borrowed conception, adapting it to the needs of peaceful agitation and using it, at one and the same time, as an agency in training the Irish people in nationhood and demonstrating that nationhood to his opponents and to the world.

In what sense was he mistaken and in what undeniably right in his reliance on purely non-violent methods?

In relation to the immediate attainment of Repeal, he completely failed and in his belief in the immediate efficacy of his methods to that end, he was in error : that is a historic fact. The reason for the failure is plain : Great Britain would hear of no Repeal, and her decision was final. At any time in the nineteenth century, the dissolution of the Union could have come in one way only : by the military defeat of the British Empire. O'Connell's faith in the power of moral force was excessive, when considered in relation to the immediate attainment of objectives. He was misled by the false analogy of the Emancipation triumph ; he forgot that in 1828, he enjoyed the support of a wide section of English opinion, which included the parliamentary Radicals to a man ; he forgot that Emancipation was a much less terrifying prospect to most of its opponents than Repeal became ; he forgot that constitutional practice demanded the admission of the duly-elected Member for Clare, while the very existence of the Constitution seemed endangered by the demand for Repeal. But his optimism appears in truer proportions when related to long-term results. The administration of Thomas Drummond stands proof of a measure of success in the conversion of English opinion even in his own lifetime : it represents indeed, the first twinge of the English public conscience on the score of the administration of Irish affairs. The very restiveness of the Young Irelanders was a tribute to the success of his other great aim. But the fruition was to increase with every generation that has passed since his death. The exercise of moral force was resumed by the Irish parliamentarians and the work of education, conciliation and conversion went on. The public mind of Great Britain underwent a great change within a lifetime of the tragic fall of O'Connell, and to no one is that change more due than to O'Connell's great posthumous convert, William Ewart Gladstone. "My mission is to pacify Ireland." Moral force had very nearly succeeded by 1914, and the part it played in the struggle which ended the Union on the 6th December, 1921, was decisive.

As the years pass, and the lessons of history pile up, judgments alter on the significance of many events and many men. O'Connell's reputation has had its vicissitudes. When all Europe, including Ireland, resorted to the arbitrament of arms, it was inevitable that names associated with the principle of moral suasion should come under a cloud. But the cloud passes with the storm. When O'Connell said that liberty is not worth a drop of human blood, he spoke in riddle, and the true meaning of his words has taken a hundred years to make itself fully clear. The Revolution began with a reliance on violence as a means. Unanchored in objective law, it soon became confused as to its ends. It forgot, too, that means condition ends. Faith in the underlying harmony of Nature wavered under the impact of the revolutionary wars ; the miseries of the industrial revolution, the *machtphilosophie* of Hegel, the new Darwinian biological conceptions, shattered the ideal. Nature emerged " red in tooth and claw," survival became the sole end, violence the principle of life.

It was only one year after O'Connell's death that Karl Marx announced his gospel of organised anarchism to the world. The old Harmony of Nature had now become the Principle of Revolutionary Preservation : destroy indiscriminately, place no restraint on violence, because only what is false will disappear, the true and permanent things will survive. The land-mine and the petrol-can would renew again the face of the earth. The great enemies to this beneficent process were the " reforming politicians,"

whom Georges Sorel denounces in his *Reflections on Violence* ;
they impeded the progress of Revolution by removing
political and social evils piecemeal, instead of allowing them
to pile up until they became unbearable.   Hence the Red
revolt that destroyed the Second Republic and drove the
conservatives into the arms of Louis Napoleon.   Hence
the bomb that killed Alexander II.   Hence the consistent
attacks upon the very principle of rational liberty in
every country to which this Nihilist blight has spread.   The
Revolution, we learned at school, " devoured its own
children."   It has since devoured much more : it has
devoured every single one of its ideals ; it has devoured
everything except its hate.   And that hate it vents to-day
on the tormented peoples of Europe, upon the millions of
slave-labourers and forced migrants and the masses who
try to flee westwards from it.   Of the famous trilogy,
Liberty, Equality, Fraternity, it has now only one to offer :
Equality—equality in despair.

When O'Connell spoke his hyperbole, the fullness of its
significance could not have been appreciated even by himself.   But he well knew the core of truth it contained :
liberty shrinks from the presence of violence, she shrivels
in its atmosphere.   Arms may, in certain circumstances, be
an indispensable adjunct to a campaign against oppression,
but they never cease to be a danger, for they debase the
moral currency.   Short-cuts are always tempting, and
physical force often seems the shortest of short-cuts.   To
freedom, there are no short-cuts : it must exist within
before it can exist without : it cannot be imposed.

CATHOLIC EMANCIPATION

Rev Patrick Rogers

When on 13th April, 1829, George IV gave his most ungracious assent to the Catholic Relief Bill sponsored by the Wellington ministry, Daniel O'Connell acquired the title which has ever since retained the sanction of popular usage. In his day the enthusiasm of friends and the rancour of opponents conferred on him a variety of appellations. The Irish countryfolk spoke admiringly of " the counsellor"; writers in the nationalist press lauded " the man of the people "; Tories, aroused from their complacency, denounced " the big beggarman," and Lord Shrewsbury, whom he had emancipated, went a degree farther in hailing him " king of the beggars." Today, these appellations are familiar only to the student of history. Over more than a century the people of Ireland have thought and talked of O'Connell as " the liberator." The title has not proved an entirely happy choice. Its appropriateness has been challenged, and, at the other extreme, its implications have been exaggerated. Critics of the Emancipation Act have striven to show that the concessions here gained were harmful to the cause of Irish nationalism. A measure, they argue, which rendered a minority of upper-class Catholics eligible for admission to an alien legislature and for the plums of office in the service of an alien government while at the same time the mass of the people was disfranchised, cannot be regarded as endowing the person responsible for it with the status of a liberator of his country. On the contrary, it spells his condemnation for diverting Irish political endeavour into the channel of British parliamentarianism. The O'Connell of the critics is simply a Catholic lawyer-politician whose illusory, though strangely enduring, fame rests on his achievement in forcing the English cabinet to open avenues of advancement to Catholic lawyers and politicians and their kind. Against this must be set the O'Connell of the " altars free " legend who is credited with abolishing the penal code and depriving the priest-hunter of his livelihood.

Both O'Connells are wrongly drawn. The critics have erred through short-sightedness. Their field of vision does not extend beyond the clauses of the Emancipation Act, and the figure which emerges is stunted. It is, however, less of a caricature than the legendary O'Connell, now a dim outline unlikely to survive the present generation since the teaching of Irish history is no longer neglected in our schools. In determining O'Connell's rank as " liberator " we must not be content with conclusions based solely on a legal evaluation of his achievement in 1829. Such an evaluation has to be made, but, taken by itself, it will prove inadequate for our purpose. The greatness of O'Connell arises not so much from the radical change which he effected in the law of England as from the means by which he brought this change about, his introduction into politics of the deciding factor of organised Irish democracy.

The Catholic Relief Act of 1829 was the outcome of a very determined campaign to obtain the repeal of certain disabilities imposed by law on the Catholics of Ireland and Great Britain. By the beginning of the nineteenth century, when the Anglo-Irish parliamentary union came into force, the Irish Catholics had advanced a considerable way towards complete emancipation. Subject to a few humiliating but comparatively unimportant restrictions they enjoyed freedom of worship, and they were allowed to provide their own schools. The relief acts of 1792 and 1793, passed by the Irish parliament in the last phase of its existence, removed most of the social and economic barriers which had hemmed them in. With respect to the acquisition and disposal of land they were placed on an equality with Protestants. They could become barristers and solicitors, members of grand and petty juries and of corporations. They were made eligible for appointment to the magistracy and to all except specified positions in the government service, and, if possessed of a forty-shilling freehold, they were entitled to vote at parliamentary and municipal elections. In the interests of Protestant ascendancy, however, important disabilities were retained. Catholics were debarred from membership of both houses of the Irish parliament, from the higher offices in the civil administration and from the posts of sheriff and sub-sheriff of counties. A Catholic lawyer could not be admitted to the inner bar nor to the judicial bench. In the Irish military establishment, promotion for a Catholic officer ended with the grade of colonel. A Catholic student was allowed to graduate in Trinity College, Dublin, the only institution in the country which provided university education, but not to hold any of its scholarships nor positions of emolument. Of their nature these disabilities primarily concerned Catholics of the upper and middle classes, but exclusion from the legislature had far-reaching consequences. Owing to the wide interpretation given to the term " forty-shilling freehold " very many Catholic tenants—their number has been calculated as 30,000—were enfranchised. The practice of subletting farms was encouraged by landlords anxious to increase the number of voters on their estates with the result that the county electorate became predominantly Catholic. The anomaly of withholding from this electorate the right of being represented by Catholic members was the fundamental defect for which men differing so widely in outlook as Grattan and Wolfe Tone condemned the relief act of 1793.

During the seven years of life which remained to the Irish parliament the Catholics twice entertained hopes that the defect would be removed. After the outbreak of war with revolutionary France the aristocratic Whigs offered their support to Pitt's Tory government, and their leader, the duke of Portland, was given charge of the department of home affairs which included the Irish administration. In December, 1794, one of the Portland Whigs, Earl Fitzwilliam, became lord-lieutenant of Ireland. Fitzwilliam, a popular Irish landowner, was believed to share his friend Grattan's views on the necessity of complete emancipation, and his appointment led to a revival of agitation among the Irish Catholics. When he arrived in Dublin in January, 1795, the agitation had reached such a pitch that he thought it advisable to support Grattan in bringing a comprehensive relief bill before parliament. Unfortunately in this he showed himself guilty of a twofold error of judgment. He took for granted the approval of the English cabinet, and he underestimated the influence of the ascendancy diehards led by Lord Chancellor Fitzgibbon and John Claudius Beresford. The Fitzwilliam episode, as the events of his short tenure of office came to be known, makes a complicated story of intrigue and clashes between two great family-connections into which it is unnecessary to digress. Pressure was brought to bear on the king and the prime minister with results fatal to the Catholic cause and the peace of Ireland. It proved no difficult matter for the ultra-Protestant faction to persuade George III that he could not sanction the admission of Catholics to parliament without violating his coronation oath and to arouse Pitt's jealousy of his Whig allies. Portland became alarmed and instructed Fitzwilliam that consideration of the Catholic question would have to be postponed indefinitely. In March, Fitzwilliam was removed from office. The change of policy which this was taken to denote was not lost on the Irish parliament which had been on the whole favourably disposed towards emancipation.[1] At the beginning of May, Grattan's relief bill was rejected on its second reading in the commons by 155 votes to 84. The Catholics had suffered their first disillusionment, and many of them, despairing of constitutional methods, joined the societies of United Irishmen which by this time were in process of conversion into a revolutionary organisation. Henceforward the question of emancipation held little interest for the Irish parliament, and the next three years witnessed the establishment of a regime of savage coercion which hastened the outbreak of rebellion.

The rebellion failed, but its seriousness gave Pitt the opportunity of introducing the scheme, long favoured by him, of a union of the British and Irish parliaments. The recent trend of events had deepened his conviction that union was an essential safeguard for the integrity of the

[1] W. E. H. Lecky, *History of Ireland in the eighteenth century*, iii, p. 287.

empire and that it would prove successful only if accompanied by the grant of emancipation. In the first place, he desired a union " not with a party but with the Irish nation," and for this the good-will of the Catholics would have to be secured. In the second, he hoped that their chief temptation to disloyalty would thereby be removed. An imperial parliament which offered them representation through members of their own religion must, it seemed to him, have claims on their allegiance which they could not be expected to concede to a national but exclusively Protestant parliament with a freshly inscribed record of persecution to its discredit. Moreover, the established Protestantism of the British constitution had nothing to fear from such a concession. Catholic members would never form other than an inconsiderable minority in the imperial parliament, while discretion in the use of government patronage could prevent the appointment of Catholics to offices for which they might be eligible in law. The scheme was well conceived from the view-point of an English statesman and might have had a temporary measure of success, though the rising spirit of nationality would never have allowed the Irish people to accept it as the final settlement of their political aspirations. It was not put to the test. Circumstances deterred Pitt from advocating emancipation as the corollary of the union. He had every reason to fear the hostility of the king, whose conscience remained as scrupulously Protestant as it had been in 1795, and his position was further weakened by the cleavage of opinion in the Irish administration. The lord-lieutenant, Lord Cornwallis, and the chief secretary, Lord Castlereagh, were in favour of wide concessions to the Catholics, but Fitzgibbon, now earl of Clare, insisted on a union " unencumbered with the doctrines of emancipation." In the long run, Clare's influence prevailed, and Pitt consented to the drafting of a bill of union which retained the disabilities on Catholics. At the same time, the Irish Catholics were led to believe that emancipation was not far distant. Cornwallis and Castlereagh were authorised by the cabinet to win their support for the bill, and, while no specific

promise was given, the negotiations conducted with the
leading Catholics created the general impression that the
disabilities would be abolished by act of the united parliament. The majority of the bishops and of the nobility
commended the union.[1] The parochial clergy for the most
part remained silent, but Catholics of the professional
classes were loud in their denunciations. It was at a protest
meeting of the Dublin Catholics held in the Royal Exchange
in January, 1800, that O'Connell delivered his first political
speech. He repudiated the assertion that the Catholics
of Ireland were prepared to support the union in the hope
of gaining emancipation from the British parliament.

" They will show every friend of Ireland," he continued, " that the Catholics are incapable of selling their
country. They will loudly declare that if their emancipation were offered for their consent to the measure—
even were emancipation after the union a benefit—they
would reject it with prompt indignation."[2]

The occasion for indignation was not to arise until almost
twenty-nine years had passed. After the union was safely
carried, Pitt proposed measures for the admission of Catholics
to parliament and the high offices of government, together
with a scheme for the state payment of the Catholic clergy.
He met with uncompromising opposition from Lord
Loughborough, the English lord chancellor. Loughborough
took the obvious course of appealing to the king, whose
confidence he possessed, and the king responded as he had
done six years previously. At the court levee of 18th
January, 1801, he announced that he would regard as his
personal enemy any minister who proposed concessions to
the Catholics, and later he wrote to the speaker of the

---

[1] Among the Catholics the chief supporters of the union were Archbishop
Troy of Dublin, Bishop Moylan of Cork and the earls of Kenmare and Fingall.
The other three archbishops and twelve of the bishops either wrote or signed
petitions in its favour; seven seem to have expressed no opinion, and only
Bishop Young of Limerick opposed it.
T. A. Burke, " The Irish Catholics and the legislative union, 1800 " in
Bulletin of the Irish committee of historical sciences, no. 33. (May, 1944.)

[2] J. O'Connell (ed.), *The select speeches of Daniel O'Connell* (Dublin, n.d.),
i, p. 9. (Hereafter referred to as *Select speeches*.)

house of commons that Pitt must not even broach the subject. The situation was made more difficult for Pitt by the king's mental condition, which had recently been giving his physicians considerable anxiety. There seemed imminent danger of a return of the insanity which had brought about a constitutional crisis in 1788, and George, who was unpleasantly aware of this, put the blame on the prime minister. Pitt resigned office, but made it clear that in future he would cause his sovereign no worry over the Catholic question. George III's reason was saved for the time being, and the Irish Catholics were again disillusioned.

The position of the Catholics of Great Britain was even more unsatisfactory. In England and Wales since 1791 and in Scotland since 1793 they had been permitted to practise their religion, to establish schools, to enter the legal profession and to acquire and dispose of real estate,[1] but they remained excluded from parliament, from voting at parliamentary and municipal elections and from holding any position under the crown or in corporations. The legal basis for these disabilities was provided by three statutes enacted in the reign of Charles II and implemented by subsequent legislation.[2] The Corporation Act of 1661 (13 *Chas. II*, 2, c. 1), though intended by the "cavalier" parliament to exclude Protestant nonconformists from the control of towns, had an equally penalising effect on Catholics. Each person elected or appointed to office in a corporation was obliged to take the oath of allegiance and abjuration and the oath of supremacy and to receive " the sacrament of the Lord's Supper according to the rites of the church of England "—conditions which no Catholic could accept in their entirety without a practical denial

[1] The clauses of the 1791 relief act which dealt with education were vaguely phrased and almost contradictory, but in practice Catholics were allowed to establish schools of their own. Their position with regard to acquiring and disposing of property was explained by Sir Robert Peel in his speech of 5th March, 1829 : " The penal laws as to property still survive, and the Roman Catholics are only relieved from their operation upon taking the oaths with certain formalities which are required by the several acts which relate to this subject." Hansard, *Parliamentary Debates*, xx, 757.

[2] There were earlier penal enactments against Catholics which these statutes re-imposed.

of his religious faith.[1] The other two statutes of the reign
were framed as specifically anti-Catholic measures. The
effect of the Test Act of 1673 (25 *Chas. II*, c. 2) was to make
communion with the church of England and repudiation
of Catholic doctrine a condition of eligibility to all civil
and military offices.[2] The act required of each office-
holder in the government service not only the oaths
already mentioned and the reception of the sacrament
of the Lord's Supper but subscription to the following
declaration :

> " I . . . do declare that I do believe that there is not
> any transubstantiation in the sacrament of the Lord's
> Supper or in the elements of bread and wine at or after
> the consecration thereof by any person whatsoever."[3]

The penalties for non-compliance were very severe and
included a fine of £500 in addition to forfeiture of the office
held. The " black charter of Protestantism," as the act
has been called, did not affect the position of Catholics in
parliament, but, five years later, they were brought under
the ban of the law. The Test Act of 1678 (30 *Chas. II*,
2, *c.* 1) declared that, before admission to parliament, each
peer and member of the house of commons was obliged
to take the oaths of allegiance and supremacy and to testify,
also on oath, his disbelief in transubstantiation and his
firm conviction that

> " the invocation or adoration of the Virgin Mary or
> any other saint and the sacrifice of the Mass, as they are
> now used in the church of Rome, are superstitious and
> idolatrous."[4]

[1] The oath of allegiance and abjuration was offensive insofar as a person
was made abjure " as impious and heretical the damnable doctrine that
princes which be excommunicated or deprived by the pope may be deposed
or murdered by their subjects or any other whatsoever." The oath of
supremacy could not be taken by a Catholic because it denied the spiritual
and ecclesiastical authority of the pope within the realm of England. Reception of " the sacrament " was equivalent to a declaration of adherence to the
established church.

[2] C. Grant Robertson, *Select statutes, cases and documents* (London, 1923),
p. 81.

[3] Quoted in Grant Robertson, p. 84.

[4] Quoted in Grant Robertson, p. 87.

Failure to make these declarations was attended by the penalties decreed in the earlier Test Act. From 1st December, 1678 to 28th April, 1829, no Catholic sat in either house of parliament.[1] The constitutional changes which followed from the Protestant Revolution of 1688 led to an alteration in the forms of the oaths, but, as was only to be expected, the clauses unacceptable by Catholics were retained.[2] During the reign of William III the Catholics were deprived of the last vestige of political influence through the restriction of the franchise to persons who took the oaths of allegiance and supremacy.[3] Socially, the grievance which caused them most humiliation was imposed in 1752. In accordance with the Marriage Act of this year (26 *Geo. II, c.* 33), no marriage was valid in civil law except it had been solemnised before a clergyman of the established church. To safeguard the rights of any children that might be born to them, Catholics were compelled, after their marriage before a priest, to repeat their vows in the Protestant parish church and observe the ritual of the book of common prayer.[4] Estates held by Catholics were subject to a double land-tax and to tithes. The latter, however, was a burden which fell equally on all occupiers of land, irrespective of their religion.

Between the legislative union of 1800 and the passing of the Catholic Relief Act of 1829, the policy of excluding Catholics from the government service was modified in one particular. The provisions of the first Test Act kept them from obtaining commissions in the army and navy, and by the 1 *William and Mary, c.* 8 the law in this matter was re-stated and extended to include promotion to the lower grades in both services. Towards the end of the eighteenth century the Catholic gentry who had abandoned

---

[1] Catholics were ineligible for election to the Scots parliament simply on the grounds of their religion. By the terms of the Anglo-Scottish parliamentary union of 1707 this direct disqualification was retained for Scots constituencies. E. Porritt, *The Unreformed House of Commons* (Cambridge, 1909), i. pp. 140, 149.

[2] Porritt, i. p. 138.

[3] By the 7 *and* 8 *William III, c.* 27.

[4] O'Connell's parents were married in the Protestant church of the Holy Trinity, Cork.

Jacobitism offered their services to the crown, and, by connivance on the part of the war office and admiralty, they were given some measure of satisfaction. The practice was adopted of permitting Catholics to serve as officers below the rank of captain in the army and commander in the navy, but, when they sought promotion, they were required to take the prescribed oaths and receive the anglican sacrament.[1] With the passing of the Irish relief act of 1793 an anomalous situation was created in the army. So long as his unit remained attached to the Irish establishment, any Catholic officer was eligible for promotion up to a colonelcy. If it were transferred to the English establishment, a Catholic officer above the rank of lieutenant could not accompany it without rendering himself liable to heavy penalties for failure to comply with the law of Great Britain. In the circumstances there were two courses open to him. He might apply for an exchange into a unit which was remaining in Ireland or he could sell his commission. During the revolutionary and Napoleonic wars many Catholics gave distinguished service as junior officers,[2] but the injustice which denied them advancement was not removed until two years after Waterloo. In 1817, as the outcome of representations made to the prince regent and the first lord of the admiralty by an Irish Catholic officer, Lieutenant Edward Whyte, R.N., the law was modified to such an extent that Catholics became legally entitled to hold commissions and to rise to the command of battalions and ships of war.[3] The enlistment of Catholics had for long been strictly forbidden,[4] but in the struggle against Napoleon the prohibition was removed, and many thousand

[1] W. J. Amherst, *The history of Catholic Emancipation, 1771–1820* (London, 1886), ii, p. 250–69, where the position of Catholics with reference to service in the army and navy is fully discussed.

[2] Among them was Daniel O'Connell's cousin, Lieutenant John O'Connell of the 43rd Regiment, who volunteered for the "forlorn hope" attack on Badajoz (6th April, 1812) where he was severely wounded. He fell in action at the storming of St. Sebastian (31st August, 1813). *Select speeches*, i, pp. 326–7.

[3] By the 57 *Geo. III, c.* 92. Amherst, pp. 264–9. Until the passing of the Emancipation Act of 1829 promotion for Catholics ended in the army with the rank of colonel and in the navy with that of post-captain.

[4] Lecky, i, pp. 416–7.

Irish Catholics joined the army or were conscripted for the fleet. Their service was made particularly irksome by the regulation which obliged them to attend divine service conducted by the Protestant chaplains.[1] A tolerant commanding officer could grant them exemption, but not all commanding officers were noteworthy for their broadmindedness.

The history of the emancipation movement during the first twenty-three years of the nineteenth century is most involved. In Ireland the direction of Catholic affairs was undertaken by a committee drawn mainly from the gentry. So long as the Addington ministry remained in power, it would have been useless to make any representations to parliament, but the recall of Pitt to office in 1804 gave the Catholics some reason for hope. Three years before, he had resigned the premiership, ostensibly at least, because of the king's refusal to allow him to carry emancipation, and they felt that in the present circumstances he would have an opportunity of introducing the measure. The Catholic Committee appointed a deputation consisting of five peers (two of them representing the English Catholics), a baronet and two lawyers to ask him to lay a statement of their claims before parliament. Disillusion once more followed. Pitt had attained his purpose when the union became law, and he no longer felt any necessity for placating the Catholics. He informed the deputation that the king's unalterable opposition to further concessions had settled the matter once and for all, and that he himself was prepared to resist any measure of emancipation brought forward in parliament. The deputation then turned to the Whig statesman, Charles James Fox, who consented to act on their behalf. With Grattan's support Fox proposed in the commons a motion in favour of Catholic relief, but the

---

[1] This injustice was condemned in the case of the Irish military establishment by Bishop Hussey of Waterford and Lismore in his celebrated pastoral letter of 1797. John Healy, *Maynooth College: Its Centenary History* (Dublin, 1895), pp. 175, 694.

Its prevalence in the British establishment drew a similar expression of opinion from Bishop Milner, vicar apostolic of the Midland district, in his pamphlet on the Catholic claims, issued in 1805.

house rejected it by 336 votes to 124. A similar motion introduced in the upper house by Lord Grenville was also rejected. The Catholic gentry had failed, and any chance of redeeming their failure seemed lost after the death of Fox in 1806.

From the beginning the Irish Catholic Committee had been divided over the question of petitioning parliament. The veteran leader, John Keogh, now living in semi-retirement at Mount Jerome, had abandoned his faith in the British parliament and regarded any overtures to that body as futile and likely to bring ridicule on the Catholic cause. He was of opinion that, for the time being at any rate, the Catholics should content themselves with the rights which, largely through his energetic policy, had been gained in 1793. It was almost a counsel of despair for which the political situation lent some justification. The gentry, chastened by their late rebuffs, sided with their former opponent, but there was one section of the Committee which refused to be discouraged. A small group of Catholic lawyers was coming into prominence by their advocacy of a " forward " policy, and with them, or rather with the ablest member of the group, the guidance of the movement for emancipation was to lie. O'Connell, whose reputation in the courts had already made him a national figure, led the opposition to Keogh. The decisive encounter took place at a meeting of the Catholic Committee summoned to consider a petition asking parliament for the total abrogation of all penal laws. An amendment was proposed to the effect that the Catholics should watch " in dignified silence " the course of events and the conduct of their friends in parliament. Keogh was not present, but the amendment had obviously been inspired by him. At the close of the debate O'Connell delivered a vigorous speech in support of the petition which, he maintained, the great majority of the Irish Catholics wished to have presented. His only anxiety for the Catholic cause arose from " the spirit of division and the miserable ambition of leadership " which seemed likely to make the Committee " the object of disgust to their friends and the scorn and ridicule of their enemies." With the wealth of invective that characterised his public utterances he called for unity in the face of a hostile administration.

" If the Catholics continue loyal, firm and undivided," he assured his audience, " they had little to fear from the barren petulance of the ex-advocate, Perceval, or the frothy declamations of the poetaster, Canning—they might meet with equal contempt the upstart pride of the Jenkinsons and with more than contempt the pompous inanity of that Lord Castlereagh who might well be permitted to hate the country that gave him birth to her own annihilation."[1]

No such defiant language had been heard at a Catholic meeting since the days of Keogh's agitation in 1793. Its boldness won over the Committee, and by an unanimous resolution the petition was accepted and forwarded to Grattan. Its rejection by parliament did not in the least dishearten O'Connell. He had gained his point in securing the Committee's approval of the continuance of agitation, and with this he was for the time content.

Emancipation, however, was not the only scheme to which he devoted his energies. The treatment of Ireland by the British parliament since the union had persuaded him that her economic interests could be served only by a repeal of that act. It was not a conviction which remained unshaken throughout his political career, but at the moment he was greatly influenced by it. He even went so far as to proclaim his willingness to abandon emancipation in favour of a campaign for the restoration of the Irish parliament. At a repeal meeting held in Dublin on 18th September, 1810, he made the startling pronouncement :

" I trample under foot the Catholic claims if they can interfere with the repeal ; I abandon all wish for emancipation if it delays that repeal. Nay, were Mr. Perceval tomorrow to offer me the repeal of the union upon the terms of re-enacting the entire penal code, I declare from

[1] *Select speeches*, i, p. 14.

my heart and in the presence of my God that I would most cheerfully embrace his offer."[1]

Before long, circumstances brought him to realise that emancipation would have to precede repeal. When emancipation did come, he was by no means so certain of the absolute necessity of re-establishing Ireland's legislative independence. However we interpret his fluctuating policy in this matter, we must not lose sight of the fact that he regarded emancipation not simply as an act of justice due to the Catholics but as an essential means towards obtaining good government for Ireland either from the British parliament or through a parliament of her own.

There is a dreary sameness about the years of fruitless endeavour which preceded the founding of O'Connell's democratic association in 1823. The Catholic Committee led a troubled existence, changing its name and constitution to safeguard itself from government hostility ; petitions were rejected by parliament with monotonous regularity, but the Catholic question was kept alive and its urgency impressed on the people by the holding of aggregate meetings in the principal towns. One episode of these years demands notice. In May, 1812, Spencer Perceval, the ultra-Protestant prime minister, was assassinated, and Lord Liverpool (the Jenkinson whose upstart pride had roused O'Connell's ire) succeeded him in office. Liverpool was opposed to emancipation, but his ministry included George Canning who at its formation gave notice that he would introduce a Catholic relief bill early in the next session of parliament. The result of a general election strengthened Liverpool's position, but Canning persevered in his intention. A bill which resembled that enacted in 1829 was drawn up with the co-operation of the English Catholic leaders and entrusted to Grattan, who introduced it in the house of commons on 12th April, 1813.[2] It had passed the second reading when an issue was raised which caused

---

[1] *Select speeches*, i, p. 24.
[2] A summary of the main provisions of the bill is given in Charles Butler, *Historical Memoirs of the English Catholics* (London, 1819), ii, pp. 257-8.

bitter dissensions among the Catholics. The proposal of a royal veto on the appointment of Catholic bishops had long commended itself to the Protestant supporters of emancipation and to the aristocratic coterie which under the title of the English Catholic Board assumed the duty of representing the Catholics in Great Britain. Both parties looked on the veto as providing a guarantee of loyalty which, they hoped, would make parliament less suspicious of the Catholic claims. Their attitude was resented in Ireland where the principle of state interference had been debated since 1795.[1] Canning was of opinion that some guarantee of loyalty should be given and, after consultation with Lord Castlereagh, he induced Grattan to insert two clauses in the bill which would have this effect. The clauses were in the nature of a compromise. They provided for the establishment of a body of lay commissioners consisting of Catholic peers who possessed freeholds valued at £1,000 a year. To this body every priest elected to the charge of a vicariate apostolic in Great Britain would have to notify his election, whereupon the commissioners' office was to transmit his name to the privy council with a certificate of his loyalty unless they had reason for refusing such a certificate.[2] A commission, similar in constitution and powers, was to pass judgment on priests elected to Irish bishoprics. In addition both bodies, with the Catholic bishops and certain Protestant officials, were to form censorship boards in the matter of examining all papal documents received in the United Kingdom.[3]

The sincerity of Canning's effort to secure emancipation cannot be doubted, but his proposals were singularly unfortunate. Their immediate effect was to fan into flame the smouldering controversy over the expediency of permitting lay interference in ecclesiastical affairs. The

[1] For an account of the veto controversy see James MacCaffrey, *History of the Catholic Church in the nineteenth century* (Dublin, 1910), ii, pp. 144–62.

[2] Butler, ii, pp. 260–1. At that time, England and Wales were divided into four ecclesiastical districts and Scotland into two. Each district was governed by a vicar apostolic who was in episcopal orders and took the title of some see *in partibus infidelium*. The English hierarchy was re-established in 1850, the Scottish in 1878.

[3] Butler, ii, pp. 261–2.

Catholics arrayed themselves in two implacably hostile camps. The English Catholic Board, whose members continued in the Cisalpine tradition of the past century, welcomed an amendment which would give the aristocracy influence in the selection of the vicars. On the other hand, Bishop Milner, vicar apostolic of the Midland district, denounced this unwarrantable infringement of the Church's liberty and issued a pamphlet in which he insisted that Catholics could never accept emancipation on such terms. He was ill-supported by the other vicars who erred on the side of over-caution, but the Irish bishops unanimously adopted his standpoint. The Irish Catholic laity was divided. As in England, the aristocratic section had no hesitation in supporting the bill. The professional classes, however, were loud in their denunciations. The Irish Catholic Board, under which title the Catholic Committee now functioned, passed a vote of thanks to the bishops for their intransigent attitude towards a measure which, in O'Connell's language, would have degraded prelates to the subserviency of gaugers and priests to the dependency of police constables.[1] Dissatisfaction expressed by so influential a body of Catholic opinion would have convinced parliament of the futility of passing the bill had not a further change in its text led Grattan to withdraw it. Charles Abbot, the speaker of the house of commons, moved, when the house was in committee, that the clause dealing with the admission of Catholics to parliament be deleted, and the amendment was carried by a majority of four. In the opinion of Grattan and his colleagues the bill had now become " worthy neither of the acceptance of the Catholics nor of the further support of the friends of emancipation," and it was withdrawn.[2]

For five years the veto controversy raged with unabated fury, and the Catholics were distracted and disedified by the intrigues of the opposing factions. The English Catholic Board appealed to Rome where their case received most sympathetic consideration from Monsignor Quarantotti,

[1] *Select speeches*,i , p. 168.
[2] Butler, ii, p. 265.

vice-prefect of the congregation *de propaganda fide*. Pius VII was Napoleon's prisoner at Fontainebleau, and Quarantotti had charge of relations with countries, such as Great Britain, which came under the jurisdiction of his congregation. On 16th February, 1814, he published his decision in a rescript addressed to Bishop Poynter, vicar apostolic of the London district. It was strongly in favour of the policy adopted by the English Board. In solemn fashion Quarantotti decreed that the mature judgment of learned prelates and divines authorised the Catholics to accept readily, and indeed gratefully, the measure which had been proposed in parliament for their emancipation[1] and to observe all the conditions attached. Far from settling the controversy, his intervention provoked the wrath of the anti-vetoists. In Ireland the rescript was declared "non-obligatory" by assemblies of indignant clergy, a view endorsed by the bishops without exception, while O'Connell reached a high level of verbal forcefulness in criticising the petty Italian ecclesiastic who interfered in what did not concern him.

When the pope returned to Rome after Napoleon's abdication, an effort was made to have the rescript withdrawn. Bishop Milner and Dr. Murray, coadjutor to the archbishop of Dublin, undertook this mission and were referred by Pius to Cardinal Litta, the recently appointed prefect of the congregation of propaganda. Counter-moves on the part of the English Catholic Board were much assisted by the course of events in Europe. Napoleon escaped from Elba and attempted to re-assume the government of France. The continent was again in turmoil. Murat, the Bonapartist king of Naples, threatened to invade the papal states, and the pope left Rome to retire to Genoa where the British fleet afforded him protection. The situation augured badly for the anti-vetoists. Pius was dependent on the good-will of Britain not only for his personal safety,

---

[1] The Latin of the rescript is most emphatic : " decretum est ut Catholici legem, quae superiore anno rogata fuit pro illorum emancipatione iuxta formam quae ab amplitudine tua relata est, aequo gratoque animo excipiant et amplectantur." Thomas Wyse, *Historical sketch of the late Catholic Association of Ireland* (London, 1829), ii, Appendix, p. xxiii.

but for the restoration of his dominions, and the papal secretary of state, Cardinal Consalvi, made no secret of his anxiety to please Lord Castlereagh. Discussions were prolonged for nearly a year. Meanwhile Irish opposition to the veto hardened. O'Connell spoke with regret of the pope's confidence in the British government and then, changing his tone, bade the Catholics stand firm in their resistance to all suggestions of state interference.

" Let our determination never to assent reach Rome. It can easily be transmitted there ; but even should it fail, I am still determined to resist. I am sincerely a Catholic, but I am not a Papist. I deny the doctrine that the pope has any temporal authority, directly or indirectly, in Ireland. We have all denied that authority on oath, and we would die to resist it. He cannot, therefor, be any party to the act of parliament we solicit, nor shall any act of parliament regulate our faith or our conscience." [1]

Curiously enough, the vetoists were also loud in their assertions that they were Catholics but not " Papists." Both parties seem to have agreed in applying the latter designation to those Catholics—if any such existed—who believed that the papal authority was unlimited in temporal as in spiritual matters.

Cardinal Litta's decision was promulgated on 26th April, 1815. In certain respects it reversed that given by Quarantotti but permitted a veto to the crown on condition that this should not develop into a positive nomination. The new solution of the problem was taken badly in Ireland. The bishops again protested and appealed for a reconsideration. Negotiations dragged on and never attained any satisfactory conclusion. Another crisis seemed likely to arise when in 1821, the year after Grattan's death, his friend, William Plunket, introduced an emancipation bill together with proposals for an indirect form of veto. As a

---

[1] *Select speeches*, i, p. 447. The oath referred to was that which Catholics had to take before they could be admitted to the bar or avail of the concessions granted them by the various relief acts.

result of the rejection of the bill by the lords the crisis was averted, but the principle at stake remained a subject of acute controversy. Obstinacy at Rome encountered obstinacy in Ireland, and the deadlock lasted until the British government, realising that only an unqualified relief bill would be accepted by the Irish people, abandoned all claim to the veto.

At the beginning of 1823 the emancipation movement in Ireland had reached its nadir. The Catholics were thoroughly disheartened. They had lost confidence in parliament. On the two occasions when they expected relief, its promise had been made dependent on conditions which they believed would enslave their clergy. The policy of the Holy See was a constant source of puzzlement and worry to them. Richard Lalor Sheil gives a depressing picture of the Ireland which O'Connell was to raise from lethargy :

> " In 1823 an entire cessation of Catholic meetings had taken place. There was a total stagnation of public feeling, and I do not exaggerate when I say that the Catholic question was nearly forgotten. . . . The country was then in a state of comparative repose, but it was a degrading and unwholesome tranquillity. We sat down like galley slaves in a calm. A general stagnation diffused itself over the national feelings. The public pulse had stopped ; the circulation of all generous sentiment had been arrested, and the country was palsied to the heart."[1]

Only a man endowed with faith in the power of democracy would contemplate an appeal to so dispirited a people, and only a man of immense energy and commanding personality could make such an appeal effective. O'Connell possessed these attributes in a high degree. Twenty-five years of frustrated effort had convinced him that agitation by the Catholics would have to take an entirely different form. The day for humble petitioning had passed and with it

---

[1] Quoted in Denis Gwynn, *The struggle for Catholic emancipation* (London, 1928), pp. 212–3.

the direction of Catholic affairs by oligarchic committees and boards. The future lay with the people. It was for them to present their case at Westminster and demand the repeal of the laws which denied them full citizenship.

The project was so bold as to be almost hopeless. The difficulties of carrying it into action seemed insurmountable. By the terms of the Convention Act of 1793 the Catholics were prevented from electing a body of delegates to speak on their behalf, and no other body would have sufficient authority to impress parliament. An even greater difficulty was presented by the attitude of the people themselves. Living, as they did, in constant dread of the landlord, the tithe proctor and the magistrate, they could scarcely be expected to risk eviction and, perhaps, imprisonment for a cause which appeared remote from the interests of the common man. Over the past quarter of a century they had been surfeited with talk about Catholic emancipation. They were told, or had read in the papers, accounts of debates in the house of commons, of petitions ignored, of relief bills which, if passed, would make their clergy agents of the government. They had flocked to aggregate meetings to hear lawyers, and sometimes priests, denounce a veto which to many of the audience was incomprehensible. And amongst themselves they expressed grave doubts if Catholic emancipation—in the highly improbable event of its attainment—would be of any practical benefit to them. That Catholic gentlemen should be allowed to enter parliament or hold high rank in the army or become judges was unquestionably an object worth striving for—by Catholic gentlemen; but it held little appeal to the Catholic who cultivated his little patch of rack-rented land or worked as a day-labourer in the town.

To the solution of these difficulties O'Connell brought the ability of a subtle lawyer and the prestige of an agitator capable of arousing the people's enthusiasm and retaining their confidence. He boasted that he could drive a coach-and-six through any act of parliament, and he went far to make the boast good. Yet it was not skill in the law, or even in evading the law, which endeared him to his fellow-countrymen, but his reckless defiance of judges and juries and the whole machinery of British rule. The law case which made his name had ended in a verdict against his client. In July, 1813, he defended the newspaper proprietor, John Magee, who was charged with a libel on the duke of Richmond, a former lord-lieutenant of Ireland. From partisan judges and a packed jury there was no chance of obtaining an acquittal, and O'Connell turned his speech for the defence into an impassioned arraignment of the ascendancy clique who were misgoverning the country. Robert Peel, the new under-secretary for Ireland, who was present in court, found it hard to restrain his indignation. In a letter to Lord Whitworth, the viceroy, he described O'Connell's four-hour tirade as " a libel, even more atrocious than that which he had to defend, upon the government and the administration of justice in Ireland."[1] In years to come O'Connell was to afford him more cogent grounds for indignation. Magee was sentenced to fine and imprisonment, and O'Connell became the champion of his oppressed country. His supremacy was not undisputed. Catholics of a conservative turn of mind disapproved of his pugnacity. His stand on the veto question led to the secession from the Irish Catholic Board of the aristocrats and, what was of greater moment, to a serious difference of opinion with Sheil whose ability as lawyer and agitator was second only to his own, but he kept the admiration of the people. Ten years after the Magee trial, whatever hopes of emancipation they retained were centred on him.

A reconciliation with Sheil took place early in 1823, and in May of this year O'Connell founded the Catholic Association of Ireland for the purpose of adopting " all such legal and constitutional measures as may be most useful to obtain Catholic emancipation."[2] In its original form the Association resembled the now defunct Catholic Board. It disclaimed the right to act as a " representative or delegated body " and admitted to membership any

[1] Michael MacDonagh, *Daniel O'Connell and the story of Catholic emancipation* (Dublin, 1929), p. 64.
[2] Thomas Wyse, *Historical sketch of the late Catholic Association of Ireland* (London, 1829), ii, Appendix, p. xxxvii.

person, Catholic or Protestant, who paid an annual subscription of one guinea. The Catholic clergy were to be
ex-officio members without payment of subscription. For
seven months the Association barely managed to keep in
existence. The spell of depression overhung all its forty-
seven members except the founder. "At last," O'Connell's
son wrote, " upon Wednesday the 4th February, 1824, the
spell was broken."[1] O'Connell brought forth his long-
considered plan for making the Association a nation-wide
movement, and persuaded his bewildered and diffident
colleagues to adopt it. A new class of associate members
was to be formed of persons willing to subscribe one shilling
a year " Catholic rent." It was calculated that the
Catholics in Ireland numbered seven millions and, if only
one million of these were enrolled, their contributions would
produce a yearly income of £50,000. Part of this money
was to provide the Association with a campaign fund;
part would be directly expended on the people's behalf in
furnishing legal redress against their oppressors, and the
remainder was to be devoted to religious and charitable
purposes. O'Connell drew up the following scheme of
disbursements :

For parliamentary expenses	£5,000
the services of the press	£15,000
law proceedings in preserving the legal privileges of the Catholics and prosecuting Orange aggressors	£15,000
the purpose of education for the Catholic poor	£5,000
educating Catholic priests for the service of America	£5,000

The surplus of £5,000 was to be allowed to accumulate as
a fund for the building and repair of Catholic churches and
schools.[2]

The scheme met with ridicule at first. John O'Connell,
then a schoolboy, was often annoyed by jeers at his father's

[1] *Select speeches*, ii. p. 274.
[2] Ibid.

" penny-a-month plan for liberating Ireland." But it appealed to the two most important classes in the country— the priests and the men on the land. The clerical tradition of non-intervention in public affairs was dying out. The new generation of priests educated in Maynooth and inspired by the example of Dr. Doyle, bishop of Kildare and Leighlin, became O'Connell's most valued allies. They presided over parish branches of the Association and super-vised the collection of " Catholic rent " at the church doors after Sunday Mass. The people were roused from their torpor when it was brought home to them that the Association catered for their individual needs. Thomas Wyse, who constituted himself historian of the movement, could write with truth :

> " The feeling of the people was awakened. They saw, in their own words, that ' something was to be done for *them* also.' It was not a cold question of distant and doubtful advantage, the readmission of the peerage or the gentry to the privileges of their order, the extension of legal honours and emoluments to the Catholic bar-rister ; but it was the strong and home assurance which every peasant soon had of instant protection against local wrong, the redress of the law against the law, the assisting hand in distress from a body in which he found the interpreter of his own sufferings and the conviction that, whilst others still sought their emancipation, his emanci-pation had already begun." [1]

Underlying all this was their implicit trust in O'Connell. An index to the success of his scheme is given by the increase in the " Catholic rent " from £100 a week in the summer of 1823 to £1,000 a week at the beginning of 1824.

Within two years the Catholic Association had attained such proportions that the government was perturbed. An act was passed for its suppression,[2] and O'Connell got ready his coach-and-six. The New Catholic Association,

---

[1] *Historical sketch of the late Catholic Association,* i, p. 205.
[2] "An act for the suppression of unlawful associations in Ireland," (6 *Geo. IV,* c. 4).

which he established in July, 1825, was directed, according
to its published constitution, " merely for the purposes of
public and private charity " the first of which was the most
laudable one of " promoting public peace and tranquillity
as well as private harmony among all classes of his majesty's
subjects throughout Ireland,"[1] and the " rent " was professedly assigned to the support of a whole range of charitable
causes. No one was deceived. The law was respected and
the agitation continued as before.

The same year saw the failure of the last attempt made
by the Protestant supporters of emancipation to manoeuvre
a relief bill through parliament. Sir Francis Burdett, the
Radical member for Westminster, played Grattan's role.
He was persuaded that without " securities " the bill would
never pass. A re-introduction of veto proposals was out of
the question, but he substituted for them two measures
popularly known as " wings " because " it was hoped by
their aid to float emancipation over the anti-papist prejudices of both houses of the legislature into the haven of
the statute book."[2] These subsidiary measures comprised
a plan of state payment for the Catholic clergy and the
disfranchisement of the Irish forty-shilling freeholders by
raising the voting qualification to a ten-pound freehold. In
a moment of weakness O'Connell agreed to the " wings."
He may be excused for thinking that the disfranchisement of
the rank-and-file of his followers was not too high a price
to pay for emancipation. The Irish forty-shilling freeholders had been the bond-slaves of the landlords. On
election day they were mustered in droves and escorted by
bailiffs to the polling booth to vote in accordance with the
instructions given them. A vote cast against the landlord's
candidate meant the eviction of the voter from his holding.
O'Connell did not fully comprehend how far his agitation
had changed the spirit of the people. He had forged a
weapon the keenness of which was yet hidden from him.

Burdett's relief bill was rejected in the house of lords
and the " wings " had to be abandoned. In the following

[1] Wyse, ii, Appendix, p. xlii.
[2] MacDonagh, p. 145.

year writs were issued for a general election. In Waterford the leaders of the Association—among them Thomas Wyse—decided to oppose the return of Lord George Beresford who was bitterly anti-Catholic. O'Connell disapproved. The Beresfords were the most influential family in Ireland and exercised complete dominion over the constituency. Wyse and his friends insisted on a contest, and O'Connell reluctantly gave way. The Association included many liberal-minded Protestants, and one of these, a Co. Waterford landlord named Henry Villiers Stuart, accepted nomination as its official candidate. For the first time since they had been given the vote in 1793, the Beresford tenants were exhorted to defy their master. They were not asked in vain. Some weeks before the election O'Connell visited Waterford. He was amazed by the changed attitude of the people. The slave mind was gone. In its place was an independence and a daring which banished his misgivings. These men were not to be coerced by threats of eviction. They showed their determination, at all costs, to stand by the Association, and O'Connell became the most enthusiastic speaker at Villiers Stuart's meetings. The contest was a remarkable one. The agents of the Association took elaborate precautions to maintain order, and the resolute and disciplined conduct of their party puzzled the authorities, who were accustomed to very different scenes at election meetings. There was little evidence of drunkenness, which in itself was cause for amazement. In the days before Father Theobald Mathew began his total abstinence crusade, the excitement of an election provided an excuse as well as an occasion for excessive drinking, but few Catholic voters were so deficient in loyalty to their cause, or so unresponsive to the warnings of their priests, as to offend in this manner. The polling went heavily against Beresford. Before the close of the fifth day of voting he retired from the contest, and Villiers Stuart was declared elected. Protestant ascendancy had suffered its first defeat at the hands of Irish democracy. The general election was too far advanced for the adoption of like tactics in many other constituencies, but the Association secured the return of its candidates in

Louth, Monaghan and Westmeath. No Roman proprietor of a *latifundium* could have been more appalled by news of a slave rising than the Irish landlords were by the election returns. Their serfs had revolted, and the most disconcerting aspect of the revolt was its absence of violence. Coercion acts and the employment of police and military were useless when the people would not fight, and the landlords resorted to eviction. They gained nothing beyond the satisfaction of turning recalcitrant tenants out on the roads. O'Connell established an Order of Liberators and opened a special fund for the relief of those penalised, and the revolt became widespread.

The phenomenal development in Irish politics stiffened the government's determination to make no concessions. In January, 1828, a new Tory ministry was formed with the duke of Wellington as premier and Sir Robert Peel as home secretary and chief adviser on Irish affairs. Its declared anti-emancipationist principles drew from the Catholic Association a resolution to oppose the return to parliament of every government supporter. Opportunity for action came in the summer. William Vesey Fitzgerald, one of the members for Co. Clare, was appointed to the presidency of the board of trade and had to seek re-election. He was no Beresford but a popular landlord in the county and a sincere advocate of emancipation. With some reluctance the Association looked for a candidate to oppose him. Major MacNamara, a Protestant landlord, was approached but declined nomination on the grounds of his friendship with Vesey Fitzgerald. At the suggestion of Sir David Rosse, another Protestant member of the Association, O'Connell was persuaded to contest the seat. It was an unprecedented step though, many years before, such action had been proposed by John Keogh as the most effective means of making the English people realise the injustice of excluding Catholics from parliament.[1]

The Clare election was the most memorable episode in the history of nineteenth-century Ireland. The discipline

---

[1] W. J. Fitzpatrick, *Correspondence of Daniel O'Connell* (London, 1888), i, p. 160.

introduced at Waterford was now perfected. The Association's voters were pledged to abstain from whiskey and to avoid giving or taking provocation, and so scrupulously did they observe the pledges that the large forces of police and military drafted into Ennis stood by inactive throughout the contest. The " sobered and desperate enthusiasm "[1] of the forty-shilling freeholders carried O'Connell to victory. When the poll closed on 5th July, he had received 2,057 votes against 982 cast for Vesey Fitzgerald.

O'Connell was member for Clare, but he had given his solemn word that he would never take the oaths required of a member on admission to parliament. The government found itself in a dilemma. What had happened in Clare would be repeated in most Irish constituencies at the next general election unless the forty-shilling freeholders were deprived of their votes. But in the present state of the country disfranchisement without emancipation would almost certainly lead to civil war. The Catholic Association was solidly behind O'Connell ; the ascendancy landlords had formed Brunswick Clubs and were arming the Orangemen in defence of the Protestant constitution, and Lord Anglesey, the viceroy, gave his considered opinion that in the event of civil war neither police nor military could be wholly trusted. Moreover, the problem had ceased to be one of purely British interest. Public opinion in the United States and in France was strongly on the side of the Irish Catholics, and O'Connell had attained international reputation as the protagonist of the Church.

Faced with a situation of steadily increasing gravity Wellington and Peel surrendered. Parliament met on 5th February, 1829. The king's speech proposed two matters for consideration—the restoration of order in Ireland and the removal of the disabilities imposed on his Catholic subjects. On the following day Peel introduced a bill for the suppression of the Catholic Association. O'Connell, confident that emancipation would follow, took the advice of the Whigs and urged the Association to dissolve itself

---

[1] The phrase was used by Peel in a letter to Sir Walter Scott describing the Clare election. MacDonagh, p. 171.

voluntarily as a concession to anti-Catholic prejudices. Some members demurred but Sheil overruled their opposition. Before the bill passed the commons, the Association held its final meeting which concluded with a richly-deserved tribute to O'Connell.

"That as the last act of this body on the point of dissolution we do declare that we are indebted to Daniel O'Connell, beyond all other men, for its original creation and sustainment and that he is entitled, for the achievement of its freedom, to the everlasting gratitude of Ireland."[1]

It was a declaration which expressed nothing more than the truth.

On 5th March Peel laid his scheme of emancipation before parliament. He had prepared two bills, one for Catholic relief, the other for raising the property qualification for the franchise in Ireland to a ten-pound freehold. In a speech which lasted for four hours, he explained the reasons which had led him to change his views on the Catholic question. He reminded the house that since 1812 successive cabinets had been nearly equally divided over the problem of emancipation, and this division of opinion had been attended with consequences most unfavourable to the administration of Irish affairs. Scarcely a year had passed since the union without the adoption of measures outside the ordinary course of law.[2] At the present juncture the government was forced to choose between alternative lines of policy—permanent, unqualified resistance to concessions or emancipation which would necessarily include admission of Catholics to parliament.[3] On behalf of the ministry he submitted the latter alternative in the form of a Roman Catholic Relief Bill which would place the Catholics of Great Britain and Ireland on an equal footing. His skilful

---

[1] Wyse, ii, Appendix, p. ccxci.
[2] Hansard, *Parliamentary debates*, xx, 741–2.
[3] Peel was insistent that without this provision any grant of relief would be useless and, perhaps, dangerous. "There is no intermediate position, defensible upon principle, between the maintenance of the present civil disabilities in Ireland and their complete removal." Hansard, xx, 757.

presentation of the case won over all but the Tory diehards, and with the assistance of the Whigs he conducted the bill successfully through all its stages. On 30th March it passed the commons by a majority of 320 to 142 and next day was brought before the lords. As in duty bound, Archbishop Howley of Canterbury and Archbishop Beresford of Armagh led the opposition, but Wellington's portentous speech on the horrors of civil war proved the deciding factor. The division on the third reading showed a majority of 105 for the bill.

The government experienced no difficulty with the measure for disfranchising the forty-shilling freeholders. O'Connell did his utmost to build up an opposition from the Whigs and Radicals but failed.[1] In each house the anti-government minority amounted only to seventeen.[2]

The Catholic Relief Bill had yet to receive the royal assent. George IV had inherited the bigotry, though not the scrupulous conscience, of his father, and he swore that nothing would induce him to sanction so iniquitous a surrender to Romanism. Wellington would take no refusal, and on Monday, 13th April, the tearful and protesting monarch signed the bill which then became law as the 10 *Geo. IV, c. 7.*

It remains to examine the extent to which the Catholics were emancipated.

In his speech of 5th March, Peel described the bill as founded on two principles :

" the abolition of civil distinctions on account of the religious creed of the Roman Catholics, and the maintenance, intact and inviolate, of the integrity of the Protestant church, its worship, its discipline and its government." [3]

It must therefore, be considered under two aspects—the repeal of disabilities placed on Catholics and the provision of safeguards for Protestantism.

---

[1] Wyse, ii, Appendix, p. cccxxxiii.
[2] *Correspondence of Daniel O'Connell*, i, pp. 174, 178.
[3] Hansard, xx, 756.

The " emancipation " clauses may be briefly summarised as follows :

i. the declaration against transubstantiation imposed by the test acts of 1673 and 1678 was no longer to be required except from persons appointed to the offices of regent, lord chancellor of England, lord chancellor of Ireland, lord-lieutenant of Ireland and high commissioner to the general assembly of the church of Scotland.[1]

ii. Catholics were declared eligible

(a) to sit and vote as peers in the house of lords and as members in the house of commons,

(b) to hold all posts in the government service and all places of trust or profit under the crown except those mentioned above,

(c) to vote at parliamentary elections,

(d) to exercise all other franchises and civil rights on condition that they took the oath which the present act substituted in their case for the oaths of allegiance, supremacy and abjuration.

The oath prescribed by the act was unusually long and included clauses offensive to Catholic susceptibilities. The lawyers who formulated it had obviously been instructed to provide against all the possible dangers to church and state that the most disaffected Catholic could plan or the most suspicious Protestant imagine. In addition to pledging his allegiance to the king and the Protestant succession, a Catholic was called on to make these solemn denials :

[1] The declaration was finally abolished by the 30 *and* 31 *Vict.*, *c.* 62 (1867), but the second section of this act stated that Catholics remained ineligible for the offices from which the relief act of 1829 excluded them. In the same year, however, Gladstone got the law altered with respect to the lord chancellorship of Ireland in order to permit the appointment of the Irish Catholic lawyer, Thomas O'Hagan. He later failed to obtain a similar concession in the case of the lord chancellorship of England which he wished to confer on Sir Charles Russell. The Government of Ireland Act, 1920 (10 *and* 11 *Geo. V*, *c.* 67) removed the disqualification which prevented a Catholic from becoming lord-lieutenant of Ireland, and the last person to hold this position before the establishment of the Irish Free State was an English Catholic, Lord FitzAlan of Derwent. Catholics are still debarred from occupying the offices of regent, lord chancellor of England and high commissioner to the church of Scotland.

" I do declare that it is not an article of my faith and that I do denounce, reject and abjure the opinion that princes excommunicated or deprived by the pope or any other authority of the see of Rome may be deposed or murdered by their subjects or by any person whatsoever ;

" And I do declare that I do not believe that the pope of Rome or any other foreign prince, prelate, person, state or potentate hath or ought to have any temporal or civil jurisdiction, power, superiority or pre-eminence, directly or indirectly, within this realm. . . .

" And I do solemnly swear that I will never exercise any privilege, to which I am or may become entitled, to disturb or weaken the Protestant religion or Protestant government in the united kingdom."[1]

The first of the above declarations was a repetition of the abjuration clause in the oath of allegiance. The second was worded in the same terms as the oath of supremacy except for the substitution of " temporal or civil " in place of " ecclesiastical or spiritual." This change made the declaration, if not acceptable to Catholics, at least permissible for them to take in good faith.

The " safeguards for Protestantism " were framed with a view to reassuring the troubled conscience of parliament and forestalling objections to the bill. Only two had any political significance, and this was extremely slight. The five high offices of state already mentioned were reserved for Protestants, while Catholics in holy orders were made ineligible for membership of the house of commons.[2] A " safeguard " which can be described as rather ludicrously

---

[1] Quoted in Grant Robertson, pp. 318–9. Only Catholics took this oath. The oaths of allegiance, supremacy and abjuration (consolidated in one formula in 1858) were obligatory on Protestants entering parliament until 1866. The Parliamentary Oaths Act of this year (29 *Vict.*, *c.* 19) abolished all existing oaths for peers and members of the commons, and substituted an oath of allegiance to the crown and the Protestant succession which had to be taken by Catholics and Protestants alike. Two years later, by the 31 *and* 32 *Vict.*, *c.* 72, the present oath of allegiance was imposed in its stead. Porritt, i, pp. 148–9. The 1829 oath could not be required of any Catholic after the passing of the Promissory Oaths Act, 1871 (34 *and* 35 *Vict.*, *c.* 48).

[2] This disability remains in force. It is only fair to add that clergymen of the church of England are equally ineligible for election to the commons. Porritt, i, pp. 126–7.

superfluous prevented the appointment of Catholics to
" any office, place or dignity of, in or belonging to the
united church of England and Ireland or the church of
Scotland." Of some practical importance were the refusal
of advowsons to Catholic patrons of benefices[1] and the
maintenance of the universities of Oxford and Cambridge
and the public schools as exclusively Protestant institutions.
The church by law established was saved from affront
as well as from injury by regulations governing the conduct of the Catholic clergy. No priest might conduct a
religious service except in a Catholic church or in a private
house, and the wearing of Catholic vestments and religious
habits was forbidden outside such places. The penalty for a
breach of the law in either matter was a fine of £50. In
accordance with the terms of the relief act of 1791, each
Catholic church had to be registered at the quarter sessions
and registration would not be given if the building were
adorned with a steeple or bell. A Catholic bishop or dean
who took as his territorial designation the title of an Anglican
diocese in England or Ireland rendered himself liable to a
fine of £100.[2] The privileged position of the state religion
was further emphasised by a clause which affected the laity.
Judges and other civil dignitaries were prohibited under
pain of fine and forfeiture of office from attending in
ceremonial dress at religious functions other than those
of the established Churches.[3]

[1] Among the Catholic nobility, the duke of Norfolk was patron of five
livings, the earl of Shrewsbury of eleven and Lord Petre of three. On the
disposal of the right of patronage see Lilly and Wallis, *A manual of the law
specially affecting Catholics* (London, 1893), p. 43.

[2] This provision was re-stated and extended by the Ecclesiastical Titles Act,
1851 (14 *and* 15 *Vict., c.* 50) which imposed a fine of £100 on a Catholic bishop
who took his title from any place in the United Kingdom. The act, which
had been intended as the government's counter-move to the restoration of
the English Catholic hierarchy in 1850, became a dead letter and was formally
repealed during the first Gladstone ministry by the 34 *and* 35 *Vict., c.* 53. The
original provision respecting ecclesiastical titles was unrepealed by the Catholic
relief act of 1926 (16 *and* 17 *Geo. V, c.* 55), and presumably can still be enforced
in England. The terms of the Government of Ireland Act, 1920, make it
inapplicable to Northern Ireland.

[3] On New Year's day, 1842, O'Connell drove to Marlborough Street pro-
Cathedral, Dublin, in his robes of office as lord mayor of the city, but complied
with the law by laying them aside before entering to assist at Mass. This
provision of the Emancipation Act was repealed by the Office and Oath
Act, 1867 (30 *and* 31 *Vict., c.* 75).

These enactments may be dismissed as likely to cause only mild annoyance to Catholics, but the very severe restrictions placed on religious orders of men fall into a different category.[1] They virtually constituted a new penal law, the purpose of which was unequivocally stated to be "the gradual suppression and final prohibition, within the united kingdom, of Jesuits and other religious orders, communities and societies of the church of Rome."[2] Every Jesuit and other male religious living in the kingdom at the date of the commencement of the act had to register himself at the office of the clerk of the peace for his district under pain of a fine of £50 for each month during which he remained unregistered. Any religious who came into the kingdom after this date was deemed guilty of a misdemeanour punishable by banishment for life.[3] A residence licence might be granted to an unregistered member of an order, but not for a period exceeding six months nor by authority of a Catholic secretary of state. The administering of vows in religion was made an indictable offence. Had these restrictions been enforced, a fresh chapter in the persecution of the Catholic Church would have opened. Enforcement was left at the discretion of the attorney-general, and fortunately no occupant of this post seems to have been perturbed by the growth of monasticism.[4] The only serious consequence of the legislation against religious orders was to place them at a grave disadvantage in establishing title to bequests. For years after 1829, bequests and trusts intended for the collective benefit of an order were held to be invalid on the ground that the law of

[1] When the bill was before the lords, an Irish peer, the earl of Mount Cashel, expressed the view that "if the government were disposed to prevent the increase of Jesuits, they should also take measures against female Jesuits." He declared himself in favour of making the penal clauses applicable to religious orders of women and, in particular, to the Sisters of Mercy whom he accused of widespread proselytising activities, but the house was not prepared to support him. Hansard, xxi, 567–8.

[2] Clause xxviii of the Catholic Relief Act, 1829. In this matter the act contrasts unfavourably with the relief act of 1791. Amherst, i, p. 182.

[3] Provision, however, was made for legalising the return to the united kingdom of religious who were British subjects living abroad.

[4] O'Connell described the clauses against the religious orders as "unexecutable." *Correspondence of Daniel O'Connell* (London, 1883), i, pp. 177–80.

England did not presume the existence of any such institutions.[1]

The omissions in the act proved more galling to Catholics than any restrictions which it imposed. The marriage law was unchanged; funds in support of Catholic charities were not given recognition in the courts, and legacies and bequests for the celebration of Masses remained void as intended for " superstitious uses." The law in the first two matters underwent considerable modification within the next few years,[2] but almost a century was to elapse before Catholics attained the status of complete equality with their fellow-subjects. On 15th December, 1926, the royal assent was given to a relief bill promoted by two Catholic members of the Conservative party, Captain Blundell and Lord FitzAlan of Derwent, and introduced by a Protestant Conservative, Denis Herbert.[3] By this measure, all the disabilities and restrictions under which the Catholics of Great Britain laboured were repealed except in the particulars already noted.

O'Connell expressed his satisfaction with the concessions made in 1829. When the emancipation bill was before parliament, he commended it as " very good, frank, direct, complete, no veto, no control, no payment of the clergy "[4]— " an excellent one in every respect."[5] His sole criticism was levelled against the provisions respecting ecclesiastical titles and religious orders, and these he denounced as so " foolish and abortive " that he could drive a coach-and-six, or alternatively ride a troop of horse, three times through them.[6] With the passing of the bill his enthusiasm reached greater heights. On the day after it became law, he headed

---

[1] Lilly and Wallis, pp. 145-7.

[2] The Roman Catholic Charities Act, 1832 (2 *and* 3 *Will. IV, c.* 115), granted protection to trusts approved for certain Catholic purposes, and the Marriage Act, 1836 (6 *and* 7 *Will. IV*, c. 85) established the validity in civil law of marriages solemnised before a Catholic priest in a church registered for this purpose.

[3] "An act to provide for the further relief of H.M. Roman Catholic subjects," (16 *and* 17 *Geo. V, c.* 55). The act did not apply to Northern Ireland where, under the constitution established in 1920, no such disabilities and restrictions existed.

[4] *Correspondence of Daniel O'Connell*, i, p. 174.

[5] Ibid. i, p. 178.

[6] Ibid. i, pp. 174, 177.

a letter to his cousin, James Sugrue, " the first day of Freedom."

" I cannot allow this day to pass," he wrote, " without expressing my congratulations to the honest men of Burgh Quay on the subject of the relief bill. It is one of the greatest triumphs recorded in history—a bloodless revolution more extensive in its operation than any other political change that could take place. . . . It is clear that without gross mismanagement it will be impossible to allow misgovernment any longer in Ireland." [1]

To appreciate his enthusiasm we must again take into consideration the view-point from which he regarded the problem of emancipation. A month previously he had reminded Sugrue

" How mistaken men are who suppose that the history of the world will be over as soon as we are emancipated ! Oh ! *that* will be the time to *commence* the struggle for popular rights." [2]

For O'Connell, emancipation was not an end in itself but the first step towards obtaining just treatment for Ireland. The Irish Catholics had now been granted representation in the imperial parliament through members of their own faith, and, unless these members failed in their duty, he foresaw the end of misrule. It was an unduly optimistic interpretation of the possibilities inherent in the relief act and it evidenced a naïve trust in parliamentary agitation. Before ten years had passed, he was thoroughly disillusioned. The Irish members who constituted his following proved for the most part worthless as advocates of their country's interests, and the Whig government, on the rare occasions when it fathomed the causes of Irish discontent, was curbed in its efforts at reform by a hostile majority in the house of lords. By 1840, O'Connell was fully convinced that Ireland would never obtain justice from the imperial parliament and that the time had come for a new policy

---

[1] Ibid. i, pp. 180–1. The " honest men " were the Catholic Association.
[2] Ibid. i, p. 176.

and a changed allegiance. Emancipation had not attained
the end for which he had hoped. Nevertheless, failure in
this respect does not deprive him of the title he cherished.
He had begun the process of liberating the people of Catholic
Ireland from their sense of inferiority. He had taught them
the first lesson in self-reliance. The process had to be
continued; the lesson needed repetition before the full
force of Irish democracy was made into an effective instrument. In the year preceding his death, two men were
born—one in a poor cabin at Straide in Mayo, the other
in a gentleman's house at Avondale in Wicklow—who would
complete the task he had left unfinished. On Davitt and
Parnell and on their successors in the leadership of the Irish
nation fell the mantle first worn by the liberator.

REPEAL OF THE UNION

Michael Tierney

A very popular way of looking at our history is to conceive of it as having been guided in all its many phases by one true doctrine, the doctrine of Nationality, all other explanations being dismissed as aberrant. This one true doctrine is often believed to be of immemorial native origin and is invoked with equal rigour to explain the course of events in the twelfth, the seventeenth, or the nineteenth century. Thus construed and invoked, it makes nonsense of a great part of our history ; for in this rigid form it is a product of the late eighteenth century and was first popularly preached only a little more than a hundred years ago. Thomas Davis, its earliest and most influential champion, stated emphatically in 1844 that it " had been made in the Historical Societies of Dublin, and belongs to Trinity College Protestants and a few Roman Catholics of T.C.D." Its formulation is in fact a curious product of that reaction of the English in Ireland against English rule which has had such a strange influence on the recent relations between the two countries.

One consequence of the drastic application of this doctrine to Irish history has been the setting-aside or the condemnation as somehow irrelevant of the greatest Irish political figure because he cannot be fitted into it. O'Connell was no more a nationalist in the doctrinaire sense than he was a republican. Yet it will probably be the permanent judgment of history that no two men have done so much to create and ultimately to liberate the modern Irish nation as he and that other very different but equally opportunist genius of action, Michael Collins. To Davis and the men of his generation it was obvious that O'Connell could not be a nationalist in their sense ; he had lived his long life and done his immense work before the idea of nationality was " made " in Trinity College. Though, like Grattan, and many others before him, he often made speeches about the Irish nation he had not the rigid semi-Hegelian idea of what he meant by the word which became common-place afterwards. No Irish nationalist of later times could have talked, for instance, as he did in his Reform speech at Bath in 1832 : " we only want a parliament to do our private business, leaving the national business to a national assembly." He could not have been in the remotest degree conscious of the horror such an appellation for the Imperial Parliament would have aroused in the breast of the most moderate Home Ruler.

It is one of the many paradoxes of Irish history that this doctrine, which was destined to have so fatal an influence on his own reputation, was first effectively set going in a journal founded to assist him in his last great campaign for Repeal. Like O'Connell himself, the " Young Ireland " movement was to be afterwards labelled as a failure because of its association with the abortive attempt at rebellion in 1848. In the intellectual sense it was anything but a failure, and there is nothing extravagant in the view that we are still largely living on its ideas. In his great opening speech during the Treaty debate of 1921–2, Arthur Griffith spoke of Davis as " the prophet I followed throughout my life, the man whose words and teachings I tried to translate into practice in politics " ; and much of our subsequent history might be explained as a quarrel over the title to Davis's heritage. From the *Nation* the doctrine of nationality passed on to the Fenians, and then by different ways to the Irish Party and to Sinn Féin. The intransigence, the un-willingness to compromise or bargain, and the cult of physical force which have been so marked a feature of our politics during the past half-century all undoubtedly derive from the influence of the *Nation* ; and it should not be forgotten that the modern veneration for Wolfe Tone began in 1844 with the erection of the monument over his grave in Bodenstown, for which Davis composed the inscription.

O'Connell did not anticipate, and could not have antici-pated, the doctrine of nationality, nor is it probable that he would have wished to do so. Nevertheless, he did anticipate far more in the conduct of later nationalist politics than he is usually given credit for. The Catholic Association which he founded in 1823 was in many striking ways a forerunner of the Sinn Féin movement of nearly a century later. He was the inventor of the Arbitration Court, and his plan for the calling of a Council of Three Hundred was to serve long afterwards as a model for the first Dáil Eireann. He was also a pioneer in his views on land legislation ; his proposals at the time of the Devon Commission included fixity of tenure and " an absolute right of recompense for all substantial improvements." The Federalism which seems to have been in his mind the practical form of Repeal was simply an earlier version of what Professor Galbraith was later to christen " Home Rule." Nor does this exhaust the immensity of his influence. His Catholic Association became the immediate model for the organisers of the Reform movement in Great Britain ; indeed he was himself one of the chief leaders of that movement, and in 1830 Cobbett, with whom he had previously quarrelled, declared that he was the only public man to retain the confidence of the English Radicals. It is no exaggeration but the literal truth that without him the great Reform Bill of 1832, with all its enormous consequences, could not have been carried.

What is true of the Reform Bill is equally true of the Repeal of the Corn Laws, a measure destined to have even greater effects. The agitation which forced Peel to break up the Tory party and adopt the principle of Free Trade was once more inspired by O'Connell's methods and backed by his vigorous support, founded on one of his most passionate convictions. His abhorrence of the Corn Laws was only equalled by his hatred of slavery, and here once more his alliance with the English Radicals was decisive in forcing the passage of the Slavery Abolition Act. He differed, of course, from his English friends in two important respects. In the first place he was a convinced and thoroughgoing Catholic. "I am for justice," he said, "in the name of humanity and according to the law of the living God." In the second place he was no doctrinaire Radical or Free Trader. (He once called the great Nassau Senior " that intelligent but wrong-headed man.") His criticism of the measure by which the Whigs extended to Ireland the English poor-law system with the cruelty of its workhouses has led to his being accused of hostility to social reform. Perusal of such a book as *The Bleak Age* by J. L. and Barbara Hammond (who can scarcely be called extreme Conservatives) should be enough to show the fallacy in this accusation. O'Connell's opinions on this subject or on Trade Unionism were no more the product of intellectual fashion than was his hostility to slavery in all its forms. They were the result of masterly independent thinking based upon wide experience and a powerful grasp of realities. No one who studies his writings and speeches can doubt that had he been given an opportunity he would have conferred immense benefits as a legislator both on Ireland and on England.

The opposition to physical force, for which he was afterwards and is still most strongly criticised, was based on two arguments, one practical, the other theoretical. The practical argument was the simple one of the military discrepancy between the two countries. It is, indeed, too often forgotten how different the situation in this respect before the Famine was from what it is to-day. At that time Ireland had a population of eight millions to Britain's eighteen. In reality this comparatively much greater Irish strength was, however, all to Ireland's disadvantage from the military point of view. It may be stated as an historical axiom that the Industrial Revolution did not produce its full effects in warfare until the American Civil War. Nevertheless the financial and industrial resources of Great Britain were even in O'Connell's time quite as much out of proportion to those of Ireland as they are to-day. Executive controls were then far simpler and more massive than now, but for that very reason they were less vulnerable to the kind of attack of which Collins was to prove himself such a master. O'Connell's clear and penetrating intelligence was quite as capable of grasping the essentials of a military situation as was that of Collins himself. History has entirely vindicated the rightness of his view; and it must always be remembered that the success afterwards achieved by Collins was only to a very minor extent a military success. Collins won a substantial victory by limiting military action to a carefully narrowed field and by combining it with skilful political action. His military tactics were in reality those of the Tithe War and the Land War differently applied. It should be also emphasised that nothing could be further from O'Connell's temperament than the " blood-sacrifice " *mystique* which was to inspire the Rebellion of 1916.

Even stronger than his practical reasons for condemning resort to physical force was his doctrinal belief in the efficacy of moral agitation. It is almost the orthodox procedure to dismiss this belief as entirely wrong ; but we should do better to try to understand it. O'Connell was in this respect the exact antithesis to Pearse, who believed that bloodshed has a positive moral value in itself and must be resorted to in every generation, irrespective of success or failure. For Pearse success lay, not in military victory, but in the maintenance of a tradition of violent opposition to alien rule. It may be conceded that from a purely positivist standpoint both leaders were illogical ; but O'Connell's illogicality lay in the exaggeration of a Christian virtue, Pearse's in that of a pagan virtue. Christian morality does not, of course, prohibit all recourse to violence, as O'Connell himself was to recognise in 1845 when, in response to a singularly foolish as well as callous pronouncement on the Famine from the Duke of Cambridge, he declared that if the people were to be left to feed on grass or eat mangel-wurzel " it would be the duty of every man to die with arms in his hands."

Recent experience of the plight to which civilisation and humanity can be reduced by the practice of a doctrine of pure force makes us in this generation perhaps readier than were our immediate forbears to sympathise with O'Connell in his view that no political end justifies bloodshed. At the same time, while no longer dismissing it as utterly contemptible, we should be clear as to the kind of exaggeration this view implies. O'Connell was in truth a new phenomenon in Europe : a Catholic Radical. His belief in the supreme efficacy of moral force did not come to him entirely from Catholic teaching. It was, of course, partly that and partly derived from his own experience in the terrible prelude to the Union ; but it also owed something to his early reading of Tom Paine and Godwin and to his friendship with and admiration for Jeremy Bentham. He was proudly conscious of being a chief standard-bearer in a new kind of democratic policy. The resounding successes of that policy between 1823 and 1832, when it brought about Emancipation in Ireland and Reform in England, were enough to harden into a doctrine what had been at first the combined outcome of temperament, training, and experience. We must not, of course, fall into the error of attributing to his vigorous manhood the extreme form in which the doctrine was imposed during his own senility by his incapable son upon the sorely-divided Repeal Association. Neither should we fail, however, to recognise that John O'Connell was only driving to the extreme of futility a view always held with strong conviction by his father.

The real difference between the old leader and the young malcontents was more subtle than the mere abstract quarrel as to whether the sword should or should not be stigmatised, into which Meagher's oratory seemed to turn it. "John Mitchel," said Arthur Griffith in his eloquent preface to the *Jail Journal*, "met the crisis of 1848 with a policy. Practical Posterity, from its easy chair, has pronounced the policy extravagant and impossible : even, in unctuous moments, reprehensible. Let the Censor stand in the Censored's place and declare what its wisdom would have counselled a people whose life was assailed." Griffith's plea cannot exempt historians from the sombre but salutary task of exercising their judgment on persons who have had the making of history. In this instance the answer surely is that the crisis came, not in 1848, but in 1845 with the onset of the Famine, or even in 1844 with the embarrassing victory over Peel, the decision of the House of Lords and the release from Richmond. And the sad and sober truth is that the young men were terribly inclined to meet that crisis, not with a policy but with abstractions untranslatable into the necessary deeds. It may even be suggested with some justice that their devotion to military abstractions was in part responsible for the most extravagant pacifist utterances of O'Connell at that time and for his son's fatal test which split the Repeal Association.

The impression is easily gained from the literature of the 'forties that Ireland was then and had long been a land sunk in craven peace and that it was the " Young Irelanders " who first preached violent resistance to oppression. The reality was far otherwise. Making due allowance for O'Connell's exaggeration of moral force, it must be said that most of his life had been spent in a prolonged effort to substitute intelligent political action for the endemic violence which, while by no means unjustified, was worthy of his condemnation because of its costliness and futility. During much of the 'thirties Ireland was the theatre of an irregular war not much less ferocious than the struggle from 1918 to 1921. This was the Tithe War, which only came to an end with the passage of the Tithe Commutation Act in 1838. The resistance to tithes was organised by the secret societies so well described in the second chapter of Davitt's *Fall of Feudalism in Ireland*. Such was the power of the Whiteboys during this period that in 1834 their combination was said " to surpass Dublin Castle in vigour, promptitude and efficacy," so that it was " more safe to violate the law than to obey it." O'Connell never concealed his strong objection to the secret societies, which was founded alike on moral principles and on his belief that they merely served as a weapon to a coercive Government. He was nevertheless continually charged in England with responsibility for their deeds because he also vigorously denounced the oppression which provoked them. In certain ways, while his own attitude was less equivocal, his position with regard to this popular violence was not entirely different from Parnell's with regard to " Captain Moonlight " at a later date.

Thus he defended some of those accused of murder in the Tithe War while making it clear that he believed in his clients' innocence. The same judgment must be passed on his conduct of the Repeal agitation in 1842-3. His language was calculatedly defiant, and found its militant echo in the songs of a populace not yet by any means inured to reform by moral force. It is quite clear that he hoped to secure Repeal, as he had secured Emancipation, by bringing about a state of affairs in which Sir Robert Peel and his colleagues would find themselves incapable of governing Ireland. This policy of calculated risk had been successful against both Peel himself and that even more formidable character, Wellington, in the years from 1825 to 1829. Its weakness lay in its failure to take account of two factors : O'Connell's advanced age and the lack of anything comparable to the support which the English Whigs and Radicals had given to Emancipation. The second of these factors was to prove of less importance than the first. As things turned out, the Repeal movement got a much more formidable measure of support in Ireland itself than even Emancipation had achieved. Furthermore, O'Connell's years of cordial collaboration with the Whig reformers in England, for which rigid nationalist opinion has so often condemned him, had had a certain effect in " softening " advanced English opinion in favour of Irish self-government. Indications are not lacking that if it had not been for the operation of the other factor—his own old age—O'Connell might have been able to turn to very effective use the substantial victory presented to him by the reversal of his sentence in the House of Lords in 1844. Shaw-Lefevre, a good judge thoroughly familiar with all the circumstances, states his opinion that " in his earlier days there can be little doubt that he would have made great use of this victory."

Good historians have sought to throw doubt on the view that O'Connell, while in Richmond or even earlier, was beginning to suffer from the softening of the brain which later caused his death. It is true that in the two years of life which were left to him he occasionally did show flashes of his old fire and give evidence that his old political skill had not altogether decayed. This, however, is only what might have been expected. The ordinary view is proved not merely by his pathetic one-sided love-affair, while in prison, with the daughter of a Protestant merchant from Belfast, but with equal force by the rambling incoherence of his pronouncements on policy after his release. The country's great misfortune was that there was nobody now to take over from him with the same decisive, if a little callous, resolution with which he had taken over from Grattan or with which Parnell was later to take over from Butt. This was the true crisis, to which none of the " Young Ireland " group proved adequate. Their real difference from O'Connell did not lie in their advocacy and his rejection of physical force. It lay in the fact that he had shown himself able to utilise the existence of violence while condemning it ; they made splendid speeches advocating it, or rather refusing to repudiate it, but were incapable of organising or provoking it. All sides were in fact in complete agreement as to the constitutional character of the Repeal movement and the absolute necessity of confining it to peaceful channels ; but the younger men, even while admitting and insisting on this agreement, insisted also on paying rhetorical tributes to the idea of force. Nowhere was this tendency of theirs shown more curiously than in the course of Mitchel's one brush with O'Connell in Conciliation Hall. The speech of the young orator was remarkable for the equal fervour with which he disclaimed all idea of violence and at the same time praised the Volunteers of 1782 and the United Irishmen. O'Connell was moved to reply. " What can this man's object be ? " he exclaimed. " He purports to be a man of peace, and yet he preaches of war ; he affects to advocate moral and tranquil courses, and yet his speech has the direct tendency of instigating the country to anarchy and violence." It is surely difficult, even if only in point of tactics, not to sympathise with the old agitator, in spite of the grace and vigour of Mitchel's style.

In order to judge O'Connell fairly, we must always keep a grasp on the fact that he was the very antithesis of a doctrinaire. He based Ireland's claim to self-government not on the abstract principle of nationality, but on simple justice, the faith of treaties and the historic right of the Irish Parliament as vindicated in 1782. Less doctrinaire than Grattan himself, he insisted that all English policy towards Ireland had been one long series of injustices, culminating in the breach of the Treaty of Limerick and in the shameless bribery by which the Union had been bought. The great speeches in which he set forth this claim before the House of Commons in 1834 and before the Corporation of Dublin in 1842 are among our most important historical documents and deserve to be much more widely known and studied than they are. But these speeches are only the culminating points in a lifetime's agitation, and in a sense all his political oratory was devoted to the one great object. The long series began with his first public speech in protest against the Union, delivered on 13th January, 1800, before a meeting of the Catholic citizens of Dublin in the hall of the Royal Exchange. Two days later, the Irish Parliament was to meet for its last session. Years afterwards, we are told, O'Connell frequently declared that this maiden speech of his should be looked upon as the textbook of his entire political life. It was remarkable for the emphasis with which the young man of twenty-five expressed his personal preference for Irish independence even if it were to involve the continuance of Protestant Ascendancy or the revival of the Penal Laws. " If the alternative were offered him of the Union or the re-enact-ment of the penal code in all its pristine horrors, he would prefer without hesitation the latter as the lesser and more sufferable evil . . . he would rather confide in the justice of his brethren, the Protestants of Ireland, who have already liberated him, than lay his country at the feet of foreigners."

Ten years afterwards, when O'Connell was already famous as an advocate, and when the disastrous economic and social effects of the Union had made themselves widely felt, the Protestant Corporation of Dublin went so far as to pass a resolution in which the appalling decay of the city was made the basis of a demand for Repeal. In September, 1810, O'Connell was invited at an aggregate

meeting of freemen and freeholders to speak in support
of a petition to the King. This time he was addressing a
Protestant audience, and his speech not only re-affirmed
his preference for independence—" the King, Lords and
Commons of Ireland "—over Emancipation, but called
for united action by Protestants, Catholics and Dissenters
to secure Repeal. " The Protestant alone could not expect
to liberate his country—the Roman Catholic alone could
not do it—neither could the Presbyterian—but amalgamate
the three in the Irishman and the Union was repealed."
Thus O'Connell was advocating Tone's political formula
in order to restore the Parliament which Tone had repudiated. The same policy is advanced in a remarkable
"Address to the Catholics of Ireland" issued on 1st January,
1821. There he advises his co-religionists to discontinue
the petitions to Parliament which, although presented by
Grattan and Plunket, had failed to secure redress. The
alternative he now offered was agitation for Repeal and
Reform at once.

" By continuing our separate and exclusive labours,"
he wrote, " we do the work of our worst enemies, and keep
up a perpetual line of distinction—a constant wall of
separation between sects and parties in Ireland. Let us
rather endeavour to amalgamate the Catholic, the Protestant, the Presbyterian, the Methodist, the Quaker, into
the IRISHMAN—and, forgetting our own individual wrongs,
let us call upon Irishmen of every description to combine
in a noble struggle for the natural and inherent rights of
our now wretched country. Let that struggle be confined
within the most peaceable and constitutional limits. Let it
have for its object the restoration of the constitution—and
for its sole guide, the principles of the constitution ; let us,
in a word, join heart and hand in the pursuit of constitutional reform." This address gave rise to a controversy
between O'Connell and Sheil (which proved short-lived)
and, in reply to Sheil, O'Connell reiterated his belief that
it was futile to expect relief from an unreformed Parliament.
The period from 1823 to 1829 was the final phase in the
fight for Emancipation, in which the organisation of the

Irish Catholics displayed its most impressive efficiency; but it was in the second part of this six-year period, after his visit to London and very friendly reception by the Radicals in 1825, that O'Connell became also a leader in the movement for Parliamentary Reform. On the very eve of Emancipation he once more declared that "to accomplish Repeal I would give up every other measure, and my exertions for such an object would meet with the co-operation of all sects and parties in Ireland."

A further series of public addresses in 1829 and 1830 set forth a list of reforms for which he intended to work in his new capacity as leader of a Parliamentary party. Foremost among these was once more Repeal, but they included also the reform of the franchise and the secret ballot. In the most elaborate of them he declared himself "a thorough Benthamite" and announced that "he entirely concurs in the benevolent plans of that illustrious man." Among the plans in which he thus concurred were schemes for sweeping reforms in the whole legal system, for the abolition of tithes, sinecures and grand juries and for the radical amendment of the subletting act and the libel laws. Unfortunately the Whigs, whom he helped into power in 1830, were by no means prepared to go the whole way with him, and even less in Ireland than in England. The new Chief Secretary, Stanley, afterwards to win literary fame as Lord Derby, the translator of the *Iliad*, was next to Peel his most formidable opponent. Instead of reform—or rather along with a Reform Act which O'Connell denounced as inadequate and illusory—Ireland got the most comprehensive measure of repression she had yet experienced : the ill-famed Coercion Act of 1833, in opposing which O'Connell reached his greatest heights as a Parliamentary debater.

It was during the fierce interchange with Stanley on the Coercion Bill that he gave what was perhaps the earliest indication of his readiness to abate the claim for Repeal in return for substantial justice to Ireland from a Union government. " I have ever been and still am most attached to a British connexion. Such an avowal may be turned against me in Ireland, but I risk everything rather than

abandon the truth. As long as I saw the utility of the
connexion—and an immense utility may exist—I should
prefer seeing this House doing justice to my fellow-countrymen, rather than that it should be done by a local legislature. . . . If I thought that the machinery of the present
government would work well for Ireland, there never lived
a man more ready to facilitate its movements than I am.
The only reason I have for being a Repealer is the injustice
of the present government towards my country." A private
letter of the same period serves as a commentary on this
apparent retreat. Written after the retirement of Stanley
from the Chief Secretaryship towards the end of 1833, it
deals with the prospect of getting some real measures of
Irish reform from the Whigs. " Lastly," it declares, " but
first in order of magnitude, there is the Repeal of the Union.
We can never thrive without Repeal. . . . But may not
the Repeal be dispensed with if we get beneficial measures
without it ? This is a serious question, and one upon which
good men may well differ ; but it is my duty to make up
my mind upon it, and I have made up my mind accordingly
—that there can be no safety, no permanent prosperity for
Ireland, without a Repeal of the Union. That is my firm,
my unalterable conviction." It is clear that in this frame
of mind O'Connell could not have been eager to press
Repeal upon the House of Commons. That odd character,
Feargus O'Connor, who afterwards became a leader of the
Chartists and who was at this time figuring as a kind of
parody of O'Connell, tried to force his hand ; but it was
not till 1834, when Stanley had retired from the Chief
Secretaryship, that he consented to propose a formal motion
on the subject. It was the first of the long series of attempts
to achieve Irish self-government by Parliamentary action,
which ended in the abortive Home Rule Act of 1920, and
incidentally in Partition. Naturally it was a total failure,
remarkable merely for the power and logic of O'Connell's
plea. Its real result was to confirm him in his policy of
seeking justice as an alternative to Repeal. Under a Whig
administration, justice, he believed, was to some extent at
least attainable, while Repeal clearly was not.

The General Election of 1835 resulted in a Parliament in which O'Connell, with forty-four Repealers and twenty-two Irish Liberals, held the balance of power. The famous Lichfield House Compact, between O'Connell, Lord Melbourne and Lord John Russell, gave Ireland the first real attempt at good government she had known for a century and a half. The new policy had a double aspect : to secure that Ireland was governed with justice and impartiality, and to put through Parliament legislation for the abolition of tithes, the appropriation of the surplus revenues of the State Church to meet some of the needs of the people, the reform of the corrupt and antiquated corporations in the cities, and finally the extension of the franchise. During the five years from 1835 to 1840 there existed the friendliest relations between O'Connell and the Whig Government. The Irish leader and his party sat on the Government side of the House of Commons, and it is not improbable that but for the hostility of the King and the House of Lords and their own generally weak position in England, the Whigs would have given him a seat in the Cabinet. As is well known, the Whig administration in Ireland was highly successful, mainly owing to the character, ability and energy of the Under-Secretary, Thomas Drummond. Their legislative policy was comparatively a failure : they succeeded with great difficulty in effecting a not very satisfactory settlement of the tithe question, and their reform of the corporations was, if anything, rather too sweeping. The franchise they did not touch at all, and their Poor Law was so far from being what O'Connell wanted that he merely refrained from opposing it. Throughout their tenure of office, they were harassed and impeded by the able tactics of Peel, who had the advantage of an overwhelming majority in the Lords, and the support of William IV while he lived. The old King's blatant enmity goes far to explain, if it does not exactly justify, O'Connell's sentimental outbursts of praise for the young Victoria.

It was during this Whig régime that he most openly advocated the policy of accepting reforms instead of demanding

Repeal. In January, 1836, he said to the Dublin Trades Union : " I go to England to work out justice to Ireland. If I get that justice, do you consent that I abandon Repeal ? I have put that question to the men of Kerry, and received an answer in the affirmative. I put the same question in Tuam, and got the same reply. I put the same question in Moate, and got the same reply. I put it also to the honest men of the Queen's County, and they gave me the same answer. I now put that question to you. I want you to strengthen me with your authority, that I may go and tell the English people that I am authorised to make that bargain with them. Have I your authority ? I promise you I will make no niggard bargain for you. You shall have full twenty shillings in the pound of the real national debt of justice. You shall have for your trades employment, agriculture in Ireland must be encouraged, manufactures must be extended, the corporations must be opened, and the blessings of equal law must be secured to all." This was good Radical and Benthamite policy, and he went straight from Dublin to be the guest of the Radicals of Liverpool and Birmingham, at both of which places a thousand persons sat down to banquets in his honour. But the characteristic attitude of the English people to this demand for a real Union between the two countries was summed up by Lord Lyndhurst, himself the grandson of a Catholic peasant from the County Clare, who said that " the Irish were aliens in blood, in language, and in religion."

Two years' experience of this policy of collaboration were enough to prove to O'Connell that it was unlikely to be fully successful. Though he never withdrew his support from Melbourne, he felt compelled to change his tactics in Ireland, and in August, 1838, he founded the Precursor Society, whose object was stated by him to be " to procure from the British legislature full justice to Ireland." Once more he demanded "full participation with Great Britain in all franchises, privileges, and rights, civil and religious." In the next month, in a letter to the people, he reiterated the Irish claim for corporate reform, an unrestricted franchise, fair representation in Parliament and the abolition of

State provision for the Protestant Church. The remainder of his life was to be dedicated to the securing of these four aims. " Should these grievances be redressed by the United Parliament, I shall be content to be bound by that statute. If they or any of them remain unredressed, then I devote the entire residue of my life to the Repeal of the Act of Union and the restoration of a domestic legislature for Ireland." His zeal and energy as a reformer had brought him into close and cordial relations with the most advanced liberal statesmen in England, though he was never fully admitted into aristocratic Whig circles. He had aided mightily in bringing about the reform of Parliament, and had broken the first Reform Government because of its reactionary attitude to Ireland. For seven years no government could be formed in England without his support. Men like Melbourne and Russell were quite sincere in their desire " to blot out the Channel," and O'Connell was not unjustified in his determination to give them every opportunity to make the Union a reality. His own position seemed extraordinarily strong. *The Times* declared that he was " the real prime minister" and the Dublin *Evening Mail* humorously styled him " His Excellency Daniel O'Connell, Governor and Lieutenant-Governor of that part of the United Kingdom called Ireland." But the power of the Ascendancy party was far from being broken, and the Precursor Society was the sign of O'Connell's recognition that Reform must once more give place to Repeal.

The Repeal Association succeeded to the Precursor Society in 1840, and in the next year Melbourne's Government fell without having carried its Irish programme, as agreed on at the Lichfield House Compact, into more than partial effect. Peel's Tory Ministry was to last until 1846, and when the Whigs got once more into power, O'Connell was an old and broken man. The years between were filled with the last great Repeal campaign in which he achieved his greatest influence over the people. We have seen that in this campaign he hoped to repeat his success against Peel in 1829 ; but this time the odds against him were

DANIEL O'CONNELL. M.P.

From a portrait published 30th May, 1844.
by A. Lesage, 40 Lower Sackville Street, Dublin

[By courtesy of The National Gallery of Ireland]

vastly greater, for the Whigs were not interested in Repeal as they had been in Emancipation. Against Peel his policy was one of defiance only stopping short of open resistance ; it culminated in the retreat at Clontarf, but that was by no means the end if it had not been for the running-down of his powers, long strained to the utmost. Thoroughgoing opportunist that he was, he had in reality two policies, one of which involved co-operation with the sympathetic Whigs, the other unrestrained agitation against the Tories. To the young men who flocked to his aid after the foundation of *The Nation* in 1842 these double-faced tactics savoured almost of dishonesty. Like all intransigents, they tended to regard as questionable what in reality was only the supple reaction of a consummate politician to stubborn facts. There is some evidence, noted by Davitt in his *Fall of Feudalism*, that O'Connell was once more in close touch with the Whig leaders in 1844, two years before Peel was turned out of office on a revival of the coercion issue. This time the compact is said to have included a plan for what had begun to be known as Federalism, involving a subordinate Parliament for Ireland.

Mention of Federalism brings us to the final question as to what exactly O'Connell meant by Repeal. We must in the first place note the important point made by Dr. Denis Gwynn in his biography. O'Connell belonged to the ancient Irish race which had resisted English domination all down the centuries. Until the Stuart cause was finally and irretrievably ruined by the victory of the Anglo-Prussian alliance in the Seven Years' War, the Catholic Irish had remained loyal to the exiled dynasty and bitterly hostile to the Hanoverians and all they stood for. This hostility extended at a later date even to the Irish Volunteers who vindicated the liberties of the Protestant Parliament in 1782. We have an amusing letter, dated 1779, from a kinsman of O'Connell's then serving in Walsh's corps of the Irish Brigade in France, in which he speaks with soldierly relish of what he would do if he were in Ireland with his men. " I would kick the members and their Volunteers and their unions and their societies to the devil. I would make the rascally spawn of Cromwell curse the hour of his birth." At the same time the Stuart collapse turned the minds of many Catholics entirely from politics and towards the possibilities of wealth afforded both by smuggling and by legitimate trade. A disgusted poet of the time declared that they had turned from their longing for Ireland's legitimate King towards " butter and its makings." Such were O'Connell's immediate forbears ; and when in 1792 the first relief was given to Catholics hitherto smarting under the penal laws, they were ready enough to give allegiance to the Government and ultimately to lend their support to the Union, especially as it was coupled with a promise of further emancipation. The act of young Daniel O'Connell, therefore, in denouncing the Union even before its passage in 1800 constituted a " new departure " as far as representative Catholics were concerned.

There can be no doubt that he was partially helped towards this repudiation of his family's politics by his close study while in London of Radical literature, which had for a time almost shaken his Catholic faith and made him into a Deist. He recovered his Catholicism in full, but never lost his radicalism. His well-known attitude to the Irish language and its traditions was explicitly justified by himself on utilitarian, that is to say Benthamite, principles. In breaking with his masterful old uncle's views on politics he was thus no more going back to the traditional Gaelic attitude towards England and all its works than seeking a mere mechanical return to pre-Union conditions. His training as a lawyer and the very powerful legal bent it gave his mind came as a strong reinforcement to his radical tendencies. It was this legal bias, not any profound knowledge of history, and still less a theory of the indefectible rights of Ireland, that made him base his claim for justice to his country on the broken Treaty of Limerick and on the nullity of the shameful and dishonourable Union. Down to the very end his main argument against the Union, apart from its disastrous social and economic consequences, was its illegality, and he frequently suggested that it could be set aside by a simple proclamation from the Crown.

Because Repeal was only in a sense a special, if fundamental, case of justice, it was easy for O'Connell to narrow
his definition of Repeal to what was called Federalism, and
to conceive of and even advocate the securing of justice in
other forms. To the nationalist, the subordination of
sovereignty to such minor matters as the abolition of tithes
and the reform of corrupt and bigoted corporations seems
little short of blasphemy. Indeed, with the nationalist's
chronic tendency to talk of politics in religious terms,
blasphemy is what this kind of moderation is frequently
called. O'Connell must be acquitted of sin in this regard,
if only on the principle that there can be no crime without
a law. On the other hand, just as Repeal was a special
case of justice, so also in O'Connell's conception it included
or was coextensive with the minor reforms to which he
perforce at times subordinated it. He made it abundantly
clear that without Catholic Emancipation, manhood
suffrage, frequent parliaments and a very sweeping abate-
ment of every kind of privilege, Repeal would have meant
little to him. There were even times when he was prepared
to support single-chamber government. In all these respects
he was far in advance of Whigs like Lord John Russell.
It is not an exaggeration to say that as far as English and
Irish politics were concerned, he fully anticipated the
enlightened programme of Gladstone himself in his later
Liberal phase. The rancour aroused by his struggle for
justice to Ireland, and the self-sufficiency and complacency
of the English mind, have done much to conceal what
Liberalism at its best has owed to O'Connell.

But the story of his influence does not end even there.
Father Ventura's funeral oration, hailed at the time as a
superb example of eloquence, is nowadays apt to be dismissed as mere meaningless rhetoric. Nevertheless, it has
great value because it so splendidly sums up the contemporary impression made by O'Connell on the mind of
Europe. What most forcibly struck observers at the time
was the combination of apparent opposites which made him
at once a devout, outspoken Catholic and a most potent
advocate of reform. Ventura speaks of his triumph " in

having thus first reconciled liberty with order, independence with loyalty ; in having transformed into a principle of security and happiness that which was a principle destructive to thrones—a principle of desolation and the slavery of nations. This great pacific revolution, both in ideas and sentiments, began in Ireland, soon gained footing in England, and from England it penetrated into all parts of Europe." As a result of this revolution, says Ventura, the demagogues and Jacobins of the previous generation have been shown up in their true colours as " the supporters of that doctrine of the ancient pagans, the doctrine of the absolute supremacy of the State—a doctrine which abandons an entire Christian people to the caprice of a handful of men who call themselves ' the State ' and are the procreators of universal slavery." O'Connell, said his panegyrist, " has not merely modified, but has entirely changed the ideas of a great part of Europe. He it is who has unmasked the hypocrisy of demagogues and discredited sedition for ever." Translated into modern terms, this encomium may fairly be said to claim in advance for O'Connell that he was the creator of the Christian Democracy which is to-day, a hundred years after his death, the bulwark of Europe against the pagan doctrine of State supremacy. Considering how uncertain his reputation among his own people has been and still remains, the claim gives Irishmen something to ponder over

YOUNG IRELAND

Denis Gwynn

The total collapse of O'Connell's reputation after and since his death has been scarcely less remarkable than the unprecedented popularity and confidence which he inspired during almost his whole life time as the creator of the Irish democratic movement. Unquestionably his immense services have been disparaged with a deplorable ingratitude. Scarcely any other Irishman has been pursued with such a shameful campaign of vilification after his death ; and in consequence O'Connell's name has come to be regarded by later generations almost as a symbol of political imbecility and corruption. The explanation, of course, is that O'Connell's policy of agitation strictly within the law, and his condemnation of violence (which would at every stage of his public activities have enabled the Government to suppress his agitation) incurred the opposition of the Young Ireland movement during the last few years of his life. The history of those eventful years has been recorded particularly by two men of outstanding ability who were both involved in the controversy with O'Connell. Sir Charles Gavan Duffy's *Young Ireland* and *Four Years of Irish History* present a documented narrative in which, in spite of Duffy's scrupulous regard for accuracy and fair play, O'Connell's actions and general policy are described from a strongly prejudiced point of view. Duffy does at least attempt to write with moderation when he is in disagreement with O'Connell. But John Mitchel treats him sometimes as a scapegoat for all the political disasters of the time, and more often as the target for his own exuberant and irresponsible invective, delivered from afar, many years after O'Connell's death, and without even troubling to arrange the facts in correct chronological sequence.

" Let me do O'Connell justice, bitter and virulent as may have been the hatred he bore to me in his last days of public life." So writes John Mitchel at the outset of a sketch of O'Connell's character in his *Last Conquest of*

Ireland, in which he pours out the poison that had been accumulating in his embittered mind during some fifteen years of unhappy exile. " He had used all his art and eloquence to emasculate a bold and chivalrous nation " ; " O'Connell was, therefore, next to the British Government, the worst enemy that Ireland ever had—or rather the most fatal friend " ; " so capable at once of the highest virtues and the lowest vices—of the deepest pathos and the broadest humour—of the noblest generosity and most spiteful malignity." To Mitchel more than to any other must be ascribed responsibility for the fact that O'Connell's colossal services to the Irish people have been ridiculed and misrepresented. It was Mitchel who provided the late Sir James O'Connor with the most insulting of the caricatures of O'Connell which he strung together as a composite portrait[1] in his *History of Ireland*. " Poor old Dan ! Wonderful, mighty, jovial and mean old man, with silver tongue and smile of witchery and heart of melting ruth—lying tongue, smile of treachery, heart of unfathomable fraud. What a royal yet vulgar soul, with the keen eye and potent sweep of a generous eagle of Cairn Tual—with the base servility of a hound and the cold cruelty of a spider." This unscrupulous invective, made all the more damaging by its inclusion of tributes to the humour and the humanity of O'Connell, has for several generations provided the conception of O'Connell which has been formed by those who learned their Irish history (as I did) from the ardent disciples of John Mitchel. He did not confine his denunciations to O'Connell's political theory and practice. He created this monstrous legend of O'Connell's " treachery " and " fraud " and " meanness."

Yet Mitchel can scarcely have even seen O'Connell on more than a limited number of occasions. He was one of the latest recruits to the Young Ireland movement, and he did not become actively connected with it until the autumn of 1845. Davis died in September, 1845, and it was to replace Davis as the principal political writer on the *Nation* that Duffy invited Mitchel to give up his practice as a

[1] *History of Ireland*, 1798–1924, pp. 257–8.

solicitor in Banbridge and come to Dublin as a professional journalist. The Repeal Association had been founded by O'Connell early in 1841, when he was already a man of sixty-six ; the *Nation* had been founded by Duffy and Davis and Dillon in the autumn of 1842 ; the " monster meetings " had been held in a protracted series from the spring to the early autumn of 1843 ; the State trials had followed, and O'Connell and other leading members of the movement had been imprisoned for three months during the spring of 1844. Smith O'Brien had joined the Repeal Association in October, 1843, after the collapse of the Clontarf meeting and in protest against the coercion policy of the Tories. During O'Connell's trial and imprisonment he had acted as deputy leader of the movement and had won the confidence and admiration of all the younger men, particularly of Davis and Duffy. But a whole year more elapsed between the release of the prisoners and the death of Davis in October 1845 ; and by that time, according to Gavan Duffy,[1] John Mitchel had so far contributed to the *Nation* only one review, one leading article and half another. He had been at work on the life of Hugh O'Neill which Duffy had commissioned him to write for the " Library of Ireland," but it was not yet finished. Duffy had known him for some years as an Ulster Unitarian with nationalist views, and in the months just before Davis died he and John Martin and O'Hagan had all taken a holiday together.

So far as personal experience of O'Connell was concerned, Mitchel had not even taken any prominent part in the movement outside his own district in County Down until after the Repeal agitation had swept the country and was beginning to subside. By the time that he reached Dublin after the death of Davis, O'Connell was an old and broken man who was to die before long in Italy after a protracted illness. In the autumn of 1845, even before Davis died or Mitchel came to Dublin, O'Connell had virtually handed over the leadership to his son John O'Connell. " In the absence of the legitimate leaders," writes[2] Duffy in his

[1] *Young Ireland*, II, p. 192.
[2] *Ibid.*, p. 195.

meticulous record of the time, " Mr. John O'Connell was in undisputed control of the Association, and was deliberately destroying the labour of years, and the hopes of a generation. He played the part of a dictator at that time with a dogmatism which his great father after a life of public services rarely assumed." From that time forward a deliberate campaign was conducted by John O'Connell, to whom every contemporary writer attributes the full responsibility, with the object of driving the Young Ireland party out of the Repeal Association. No sincere historian could defend or excuse the attitude of John O'Connell. He counted upon taking over the leadership of the national organisation from his father who was already a dying man. For years the party funds of the Repeal Association had been collected as a personal tribute to his father, who had derived little benefit from the fund as he had to pay most of the election expenses and the salaries of party officials. It had become evident at this time that the appeal of O'Connell's name could no longer produce a fund adequate to maintain the party organisation ; and O'Connell's family knew, more clearly than other people, that he could not live more than a few years. That fact is, I believe, the simple explanation of the sudden decision, after the Whigs returned to office in 1846, that O'Connell's sons and dependents should accept Government office. Control of the popular movement had virtually passed into the hands of the " Young Liberator," and Daniel O'Connell's infrequent interventions in public affairs during 1846 were little more than expressions of approval and support for what his son decided. He had become a mental and physical wreck, as a result of the softening of the brain which began to afflict him in 1844. By the end of 1846 he was obviously a dying man. He left Ireland in early February, 1847, made one last pathetic appearance in the House of Commons, and was ordered to Hastings by his doctors in the hope that sea air would revive him. Then he set out on his last journey through France to Genoa, where he died on his way to Rome.

Whereas Mitchel claims that O'Connell had regarded him with " bitter and virulent hatred " during his " last days of public life," it is more probable that O'Connell had no clear idea of who Mitchel was. He would have regarded him simply as one of the latest arrivals among that group of opinionated and self-satisfied young men who considered themselves entitled to dictate the proper policy of the Repeal Association which O'Connell had created, and who would persist in criticising and denouncing the very weary old pilot who was navigating his ship through rocky courses of which they had no experience. O'Connell's public life was practically finished before Mitchel's began. It is true that Mitchel had been only a few months in Dublin before he involved Gavan Duffy and the *Nation* in a prosecution for his inflammatory article which declared that the Irish railways could be used to obstruct the movements of British troops. It was a typically defiant article, but singularly ill timed when great efforts were being made to induce the Government to spend large sums on constructing Irish railways as a remedy for distress during the famine. O'Connell, as well as his son, denounced it; and even Duffy, who had invited Mitchel to Dublin to work on the *Nation* as his assistant, was out of sympathy with it, although he had to assume responsibility when the prosecution followed. But this was one of the few occasions when O'Connell was personally aware of Mitchel's existence or activities. By the time that the Young Irelanders, led by Smith O'Brien, walked out of Conciliation Hall in protest against John O'Connell's suppression of Meagher's famous speech in defence of the Sword, the old Liberator was virtually in retirement.

The first onset of the potato blight in the autumn of 1845, and the famine that resulted in the following winter and spring, had broken the spirit of the people. In June, 1846, the Tory Government were defeated on the Corn Laws, and when the Whigs formed a new Ministry they made a strong bid for O'Connell's support by appointing his friend Lord Duncannon, who had now become Lord Bessborough, Lord-Lieutenant of Ireland. He was the first resident Irish peer who had ever been appointed to that position. John O'Connell and the swarm of party officials who had been wondering what would happen to them if the Repeal fund could not be maintained, seized the opportunity of providing for themselves by soliciting offices and paid positions under a new Whig administration which promised to reverse Peel's coercive policy. By that autumn, the potato blight had inflicted much more widespread losses than in the previous year; and there was every prospect of a more devastating famine than had been experienced hitherto. In October O'Connell was writing from Darrynane to his agent Fitzpatrick :

> My dear Friend—It would be the absurdest of all absurd things to think of a tribute in such times as these. They are indeed more awful than you have any notion of. All our thoughts are engrossed with the two topics—endeavouring to keep the people from outbreaks, and endeavouring to get food for them. I tell you danger is in our path. May the great God, in his infinite mercy, mitigate the calamity and avert the danger !

Only a few months more of life remained to him before he set out on that final journey which his doctors ordered as the only hope of keeping him alive. His correspondence, which had been so extensive, had almost ceased. Only a few letters survive from these last months, and they are concerned chiefly with his efforts to bring about a reconciliation with the Young Irelanders who had seceded from the Association. In one of them, written to Devin Reilly, who was then a young man of only twenty-three, the old Liberator points out that, in suggesting the names for a conference to achieve reconciliation, he had placed Smith O'Brien's name before his own. The others were to be Sir Colman O'Loghlen, Mr. O'Hea, Mr. O'Hagan and John Blake Dillon. It is easy for us now to argue that O'Connell as an old man exaggerated the risks of legal prosecution at that time. His letter stresses the earnest care he had taken to bring about some settlement which would not result in exposing the Repeal Association to extinction on the ground that it condoned the use of violence. Far from displaying " bitter and virulent hatred " towards

these young men, who, be believed, had confronted him
with the risks of criminal prosecution that he had avoided
so skilfully for years, this letter, written in December, 1846,
shows an astonishing degree of patience and personal
humility. He was remonstrating with one of the recognised
spokesmen among his critics, who was younger than some
of his own grandchildren. The question at issue was not
whether physical force was morally justifiable or practically
expedient. It was whether the Repeal Association could
continue to avoid suppression on the ground that it had
become an unconstitutional movement. O'Connell's whole
public life had been one long battle of wits against successive
governments which ceaselessly sought some pretext for
disbanding the political movements by which he had
enabled the Irish democracy to exert real power. The
advocates of physical force were now claiming the right to
assert their doctrine within the Repeal Association, and
O'Connell was convinced that by asserting that claim they
would deprive the democracy of its only effective instrument
of action. To Devin Reilly he expounded[1] his views with
exemplary patience :

The Repeal Association is a legal body because it
disclaims any use of force or violence to achieve the Repeal
of the Union Statute. *Because it disclaims the use of physical
force to achieve the Repeal of the Union,* every member of the
Repeal Association is at present perfectly safe from any
prosecution.

Would the members be equally safe if it were to admit
any intermixture of the physical force principle as part
of the means for obtaining such Repeal ?

I am decidedly of opinion that the members would not,
in such a case, be safe from a well-founded prosecution.

I take these propositions to be clear in law : First :
That any assembly admitting any species of physical
force as part of its means of obtaining a repeal of an Act
of Parliament is an unlawful assembly, liable to be
dispersed by any magistrate, and its members punished
by indictment.

[1] Fitzpatrick, II, p. 394

Secondly : That any such assembly is not only unlawful, but that any acts done by it in furtherance of its objects constitute a treasonable fact, rendering the members liable to conviction and execution for treason.

This opinion, in point of law, I have at repeated public meetings proclaimed.

On one occasion, in the Association, I brought down the legal authorities and quoted them, chapter and page.

It is observable that, often as I have repeated this legal doctrine, no one has had the hardihood to deny its accuracy.

It follows, if I be right, that the seceders cannot safely be admitted into the Repeal Association unless upon the fullest and most explicit disclaimer of resorting to any physical force means to achieve the Repeal of the Union.

In order to be enabled to receive the seceders into the Association again it should be ascertained whether, beyond a doubt, I am right in point of law or not.

At former periods in my struggles for advancing the popular cause my judgment in matters of law was found eminently useful, and my opinion of the state of the law was trusted to with implicit confidence. And I have the comfort to know that such confidence was never regretted, nor shown by any fact to have been misplaced.

Now my most anxious desire is to lay the foundation of perfect conciliation, or, if that be refused, to have the universal people understand who it is to whom the continuance of the dissension is justly attributable.

I stand altogether upon the law. My sole difficulty rests upon the legal objection to the admission of the seceders. . . .

(There) should be a preliminary inquiry. It would be idle to talk upon the terms upon which the seceders should be readmitted, if we are prevented by the law from readmitting them except at the peril of our lives.

I have quoted only a part of this very long letter of patient exposition, in which there was no hint even of resentment at his authority being challenged, apart from the hurt allusion to the confidence with which his judgment on legal matters had been regarded in previous conflicts. It is easy to see how wide the divergence had grown between the outlook of the veteran agitator, in the grip of the last illness which soon carried him to his grave, and the restless impatience of the young men, little older than under-graduates, who demanded the right to proclaim their views defiantly. Plainly the days of the Repeal Association had reached their end; and nothing had yet emerged which seemed capable of winning popular confidence and support. To blame O'Connell for that situation at the very end of his strenuous life is surely unreasonable.

More serious are the prevalent and generally accepted accusations that he behaved as an unscrupulous bully towards the young men who dared to criticise him; that, whereas they were frank and fearless idealists, he treated them with intolerance and with complete lack of either generosity or candour. A mass of unpublished correspond-ence in the " Smith O'Brien Papers " has lately been placed at my disposal, which throws a remarkably clear light upon O'Connell's relations with the Young Irelanders. Smith O'Brien was in many ways their acknowledged leader, because he was the only man who sided with them, whose age and distinguished public services and experience gave him the necessary authority outside their own circle. He had attained a position of quite unique influence as an independent M.P. during the most exciting phase of the Repeal Association, and his speech in the House of Com-mons on the state of Ireland had been distributed broadcast by the Repeal Association, although he still proclaimed his belief that the Union could be made beneficial to Ireland. But when the Tories prosecuted O'Connell and other leaders of the Repeal Association after prohibiting the " monster " meeting at Clontarf, O'Brien formally joined the Association and announced that he would test the legality of its claims in his own person by holding county meetings or taking part in arbitration courts. His personal prestige stood so high that O'Connell very soon nominated him as his deputy leader during the State trials and while he was in prison. O'Brien had a gift for encouraging and organising team

work, and the young men of the *Nation* found him an
immensely helpful leader, whose integrity and scrupulous
accuracy in speech brought a most welcome contrast to the
petty intrigues and the bombast of the Repeal Association.
Later, he came into more direct disagreement with
O'Connell over other matters ; and when Meagher made
his celebrated " Sword " speech in July, 1846, O'Brien was
the first to walk off the platform, followed by all the younger
men in protest against its interruption by John O'Connell.
Through all this period O'Brien received a stream of letters
from the younger men, many of them written in the closest
confidence, and these letters are preserved among the Smith
O'Brien papers.

Smith O'Brien's personal relations with O'Connell are
particularly illuminating. O'Brien had joined the Repeal
Association, after being an open critic of its aims and
methods for many years, at the time when O'Connell's
personal popularity was at its greatest height. There had
been nothing like it in Ireland, or perhaps in any country,
up to that time ; and it is scarcely far-fetched to compare
his position in the autumn of 1843 with that of Mussolini
in Italy before his march on Rome. Month after month
from spring to autumn in that year he had been the central
and directing figure in a series of colossal public demonstrations which became increasingly excited and intoxicating.
His journeys from place to place had been a succession of
triumphal processions. Every word that he spoke was
recorded in the newspapers, and every speech was jealously
noted, sentence by sentence, by a Government which was
determined to find some pretext for suppressing his agitation
but was constantly outwitted by his ingenuity. No man
could have been expected to remain a normal human being,
or to escape the growth of personal vanity, after so much
flattery and applause and sheer physical and mental exertion. Yet O'Connell, by all the evidence available, appears
to have by some miracle retained not only his sense of
humour but a genuine personal humility.

His treatment of Smith O'Brien was only one instance.
They had been opponents in politics ever since the Clare

election of 1828, which occurred within a few months of O'Brien's election as the young M.P. for Ennis. The O'Briens had represented either County Clare or the borough of Ennis, or both, without interruption for seven generations ; and Smith O'Brien's elder brother Lucius was in fact the other member for Clare when O'Connell was elected. Their father Sir Edward O'Brien had been in Grattan's Parliament as a young man and had voted with Grattan against the Union. They had an intense pride in their ancestral and patriotic tradition in Clare, and they strongly resented O'Connell's intrusion. Dromoland Castle became the headquarters of the landlords' opposition to O'Connell's election campaign ; and when after the Emancipation Act was carried O'Connell had to contest the seat again, the only public opposition to him came from Smith O'Brien, who protested against this intrusion from outside and declared foolishly that O'Connell had been elected " against the unanimous wish of the gentry of the county." For those ill-chosen words he had to fight a duel with his Protestant neighbour, Tom Steele, who had been one of O'Connell's most active supporters. And for years afterwards, in spite of his popular and radical sympathies, he had maintained an attitude of disdainful disapproval towards O'Connell's methods. When he became M.P. for Limerick he had publicly refused to attend a banquet in O'Connell's honour and had scornfully defied the implied threat that he would lose many votes if he did not go to it. Later again he had all but brought in the Tories by persisting, with Joseph Hume, in voting against Lord Melbourne's Ministry on the Jamaica Bill ; and O'Connell had felt compelled to mobilise the Limerick clergy to demand his resignation.

These were facts which a great demagogue could scarcely be expected to disregard at the climax of his own career as an agitator, when Smith O'Brien sent in his first modest subscription as a belated convert to the principles of Repeal. O'Connell's speech of welcome, when Smith O'Brien's long letter was read out at the first meeting in Conciliation Hall, might be dismissed as " blarney " in his exaggerated manner.

But the test of his sincerity followed quickly when O'Brien's delighted constituents in county Limerick organised a public banquet in his honour and invited the Liberator to attend. The State trials were impending and he had ample excuses for not travelling to Limerick, but he seized the opportunity that enabled him to go there. " Without the least affectation," O'Connell wrote to the organisers of the banquet in accepting their invitation, " I declare my conviction that no man ever deserved better of his native country than he does of Ireland. He has done the best possible service, at the fittest possible time : and certainly merits to be enrolled amongst the most pure benefactors of his native land." Nor was there any hesitation in inviting O'Brien to become an active member of committees of the Association, in which his presence was certain to encourage that critical and independent spirit which O'Connell was believed to resent. He was even invited to join on special terms which would not require his personal attendance except whenever it suited him, and he was to be consulted regularly by correspondence. For years it had been asserted that O'Connell would never allow a man of independent views or influence to hold any position of importance under him. But Smith O'Brien's whole reputation rested on his resolute independence and his outspoken sincerity, and O'Connell not only welcomed and encouraged him but appointed him almost immediately as his deputy. His action is the more striking because the growth of the Repeal Association had in fact produced all the elements of a direct challenge to his personal authority ; and at the end of that fantastic series of monster meetings he might well be expected to resent interference more than ever before.

O'Connell knew well how restless were the young men who gathered around the *Nation* newspaper, how constantly they criticised his refusal to give any account of the party funds, and how they distrusted his enormous personal influence over the masses which enabled him to override their objections at any time. Even so, he knew that they had established something analogous to a Cabinet council by their industrious work on the General Committee. They would have ample scope while he was prevented from attending to political matters during the progress of the protracted State trials; and neither Ray, the secretary of the Association, nor his favourite son John, whom he had trained for the leadership, would be there to control the young men, since they were both on trial with him. To entrust the deputy leadership to Smith O'Brien in such circumstances was an act of real magnanimity, not only towards a former political opponent whose personal attitude he had strong reason to resent, but towards the younger men who had often caused him anxiety. The trials dragged on, leaving political agitation almost in a vacuum, and the restlessness of the younger men deepened while they realised that O'Connell's energy and ardour were plainly failing. O'Brien had no personal ambition, and when the leadership devolved upon him he formed a parliamentary committee, as Duffy[1] puts it, " of the best available men, and his Committee now became the motive power of the organisation." The Smith O'Brien papers reveal how strong were the undercurrents of dissatisfaction with O'Connell among the young men. O'Brien made a point of consulting with O'Connell on all important matters, and he impressed upon Davis particularly that in O'Connell's absence they must be more careful than they would normally be in considering any action of which he might disapprove.

One might well imagine that O'Brien had been entrusted with a very thankless position and that the great demagogue would quickly repudiate him or diminish his influence as soon as he regained his freedom. An extremely delicate position did in fact arise. The trial resulted in a verdict against all the accused, but sentence was not to be passed until the next sessions. O'Connell went straight to London and was received with tumultuous ovations both in Parliament and in a succession of public demonstrations. Meanwhile the agitation was flagging at home and the younger men considered that O'Connell was compromising himself by seeking English applause. O'Brien had to perform the invidious duty of telling him to cut out further meetings

---

[1] *Young Ireland*, II, p. 50.

in England and return at once. O'Connell's reply reveals a generosity and humility which could never have been expected from any politician in such circumstances. Agreeing to return immediately, after attending a farewell Irish rally in Liverpool, he expressed doubts of the wisdom of organising a dinner in his honour in Dublin, because he believed " not one of the Irish Whigs " would attend it. But he asked O'Brien to decide and added :

If you differ with me in opinion, I will freely act upon yours in place of my own. Will you see my son John and Ray and communicate your thoughts to them ? I know you meet them constantly on Committee, else I would not ask you to take the trouble. . . .

I cannot close without offering you my most emphatically cordial thanks for the manner in which you have conducted the Repeal cause since I left Dublin. I really think your accession quite providential—nothing less. You are by your ' antecedents ' and your popular talents and your rank and religion just the *beau idéal* of the person wanted to make the cause of Repeal keep its course against the stream of persecution on the one hand and of otherwise inevitable desertion on the other. It may perhaps gratify you a little to know that I never felt half so grateful for the exertions of any other political colleague in my long experience.

Even the casual fact of your religion is most useful to the Repeal cause. It is impossible that any Protestant who calmly thinks can imagine that you would be a party to any political movement which could deprive Protestants of their legitimate station and due sway in the State. Politically speaking, I am delighted that you are a Protestant. Protestantism can never want just protection where you advise and direct.

It looks like affectation to thank you in the name of Ireland by a private letter. Yet I venture in the name of Ireland to thank you, and I can promise you that we your colleagues will never prove ourselves unworthy of your co-operation.

A succession of letters from O'Connell, written in a similar strain of gratitude and candid discussion, have been preserved among O'Brien's papers. They leave no room to doubt O'Connell's genuine sincerity in writing them, and they create an impression very different from that of the intolerant bully which has been so widely accepted. Time after time O'Connell asks O'Brien to decide some question for him which will involve committing him to definite action, while he promises to act according to O'Brien's decision. He awaits O'Brien's approval even upon such questions as whether he should go to London or not to attend Parliament; and at times he writes earnestly for a quick reply, promising that he will leave at once, if need be, or that he wishes to leave now but will not start before hearing from O'Brien. Gavan Duffy quotes at length one such letter from O'Connell to O'Brien consulting him about the plan that had been submitted by some of the Federalists, who would not yet advocate Repeal but had advanced a long way towards it. He tells O'Brien that he regards this advance by a large number of wealthy business men and influential landlords as being directly attributable to him, and he continues :

I do not hesitate to say further and to pledge myself not to assent to any plan for the restoration of the Irish Parliament, or to any of the details of any such plan, that meets with your disapprobation. *We* go together; that is, you go with me, because I certainly will not go a single step without you. . . . I will not take one single step about it without giving you *previous* intimation and consulting with you fully and deliberately.

Gavan Duffy adds a bitter comment to this letter, that " It need only be noted that these professions of a determination to act together were made ten days after O'Connell had written his public letter, declaring his preference for Federalism, on which he had not consulted O'Brien. They were made also several days after the *Nation* had opposed the scheme, when O'Brien's neutrality had become highly

important."[1]   Actually Duffy's statement is incorrect. He
had access to the O'Brien papers when he wrote his *Young
Ireland*, but he may easily have missed, among such a mass
of correspondence, another letter of O'Connell's written
three weeks earlier, in which O'Connell did definitely
consult O'Brien.

This whole Federalist episode was highly complicated,
and O'Connell's handling of it gave clear proof that he was
losing his old shrewd instinct for political management.
Duffy tells the story with more bitterness than can be justified, but he was deeply concerned in the controversy, which
led to much recrimination afterwards. Broadly speaking,
it was accepted by all the leading figures in the movement
that after the failure at Clontarf Repeal could not be quickly
attained and that the popular agitation in Ireland could not
be kept up indefinitely. The younger men, who had been
shocked by O'Connell's reckless prophecies of rapid success,
had been searching for some practicable goal to aim at for
their short-term programme. Davis particularly had been
impressed by the widespread signs of a desire for some
measure of Irish self-government which had been manifested
by those who were described as Federalists. He had himself
published an open letter to the Duke of Wellington purport-
ing to be written by a Federalist ; and he had urged strongly
that men of such views who would not yet advocate Repeal
deserved every encouragement and should be treated with
all sympathy. One of the principal figures in the group
who were working on these lines was the rich Dublin coach-
builder, Hutton : and Davis soon afterwards became
engaged to Hutton's daughter. Smith O'Brien, as a Protestant landowner who had passed through a long period
of conversion before he espoused Repeal, became the
recipient of many confidential letters from Federalists and
their friends. Davis had actually gone to Belfast to establish
contact with influential Federalists there when O'Connell
publicly expressed his approval of Federalism as an alternative to Repeal. O'Connell announced this so baldly that
Duffy, who was in charge of the *Nation* and unable to

---

[1] *Young Ireland*, II, p. 230–1.

consult at once with any of his principal colleagues, was scandalised and decided to express emphatic disagreement. He did so over his own name, and O'Connell's enemies were immensely rejoiced to find that his old authority was being publicly challenged. The controversy brought Gavan Duffy at once into great prominence as the leader of a revolt against O'Connell, although in fact the Young Irelanders, and particularly Davis and O'Brien, had been doing their utmost to encourage the Federalists without compromising their own convictions.

Duffy's account of the controversy conveys an impression of irrevocable conflict which the facts scarcely justify. He exaggerates, very naturally, the importance of an episode which affected him personally much more than it affected anyone else. O'Connell had only welcomed the Federalist proposals in their first vague outline, but he had pledged himself repeatedly to O'Brien that they must both be in full agreement. His handling was more clumsy than it used to be ; but this was not the first time that, after kite-flying, he had turned his back on some possible scheme that he had desired to test. Duffy's complaints against O'Connell are far more temperate than are the reckless diatribes of John Mitchel. But they have contributed largely, for that very reason, to detract from O'Connell's reputation as an Irish leader. His complaints concerning the Federalist controversy seem to me, at least, quite unreasonably exaggerated. Much more damaging is the account he gives of O'Connell's controversy with Thomas Davis ; and in that matter also O'Connell's side of the argument has been unfairly neglected, while his actual treatment of Davis has been grossly misrepresented. Duffy's story of the movement, so conscientiously and so fairly written, has become the basis of almost all subsequent narratives of the period ; and his point of view, which was definitely distorted by his great affection for Davis, has been accepted without question.

But in truth O'Connell had suffered considerable provocation from the restless and suspicious attitude of Davis, which constantly suggested a sense of injured innocence and of moral superiority. Conflict was certain to arise, moreover, from the fact that Davis considered it his mission to assert the rights of free discussion on religious matters within a movement which was overwhelmingly composed of Catholics. All over Ireland O'Connell was still acclaimed as the "Liberator" because of his achievement in organising the Catholic agitation, and it was inevitable that the Repeal movement should be largely a revival of the Catholic Association. But to Davis there was something almost indecent in the notion of religious, or as he would have said "sectarian," associations in relation to national politics. In the circumstances of the time it would have been impossible to keep the Catholic and the nationalist movements entirely separate ; but Davis was acutely sensitive on the question. He would insist that the principle of religious liberty was involved in petty controversies which should have been prevented from assuming any large importance. Few Irishmen have ever been so devoid of a sense of humour as Davis was ; and lack of it deprived him of a balanced perspective in politics, while it made him a prey to nervous irritation. Even Duffy, in recalling his earliest impression of Davis at their first meeting, confesses[1] that " at first sight he seemed to me somewhat arrogant and dogmatic, as men much in earnest are apt to look, but after a little the beaming earnestness of his face and the depth and piercing *timbre* of his voice in conversation mitigated my first impression." A few years later, at the time of the State trials, this earnest young man had only just reached the age of thirty, while O'Connell was sixty-nine and had for a whole year been living in a whirlwind of popular applause, which he had enjoyed with boisterous good humour. Solemnity, whether in the old or the young, was always liable to irritate him ; and it must be admitted that Davis could be portentously solemn. He had made a habit of working behind the scenes, and avoiding publicity himself with the ascetic modesty of such men who prefer to exert influence without receiving public recognition. But Smith O'Brien had[2] " positively insisted " that he must

[1] *Young Ireland*, I, p. 30.
[2] *Ibid.*, II, p. 131.

take the chair at one of the Association's weekly meetings
so that he should begin to " act a prominent part in Irish
affairs." Duffy gives some extracts[1] from the speech that
Davis made on this occasion, which must have been a striking
contrast to the cheerful manner in which O'Connell addressed his audiences. " I thank you for your cheers," said
Davis after he had been moved into the chair ; " but it
would not be candid in me to let you conceive that it was for
them I laboured. I and others work not for popular applause—if your shouts were given to our enemies and your
curses to us, we would work exactly as we are doing."

Young men who talk in that style are apt to be unduly
sensitive ; and even Duffy's usual sense of proportion for-
sakes him where Davis is concerned. Duffy tends to make
excuses for Daniel O'Connell on the ground that his son was
really responsible for the alleged conspiracy to drive Davis
and his friends out of the Repeal Association. The method
employed, he suggests, was " religious intrigue." They
were to be represented as " the secret enemies of the Church
and the Liberator." There was nothing inherently improbable in such a development, and Duffy's interpretation
of events has been generally taken for granted. But on
closer examination the evidence he produces is surprisingly
unconvincing. " Paragraphs began to appear in provincial
papers," he writes,[2] " charging Davis with anti-Catholic
sentiments. They might as reasonably have charged him
with anti-Irish prejudices. He was a Protestant with the
most generous and considerate indulgence for the opinions
of the bulk of his countrymen. But it was a point on which
the people were naturally sensitive and ready to take alarm."
There was, in fact, every likelihood of hurt feelings on both
sides, and one expects Duffy to produce instances of severe
provocation. Actually the only instance he quotes in this
first phase is the ungrateful conduct of a former school-
master, Edward Walsh, for whom Davis had obtained
employment on the staff of Conciliation Hall. Walsh had
" contributed some sweet simple verses to the *Nation*,"

[1] *Life of Davis*, p. 283.
[2] *Ibid.*, p. 269.

where an immense amount of sentimental poetry found publication. But even the *Nation* rejected many of the verses submitted to it, and Walsh wrote an aggrieved letter to " a county paper " complaining that " Davis had rejected one of his poems on account of the Catholic sentiments it contained." It seems astonishing that an editor with Duffy's long experience should seriously quote, as evidence of a political conspiracy directed by the O'Connells, this wholly unimportant complaint by a minor poet whose verses had been rejected. Duffy then proceeds to deal with the next attack " of a much graver character." But again it seems extraordinary that such importance should be attached to a book review contained in the quarterly *Dublin Review*. Not one in a thousand of the *Nation's* readers was likely to have seen even one number of the *Dublin Review* ; and its book reviews were still less likely to influence popular opinion in Ireland. It is true that O'Connell had been one of the founders of the *Dublin Review* ten years before. Mgr. Wiseman had met him during his first visit to England from Rome, when he was still rector of the English College, and he and O'Connell had agreed to launch a new Catholic review, as a counterblast to the *Edinburgh*. O'Connell, as often happened, became personally liable for financing it during the first years of its struggling existence ; but his connection with it had ceased long before the Repeal Association was founded. But Davis could never refrain from denouncing what he called sectarianism or bigotry, and he found that the *Dublin Review* in the summer of 1844 had dealt harshly and unfairly with a book written by one of his most intimate friends, D. O. Maddyn. Duffy describes the sequel and its results :

The *Dublin Review*, in noticing Maddyn's recent book, pointed out that the assailant of O'Connell was a man who had once been a Catholic but had abandoned his creed for a more prosperous one, and it treated the criticism of such a person with contempt. The reviewer was a professor of dogmatic theology, writing in a religious periodical, and no one will wonder that he insisted on this view of the transaction. But Davis, who was jealous for

his friend, and still more for religious liberty, censured
the spirit of the reviewer as destructive of Irish union.

Davis had in fact written in the *Nation* :

> If this be, as it seems, a threat, all we can say is, it
> shall be met.   The Repeal Association, under O'Connell's
> advice, censured most severely those in Cork who hissed
> a convert to Protestantism.   Neither he nor we nor any
> of our party will stand tamely by and see any man
> threatened or struck by hand or word for holding or
> changing his creed.   If this were allowed (we say it in
> warning) events would ensue that would indeed change
> the destinies of Ireland.

The reviewer, Duffy continues, " who was a strong,
passionate, but perfectly honourable man, turned fiercely
on his critic, and in a letter to the *Weekly Register*, denounced
the *Nation* as teaching anti-Catholic doctrines.   Several
instances were cited which it was perfectly possible for a
teacher of dogmatic theology to consider dangerous, but
which were innocent in design, and if they appeared in any
Irish journal of to-day would not attract the slightest censure.   The reviewer would have scorned to make any charge
which he did not believe to be substantially true, but he
was in a passion, and he was fighting for his individual will
as vehemently as for his convictions." [1] Unquestionably
Davis had shown courage, but he could scarcely have
chosen a more unfortunate or inadequate occasion for
displaying provocation.   Maddyn's book was not only
hostile but insolent towards O'Connell, and Maddyn himself
was a former Catholic who had bettered his social and
financial position by becoming a Protestant.   No one seems
to have assumed that he became a Protestant out of religious
conviction, or was in any way different from thousands of
other men or women who changed their religion to escape
the disabilities that were imposed on Catholics by law.   But
Davis in his chivalrous way would not tolerate the imputa-
tion of base motives to his friend, and he treated this quite

[1] *Life of Davis*, p. 270.

insignificant piece of book reviewing as a denial of the rights of religious freedom.

Having used the *Nation* to deliver a broadside attack upon Maddyn's critic, he was disgusted to find that O'Connell's Catholic followers began to regard him with suspicion. " We found," writes Duffy, " after a little time that it was circulated among the priests south and north that there was a dangerous spirit in the *Nation*, hostile to religion." Davis was soon writing excited letters to his friends, urging them to join with him " in defence of a sacred principle." " Davis was still in Ulster when the letters of 'An Irish Priest ' were published," Duffy continues, " and he wrote to me from Belfast :

> I have written to J. O'Connell, O'Brien, etc. by this post, to stop the lies of the bigot journals. I have done so less even on account of the *Nation* (which can be steered out of the difficulty in three weeks without any concession) than to ascertain whether the Catholics can and will prevent bigots from interfering with religious liberty. If they cannot, or will not, I shall withdraw from politics ; as I am determined not to be the tool of a Catholic ascendancy while apparently the enemy of British domination. . . .

On the same day Davis wrote to Smith O'Brien, who was in a position to influence O'Connell :

> I entreat of you to write to O'Connell requiring some disavowal, or at least a stop to the bigoted attacks on the *Nation*. I wrote that a man has as good a right to change from Catholicity to Protestantism as from Protestantism to Catholicity ; and called the State trial miracle " mock," and censured the Italian censorship. I shall do so again ; and I shall never act with a party that quarrels with such opinions. I will not be the conscious tool of bigots. I will not strive to beat down political in order to set up religious ascendancy. You, unless I have mistaken you, will subscribe to what I now say. The Federalist leaders here go entirely with me, and in fact, now or never, we Protestants must ascertain whether we are to have religious

liberty. I have written to J. O'C. on this. My defence of D. O. Maddyn (" Ireland and its rulers," part III) against the *Dublin Review* seems to have called out this attack. Is this to be endured? Is it even politic to endure it?

O'Brien did write to O'Connell. As a Protestant who had far less experience of Catholics than Davis had, he was just as likely to be sensitive to any hint of anti-Protestant bias; but he evidently thought that Davis was making a mountain out of a mole-hill. He wrote[1] to Davis with real sympathy and friendship, saying that he personally agreed much more with the opinions of the *Nation* than with those of the " Irish Priest "; " but, then, you and I should re- member that we are Protestants, and that the bulk of the Irish are Catholics." Duffy confesses that the terms of O'Brien's reply, " read a generation later, must be recog- nised as just and reasonable in their general scope : but at the moment they were probably not a little exasperating, as an answer to the warning of a danger which was imminent and which might lay the national cause prostrate at the feet of its enemies." Smith O'Brien's letter showed that even he thought Davis was unduly sensitive; and for that reason it is all the more remarkable to find what pains O'Connell himself took in writing to Davis when he might with good reason have told him that he was making himself a nuisance. Davis was asking O'Connell's protection after he had pro- voked the *Dublin Review* critic by praising a book which was deliberately insulting to O'Connell. The old man's reply[2] must be quoted in full :

My Dear Davis—My son John has given me to read your Protestant philippic from Belfast. I have under- taken to answer it, because your writing to my son seems to bespeak a foregone conclusion in your mind that we are in some way connected with the attacks upon the *Nation*. Now I most solemnly declare that you are most entirely mistaken—none of us has the slightest inclination

[1] *Life of Davis*, p. 272.
[2] *Young Ireland*, II, pp. 231–3.

to do anything that could in any wise injure that paper, or its estimable proprietor; and certainly we are not directly or indirectly implicated in the attacks upon it.

With respect to the " Italian Censorship," the *Nation* ought to be at the fullest liberty to abuse it; and as regards " the State Trial Miracle," the *Nation* should be at liberty to abuse not only that but every other miracle from the days of the Apostles to the present.

But we Catholics, on the other hand, may be permitted to believe as many of these miracles as we may adopt either from credulity or convincing proofs; at the same time I see no objection to a Catholic priest arguing any of these points or censuring, in suitable and civil terms, opinions contrary to his own.

As to the Cork attack upon a Protestant proselyte, you know that I publicly and most emphatically condemned it; as did the Catholic Press of Cork.

With respect to the *Dublin Review*, the word " insolence " appears to me to be totally inapplicable—all the *Review* did (and I have examined it again and deliberately) was to insist that a man who from being a Catholic became a Protestant, was not a faithworthy witness in his attacks upon the Catholic clergy. Now, independent of that man's religion, of which I care nothing, there never lived a more odious or disgusting public writer, with one single exception, and that is the passage in which he praises you.

The " insolence " of the *Dublin Review* consisted, as I have said, of merely stating that a pervert from Catholicity, who abused the Catholic clergy, was a suspicious witness in declaring their guilt. Would you not have a right, if a person who, from being a Protestant became a Catholic and abused the Protestant clergy, to state that his evidence against them ought to be considered as suspicious or even unworthy of belief? Yet for no greater offence than that, the *Review* is attacked, and a high and haughty tone of threatening assumed in speaking of it.

I really think you might have spared the insinuation that you and other Protestants were " pioneering the way to power," for men who would establish any sort of

Catholic ascendancy. I know this, and I declare it most solemnly, that in the forty years I have been labouring for the public I never heard one bigoted expression, not only in our public meetings but in our committees and private discussions, from a Catholic : but I have often felt amongst SOME of the Liberal Protestants I have met with, that there was not the same soundness of general liberality amongst them as amongst the Catholics.

I hate bigotry of every kind, Catholic, Protestant, or Dissent, but I do not think there is any room for my interfering by any public declaration at present. I cannot join in the exaltation of Presbyterian purity or brightness of faith, at the same time that I assert for everybody a perfect right to praise both the one and the other, liable to be assailed in argument by those who choose to enter into the controversy at the other side. But with respect to the *Dublin Review*, I am perfectly convinced the *Nation* was in the wrong. However, I take no part either one way or the other in the subject. As to my using my influence to prevent this newspaper war, I have no such influence that I could bring to bear : you really can much better influence the continuance or termination of this bye battle than I can. All I am anxious about is the property in the *Nation*. I am most anxious that it should be a lucrative and profitable concern. My desire is to promote its prosperity in every way I could ; I am besides proud as an Irishman of the talent displayed in it ; and by no one more than by yourself. It is really an honour to the country ; and if you would lessen a little of your Protestant zeal, and not be angry when you " play at bowls in meeting rubbers," I should hope that, this skirmish being at an end, the writers for the *Nation* will continue their soul-stirring, spirit-enlivening strains, and will continue " to pioneer the way " to genuine Liberty, to perfect liberality, and entire political equality for all religious persuasions.

If I did not believe that the Catholic religion *could* compete upon equal and free terms with any other religion, I would not continue a Catholic for one hour.

You have vexed me a little by the insinuations which your letter contains, but I heartily forgive you ; you are an exceedingly clever fellow, and I should most bitterly regret that we lost you by reason of any Protestant monomania.

We Papists *require* co-operation, support, combination, but we do not *want* protection or patronage.

I beg of you, my dear Davis, to believe, as you may do in the fullest confidence, that I am most sincerely

Your attached friend,
DANIEL O'CONNELL.

Among the Smith O'Brien Papers I have found the letter[1] in which O'Connell replied from Darrynane on 9th November to O'Brien's communication of the fears that Davis had expressed. Here at least one might have expected some explosion of exasperation or impatience. Not many political leaders of O'Connell's stature would have written with such gentle forbearance :

My dear O'Brien,

I entirely agree with you that if the repeal of the Union were to bring about such a state of things as would prevent any one Protestant or Catholic from believing or saying whatever he might think consistent with truth I would resist that repeal to the uttermost. In point of religion, our struggle is to obtain perfect religious freedom for all. This is the principle I have avowed and acted upon for near fifty years of my political life—perfect freedom of conscience for *all* and *every* one.

I do not believe there is the least danger of any bigotry tainting " the Association," not the least. I am thoroughly convinced that any sentiment of that kind would be scouted with unanimous execration.

It is not *so* with the newspapers—personal interests are involved in them—as long as I have been an *agitator* I have observed much acrimony amongst the public writers. They use every topic to annoy one another and to *transfer* circulation. But the course of the Association seems plain.

<hr>

[1] O'B. Papers, 1273.

It is most cautiously to avoid involving ourselves in the newspaper squabbles. We must not be identified with any of them and they will the sooner cease their mutual recrimination. I am quite sure you agree with me that the association ought not to be directly or indirectly a party to *these feuds*.

Nothing can be more impolitic or mischievous than these feuds. I do heartily wish we could put an end to them and I tender you all the assistance in my power for that purpose. The *Young Ireland* quarrel is I believe at an end. The writers at both sides in that strife were contributors to the same paper the *Vindicator*. I do believe we shall hear no more from them.

But it will be more difficult to appease the anger of the *Nation* and the *Irish Priest*. I had a letter from Davis written to my son John, on that subject and I candidly told him my opinion that in the attack on the *Dublin Review* he was much in the wrong. I have of course lost all influence with him, and you will have perceived by the *Nation* of Saturday the 2nd that the writer is in *no good temper* with me. What then can I do? I believe nothing but to keep clear of the adverse parties and obtain your assistance to keep the association quite disengaged from the controversy. I will gladly talk with you when we meet if you permit me. . . .

But the dispute continued to rankle with Davis, and he wrote a succession of private letters to warn his Protestant friends against the menace of bigotry. Suspicions were engendered for which there was little real foundation. Burke Roche (Lord Fermoy), who had been one of O'Connell's most ardent supporters at the monster meetings, wrote[1] to Davis : " If I hear much more of this damned outlandish bigotry in Conciliation Hall, I will go over and give you all a piece of my mind, which will be more useful than palatable." Men who would never have heard of the *Dublin Review* were exhorted to be on their guard against the conspiracy that Davis had detected in its book reviews.

[1] *Life of Davis*, p. 276.

To his friend, Alderman Staunton, the proprietor of the *Register* in Dublin, Davis wrote protesting vehemently against his having allowed the " Irish Priest " to publish " an anonymous letter full of illiberal principles and malicious hints." Davis insisted that " if his opinions be patronised by the Irish Catholics, the Irish Protestants must feel that religious liberty is in danger, and will take measures to preserve it. . . . I am resolved not to yield one of the points in dispute, nor to submit for an hour to such an Inquisition." The cumulative effect of these letters, which Gavan Duffy naturally quotes with full sympathy towards his friend, has created the impression that the Young Irelanders were being goaded into revolt by the obscurantism of O'Connell. Davis certainly convinced himself that manoeuvres were in progress to drive them out of the Repeal Association. His nerves became so strained that a conflict could scarcely have been avoided. There was common-sense in the letter [1] from his friend Dr. Cane, the Mayor of Kilkenny, who expostulated to him privately against his having said that " if such a view spread itself, you and a large number of Protestants would retire from the present movement." Cane pointed out that it was both " natural and likely " that such a result might be desired by their opponents, but that " if you are of the fit material for a leader, that move could neither surprise nor affright you from the national field."

The test was in fact imminent. It was Davis who had made the Protestant Repealers contemplate secession if they should consider themselves to be faced by the threat of religious bigotry. Unfortunately Davis used the word bigotry in a sense different from that of ordinary men. The question arose acutely when Peel introduced his proposals for establishing University Colleges in Cork and Galway and Belfast. It is usually assumed, as even Gavan Duffy implies, that the plan was an invention of Peel's, to sow dissension in Ireland and to give an impression of introducing reforms. But in fact the question of establishing provincial colleges had been strongly agitated as far back

[1] *Life of Davis*, p. 277.

as 1838. In that year two petitions to the Queen and to Parliament had been jointly organised by Thomas Wyse and by Smith O'Brien. They had both held public meetings, in Cork and in Limerick, which were attended by many influential men, and O'Brien himself had been able to submit more than eleven hundred influential signatures for a provincial college. Through all the subsequent years Wyse had remained an active and influential member of Parliament, and he had been able to report to O'Brien during the State trials that the project was at last progressing. But both Wyse and O'Brien had discovered, from their close connection with the first agitation for a provincial college, that the project was supported by men of very divergent views and for reasons that were scarcely compatible.

Broadly speaking, there were three different approaches to the question. There was a daring minority of Catholics, which in fact increased rapidly when the issue was debated, who held that the provincial colleges should be definitely for Catholics just as Trinity College, Dublin, was definitely Protestant. To expect any such concession from the British Government had seemed quite fantastic in the thirties, but the younger Catholics had gained confidence and now put forward bolder demands than their fathers had thought possible. More numerous were those who took it for granted that a State-endowed modern University could not have a Catholic character, but that it would at least be free of the anti-Catholic restrictions and other objections which practically ruled out Trinity College. Among these were many generous-minded Protestants, like Smith O'Brien and his friends, who believed that such a college would go far towards breaking down the old religious barriers, by educating Catholics and Protestants in the same institution. That view was also shared by many Catholics, especially of the older generation, who had never thought of a Catholic University as a possibility, and who hoped for more goodwill throughout the country as a result of " mixed education." A third view, much less widely held, was that the new College should be strictly undenominational on principle. English Radicals like Joseph Hume, who had been M.P. for

Kilkenny when the question was being agitated before, supported the project strongly on those grounds. And on that doctrinaire principle, of excluding " sectarian " influences from the University, Thomas Davis agreed with the English Radicals, though he admitted that he thought differently from his associates in Ireland.

Obviously there were all the elements of a vigorous controversy in such a situation : and O'Connell made full allowance for divergent views. But Davis had worked himself into a state of acute suspicion before the Bill was even introduced. In November, 1844, he had warned Smith O'Brien that the dispute over the " Irish Priest's " letter would have reactions on the education question.

> All this might pass for newspaper hubbub, to be frowned at and forgotten, but I know that it is part of a system for stopping the growth of secular education and free discussion, and that it has been, and is again likely to be within this month, a subject of serious debate, whether the *Nation* and 'promiscuous education' and 'independent' lay opinion should not be formally denounced by authority. The question at issue is religious liberty. I for one will not sacrifice my right to it for any consideration. We are assailed for condemning the Roman Censorship, for praising the simplicity of Presbyterian tenets, for not believing " O'Connell's miracle," for appreciating William Carleton's genius while we condemned his early offences against the Roman Catholics, and finally for resisting all sorts of religious persecution, from brickbats to defamation. If I am to be set upon for things, and the *Nation* officially denounced, or systematically run down for them, I pause ere I give any more help to put power into the hands of men with such intolerant principles.[1]

That last sentence suggests what difficulty O'Connell must have had in restraining himself from outbursts against such insinuations. The suggestion that O'Connell held " intolerant principles " was galling enough ; but there was

---

[1] *Young Ireland*, II, p. 128.

always the assumption that Davis and these young men in their twenties were " helping to put power into the hands " of veterans who had in fact created the popular movement and the vast organisation which had enabled the *Nation* to attain its influence. O'Connell was fully aware of that attitude. " I really think you might have spared the insinuation," he had written to Davis in that recent letter, " that you and other Protestants were ' pioneering the way to power ' for men who would establish any sort of Catholic ascendancy." That exasperating tone of moral superiority and righteousness does, unfortunately, appear very often in the private letters of Davis. And when one remembers the great difference in age and in status that separated them, it is really surprising that O'Connell continued to treat Davis with such patient consideration. A typical letter[1] is one written by Davis to Denny Lane some months before he died. " If anything could change my mixed feeling of admiration and censure of O'Connell into genuine hostility, it would be the vicious adulation and lying incentives proffered to him by the little stupid mercenary devils about him ; and his patronage of the vilest and weakest of them. They are trying to drive O'Brien, myself and others to secession, hoping to have the uncensored handling of public money with their gluey claws : but they shall be disappointed and beaten." Were they all really quite as wicked as he thought they were ?

Sooner or later some sort of public explosion between such conflicting temperaments was bound to occur. The inevitable " scene " took place in the debate on the Colleges Bill, and the story has been so often told that it need not be repeated in detail. For months Davis had been haunted by the belief that John O'Connell was trying to drive him and his *Nation* colleagues into resignation. There is little doubt that it was so by this time, because Davis had been fomenting suspicions which made dissension inevitable. Even Smith O'Brien was driven to exasperation by the situation that resulted. When the Colleges Bill was introduced, the conflict of views, with which he and Wyse had become

---

[1] *Life of Davis*, p. 304.

familiar six years earlier, arose at once. The Bill avoided
any subsidising of Catholic teaching by ruling out all
religious instruction. A staunch Protestant M.P. first protested against these " godless " Colleges. The Catholic.
bishops naturally protested also against "godless" education, and Archbishop MacHale's vehemence soon
encouraged John O'Connell to demand an openly Catholic
College, and to denounce any proposed compromise
as concession to paganism. When Thomas Wyse, who
had been closely concerned in the whole project,
insisted strongly on the advantages of educating Catholics
and Protestants together, John O'Connell's sacerdotal
attitude was pushed to deplorable extremes. He publicly
asked that Wyse should be compelled to resign his
seat for Waterford because of his " unchristian " attitude.
This provoked a spirited defence from Smith O'Brien as his
old friend and colleague, who favoured " mixed education "
on principle but agreed fully with the Catholic bishops that
provision should be made by each denomination for the
religious instruction of its own members. A letter to O'Brien
from Davis accepts that position reluctantly, while asserting
his private view that religion ought to be excluded from the
Colleges. The controversy was quite natural and even
healthy, but Davis was still haunted by the belief that the
O'Connells were trying to drive Protestants out of the
General Committee.

O'Brien, who was more entitled than most men to be
heard on the subject, sent a letter to the Committee ex-
pounding his own views, and was furious to learn that Davis
had refused to read it for fear of causing a crisis. He had
never been provoked, as O'Connell had, by the persistent
insinuations and criticisms of Davis, and they had been
corresponding with complete intimacy. Nor was there
anything like the same difference between their relative
positions in the popular leadership. But O'Brien lost his
temper with Davis where O'Connell had for years behaved
with absolute restraint. He wrote[1] to insist that his letter
on the Colleges Bill must now be published :

[1] *Life of Davis*, p. 289.

My dear Davis,

Being inexpressibly annoyed by the suppression of my letter on the subject of academical education, I sat down and wrote a long letter to you on the subject, but fearing lest it might give you unnecessary pain, I have since burnt it. I now enclose a note for Mr. Ray, which I shall feel obliged by your transmitting to him as soon as you have read it. . . . Feeling that I have other duties to perform as well as this which belongs to me as a member of the Repeal Association, I cannot consent to withdraw it.

I hope therefore there will be no further postponement. It is quite impossible to conceal the differences which exist on the subject of academical education. It would be base and unmanly on my part to seek to conceal the strong opinion which I entertain respecting a question in reference to which I have already taken a very prominent part. I have not the least objection that others should state their opinions with equal candour, and indeed they have done so already. There was nothing in my letter which could possibly offend anyone.

With that attitude O'Connell was at all times in full sympathy. His own views had changed as the discussion developed, and he had come to support the demand of the younger Catholics, led by his son and Archbishop MacHale, that a definitely Catholic College should be established. He stated quite openly that he wished to have two Catholic colleges, in Cork and Galway, while the new Queen's College in Belfast ought to be Presbyterian. The Irish Protestants already had all that anybody could want in Trinity College. To Smith O'Brien he wrote frankly that he hoped the Colleges Bill would be thrown out, because he believed it would be quickly replaced by a better Bill on those lines. Viewing the question now in long retrospect, one can see no reason why O'Connell should feel ashamed of holding that view. But the whole story of the controversy has crystallised around the famous incident at the Association's meeting when O'Connell at last did lose his temper with Davis on the question that had been smouldering for so long. It was tactless, to say the least, for Davis to commence his reply to Conway's speech by referring to him, with obvious irony, as " my Catholic friend, my very Catholic friend, Mr. Conway." This was more than O'Connell could stand, and he called out " It is no crime, I hope, to be a Catholic " ; adding later " The sneer with which you used the word would lead to the inference."

The sequel is well known, with O'Connell's brief outburst that " Young Ireland may play what pranks they please. I do not envy them the name they rejoice in. I shall stand by Old Ireland ; and I have some slight notion that Old Ireland will stand by me." For a man of O'Connell's excitable temper, and with his incomparable command of vituperation, the censure was probably the mildest that he ever uttered on an important occasion. And when Davis, after an impassioned reply burst into tears from sheer nervous strain, O'Connell rushed to seize his hand and exclaimed " Davis, I love you." To those of us who have been brought up on the legend that O'Connell was an intolerant bigot and a hypocritical intriguer, that phrase has seemed to add insult to injury. Yet the evidence shows undoubtedly that O'Connell, far from being intolerant towards these restless young men, regarded them with a most genuine affection. Within less than four months after that painful scene in Conciliation Hall, Davis had died suddenly after a few days' illness. O'Connell was in Darrynane when the news reached him, an old man breaking up rapidly and feeling the weight of years. There were a few close friends to whom he unburdened himself with complete freedom, of whom one was T. M. Ray, the secretary of the Repeal Association. The death of Davis came to him as a sudden shock, and in his letter to Ray one would expect to find some reference to their disagreements, some expression of regret that the young man had been so much obsessed by suspicions of the O'Connell family. The letter[1] survives, and is not easy to explain if we accept the legend that O'Connell would never allow any man of genius to work with him :

[1] Fitzpatrick, II, p. 263.

Darrynane Abbey,
September 17th, 1845.

My dear Ray,—I do not know what to write. My mind
is bewildered and my heart afflicted. The loss of my
beloved friend, my noble-minded friend, is a source of
the deepest sorrow to my mind. What a blow—what a
cruel blow to the cause of Irish nationality ! He was a
creature of transcendent qualities of mind and heart ;
his learning was universal, his knowledge was as minute
as it was general. And then he was a being of such
incessant energy and continuous exertion. I, of course,
in a few years—if years they be—still left to me, cannot
expect to look upon his like again, or to see the place he
has left vacant adequately filled up : and I solemnly
declare that I never knew any man who could be so useful
to Ireland in the present stage of her struggle. His loss
is indeed irreparable. What an example he was to the
Protestant youth of Ireland ! What a noble emulation
of his virtues ought to be excited in the Catholic young
men of Ireland ! And his heart, too ! it was as gentle,
as kind, as loving as a woman's. Yes, it was as tenderly
kind as his judgment was comprehensive and his genius
magnificent. We shall long deplore his loss. As I stand
alone in the solitude of my mountains, many a tear shall
I shed in the memory of the noble youth. Oh ! how vain
are words or tears when such a national calamity afflicts
the country. Put me down amongst the foremost contributors to whatever monument or tribute to his memory
shall be voted by the National Association. Never did
they perform a more imperative or, alas ! so sad a duty.
I can write no more. *Fungar inani munere.*

DANIEL O'CONNELL.

ENGLISH OPINION

TERENCE DE VERE WHITE

In O'Connell's day there was a fine contempt for the law of libel. Not only was it the fashion to criticise political opponents in words which would now be considered excessive if applied to a criminal convicted of half the crimes in the calendar—authors even had to submit to treatment which, in the case of Keats, is said to have brought on his consumption. Canning was eminent among Prime Ministers, but in his lifetime he was portrayed by Hazlitt as the meanest of mankind. Nowadays we spare the living; it is only when confronted with the past that our courage rises, and we are fearless in libelling the dead. But it may well be that this inhibition causes contemporary opinion to be more faithfully recorded to-day than it used to be. The old freedom produced an inflation of invective, in much the same way as the puffs preliminary of the film companies have debased the language of praise.

Extracts, selected at random, from newspaper articles and the speeches of his contemporaries, if put down without comment, could not but produce the impression that O'Connell was the most loathsome and contemptible figure that ever appeared in the public life of England. No one could believe that such consistent denunciation arose only from political hostility. And yet the truth is probably that O'Connell enjoyed considerable popularity among the masses in England, while in Europe he was one of the most honoured men of the day. The hatred which he first encountered came from the sources of power in England, the Court and the inner circle of Tories. It was purely political. Personal hostility came later and to some extent his exuberance in the use of epithets, his recklessness in abuse and slavishness in praise, were responsible for this. It estranged him from some of the best of his Irish supporters, and Newman—in whom Gladstone remarked a political narrowness—attributed the tardiness of his conversion to the antipathy which O'Connell, as the representative political Catholic, aroused in him.

Greville, who was usually calm in his judgment, wrote after O'Connell's death : " Up to the conquest of Catholic Emancipation his was certainly a great and glorious career. What he might have done and what he ought to have done after that, it is not easy to say, but undoubtedly he did far more mischief than good and exhibited anything but a wise, generous and patriotic spirit." For many years before he became one of the leading actors on the English political stage, O'Connell had attracted attention as " noises off." His first entry, heralded by the appropriate alarums, found him the object of much curiosity, some sympathy, and great speculation. His violence of language was already notorious, but many were prepared to excuse what Mackintosh described as " the rhetoric of just impatience." It was hard to blame him after " 27 years of just expectations disappointed," as Russell confided in a letter to Thomas Moore ; and, as well as this, there was considerable indignation that the Act of Catholic Emancipation did not contain any provision to enable O'Connell, who had been elected for Clare, to take his seat in parliament. In Greville's words, " They treat him with every indignity and then they complain of his violence . . . had he never been violent, he would not be the man he is, and Ireland could not have been emancipated."

Catholic Emancipation was inevitable, but it might have been postponed for a generation had it not been for O'Connell. He it was who made Peel carry through the House of Commons a Bill in violation of the prejudices and convictions of a lifetime ; who made the first gentleman of Europe sacrifice his solitary principle, when at the behest of the Duke of Wellington, he signed that hated measure of relief. In tearful anger was the signature affixed and only under extreme pressure from the Duke who hated the deed as much as his royal master. He had seen Civil War in Spain and was not going to allow that horror to break out in the King's Dominions ; but he " detested "

O'Connell, wrote Greville, " for all he has done and all he has made them do."

When the Act was passed so as to exclude O'Connell from its immediate benefit, *The Times* inquired " why so invidious a clause should ever have been suggested in a Bill professing and conferring grace." Peel was not one to excuse himself in public, and the explanation of this rebuff was only found in his papers after his death. He did not exclude O'Connell from pique but in order to win the consent of the King to the Act and to mollify conservative opinion. The Act, according to Peel, was in opposition to the popular feeling in England and a slight to O'Connell was a sop to injured prestige. In the same spirit, no doubt, when introducing the Bill to the House of Commons, Peel refused all credit for the measure which belonged, he said, to Fox, Sheridan, Grattan and Canning. No mention was made of the man who achieved what that celebrated quartet had merely recommended.

Without a doubt the greatest parliamentarian after Pitt was Sir Robert Peel. For him it seems, O'Connell had always a loathing. There is less written evidence of Peel's feelings, for he was an impersonal man who kept his antipathies on ice, but his every action in relation to O'Connell from the temper in which the Emancipation Act was passed to the prosecution which followed the collapse of the Repeal agitation in 1843, shows a determined and unrelenting antagonism. It began when Peel was the Irish Chief Secretary in 1815. It lasted until O'Connell died. Once they were to have fought a duel and some years later O'Connell apologised for his attitude at the time which the facts did not warrant and Peel was " very handsome in his acceptance " of these overtures. When O'Connell was taunted for having " crouched," he explained that his object was to propitiate Peel on the Catholic question which was then pending. In Peel's papers after he died a laconic note was found. " I had given him credit for having made the tardy reparation purely from a conscientious feeling that it was due."

But Peel never made the mistake of underrating O'Connell.

"A very clever man, but in some things a very foolish and indiscreet one," he wrote when O'Connell joined forces with Cobbett who had brought back the bones of Tom Paine from America. Not long afterwards O'Connell described his new associate as "a vile vagabond, malignant, treacherous, false," bearing out Peel's suggestion that "he took up Cobbett . . . without much reflection and having forgotten the bones." On another occasion a discussion arose as to the merits of contemporary public men and some one dismissed O'Connell as "a low broguing Irish fellow." Peel, who was present, when asked for his opinion, said : "If I wanted an efficient and eloquent advocate I would readily give up all those of whom we have been speaking, provided I had on my side this same 'broguing Irish fellow.'"

These tributes are sincere ; they come from a man who repulsed flattery and rarely dispensed praise, but it can be taken as certain that Peel disliked O'Connell for himself and for the opinions he advocated and when, in a rare burst of expansiveness, he called him "a shabby scoundrel," he was probably revealing his general opinion of the man.

The Times, though opposed to O'Connell, was a warm supporter of the Act and gave the names of those who had voted against it with the observation that "They are a poor set," while Greville, commenting on the treatment which O'Connell received, records "there is but one opinion of the wretched feeling of excluding him." Peel might have argued that liberal sentiments were all very well for those who had not to deal with the King. George IV had the obstinacy of the weak and sought immediately a mean revenge by causing O'Connell's name to be omitted from the list of Catholic Counsel called to the inner Bar under the new dispensation. As well as these insults to O'Connell, it had also been thought necessary to accompany the passage of this Act permitting Catholics to sit in Parliament with another which disfranchised the great majority of the rural population from exercising the privilege.

The tiresome Irish responded to this left-handed charity with unexpected ingratitude. "What all the damned fools said would happen, happened," said Melbourne; and Greville also remarked that "Ireland is on the point of becoming in a worse state . . . the settlement was put off too long . . . and because it was accompanied by an insult to O'Connell, which he has been resolved to avenge and which he knows he can punish." Greville was not unique in his sympathy and in many of the diaries and memoirs of the time O'Connell is mentioned as a guest at dinners in London. Creevy speaks pleasantly of him; Hyde Villiers hears that he is at the head of his profession, a man of the highest moral character, charitable to those unable to pay his fees, and a most respectable family man. Greville, meeting him at dinner, found him not especially remarkable but "lively, well-bred and at his ease." Hobhouse is asked to dine by the Speaker of the House of Commons and finds O'Connell opposite him at the table. He is still on the threshold; it has yet to be decided whether he, like Flood, will prove too old at fifty-five to be transplanted.

Before the passing of the Emancipation Act Mr. Doherty from Dublin, the Solicitor-General, confided to his English friends, "Mark my words he will turn out nothing, he will sink down gradually to his true dimensions." Villiers had heard in Ireland that he was not believed to be a man of courage or likely to succeed in the House of Commons. *The Times*, which had consistently favoured the Catholic cause, published a leading article for his benefit:

"He is fully aware that in the parliamentary walls he will not sit. But will this ranter allow us to drop him a hint? We know something of Parliament and of the talents which are necessary to procure attentions there; and we can assure him, were he in the House of Commons to-morrow, that after a few efforts in which he would receive liberal treatment (perhaps an ill-suppressed laugh or two, which would be checked by one cry of ' order '), he would be quiet enough for all the rest of his parliamentary career."

But these prophecies were unfulfilled and we find in Greville that " O'Connell is said to have made a very good speech at the bar of the House and produced rather a favourable impression." As a parliamentary speaker,

Gladstone wrote, " no one would have relegated him to the
second class, but it might be difficult to find his exact
position in the first." He considered Brougham, for one,
to be O'Connell's superior. But Jeffrey, editor of the
Edinburgh Review, a man of learning and discernment, when
he heard O'Connell speaking on an Irish measure, thought
him " indisputably the greatest orator in the House—
nervous, passionate, without art or ornament ; concise,
intrepid, terrible, far more in the style of old Demosthenic
directness and vehemence than anything I have heard in
this modern world, yet often coarse and sometimes tiresome."
The general opinion seems to have been that to hear
O'Connell at his best was to hear him in the open air
addressing a large crowd and unhampered by the rules of
court or parliament. On one point even O'Connell's
enemies are agreed. He had a voice of great range and
marvellous beauty. " The thrilling tones of O'Connell "
was how his voice was remembered by one critic in reviewing
the orators he had known. Dickens has described how once,
as a young reporter in the House of Commons, listening to
a speech of O'Connell, he was so entranced that he had to
stop writing. "Demosthenic" was the adjective used by
Jeffreys, and Bulwer Lytton has used the same expression
in verses written after hearing O'Connell speak in Ireland.

> " Then did I know what spells of infinite choice
>   To rouse or lull, has the sweet human voice :
>   Then did I seem to seize the sudden clue
>   To the grand troublous life antique—to view
>   Under the rock stand of Demosthenes.
>   Mutable Athens heave her noisy seas."

In his whole-hearted attempt to deprive O'Connell of every
merit, even Disraeli had to say : " He has not a single
quality of a great orator except a good voice." He spoke
with a brogue to which his schooldays in France had lent
some eccentric pronunciations which he never corrected.
The only rival to O'Connell in beauty of voice was his
arch-enemy, Sir Robert Peel. It is remarkable that he
did not allow Eton or Cambridge to deprive him of a

north-country accent (Carlyle said he spoke with a "'coo' in his voice.")   The modern fashion is to aim at a standardised accent. A hundred years ago men were less afraid of being individuals.   O'Connell in his youth had attended the House of Commons regularly, quite certain that he was going to be a member one day, although he had himself to have the law changed to make this possible. He had heard Pitt speaking and from him he learned " to throw out the lower notes at the close of my sentences. Most men either let the voice fall at the end of their sentences, or else force it into a shout or screech."

Hoping for no more concessions from the government, O'Connell returned to Ireland and began immediately to agitate for a repeal of the Act of Union. In the course of his campaign he described Hardinge, the Chief Secretary, as " that paltry, contemptible little English soldier, who has the audacity to pen his pitiful and contemptible name to an atrocious Polignac Proclamation."

Hardinge challenged O'Connell to a duel. He, in accordance with the vow that he took some time after the killing of D'Esterre, refused to fight. The immediate effect of this was to do great harm to O'Connell's reputation in England. At Brook's Club he was shunned by many fellow members and in parliament he was bitterly attacked. Henceforth he was always open to the taunt of cowardice.

The extent of the change of feeling towards O'Connell, after the Hardinge episode, can be gauged by an entry of Greville's in 1830. Hitherto he had written sympathetically, now he writes : " Since the beginning of the world there never was so extraordinary and eccentric a position as his. It is a moral power and influence, as great in its way, and as strangely acquired, as Buonaparte's political power was. Utterly lost to all sense of shame and decency, trampling truth and honour under his feet, cast off by all respectable men, he makes his faults and his vices subservient to the extension of his influence, for he says and does whatever suits his purpose for the moment. . . .   He cares not whom he insults, because having covered his cowardice with the cloak of religious scruples, he is invulnerable."

Not long after the events which gave rise to this denunciation the Tories resigned and Lord Grey came to power.
From the change of government O'Connell had great hopes.
He wanted to be Attorney-General because, he said, " he
longed for the opportunity of proving to the Protestants of
Ireland that when in power he could and would do them
justice." Neither Grey nor the King would hear of this,
but Lord Duncannon gave an undertaking that neither
Blackburne nor Doherty, who were unpopular in Ireland,
would be given office. In fact they were both promoted
and the Viceroy's cavalcade through the streets of Dublin
was followed by cries of " Dirty Doherty." But O'Connell
liked Duncannon and never betrayed his confidence when he
railed against the Government and renewed his Repeal agitation to such effect that the Government ordered his arrest.

King George at a levée exclaimed so loudly that
O'Connell could hear—" God damn him, what does he
come here for?" and King William, who now occupied the
throne, would have applauded the sentiment. " Billy has
been in perfect ecstasies ever since they arrested O'Connell,"
Creevy wrote to Miss Ord. " His majesty rejoices that
ground has offered for the prosecution of O'Connell"
was the more sedate manner in which the King's
secretary conveyed the same information to Lord Grey.

Despite this warfare with the Whigs, O'Connell strenuously supported the Reform Bill which they were now
attempting to pass. His reasons were not entirely disinterested, for he had hopes of better treatment for Ireland from
a parliament elected on a more popular franchise, but without any motive O'Connell was usually on the progressive
side. " He was," according to Gladstone, " as thorough
an English Liberal as if he had no Ireland to think of."

Grey was sceptical. The man who regarded Talleyrand,
Castlereagh and Brougham as the three greatest rascals in
the world was not going to be attracted by O'Connell. The
King is informed that " O'Connell is again on his good
behaviour and professing every kind of wish to assist the
passing of the Reform Bill. But he is very much mistaken
if he thinks I, for one at least, will ever have any dealings

with him, except at arm's length "; and " His Majesty was very glad to hear that you are determined never to have any dealings with Mr. O'Connell, except at arm's length, and he hopes that Lord Anglesey (the Viceroy) will adopt the same resolution."

The Reform Bill passed and was followed by one of the most severe Coercion Bills that had ever been devised to tranquillise the uneasy Irish. This was the occasion on which O'Connell referred to the Whigs as " base, bloody and brutal "—a remark which was often brought up against him during his happy relations with that Party when Melbourne was Prime Minister. Melbourne's biographer acknowledges that no man was more amenable to good treatment than O'Connell; and Russell, in his *Memoirs*, wrote that he never saw cause to complain of his conduct. When, on the formation of Melbourne's administration, O'Connell was again disappointed of office, Russell offered to resign his own seat in the Cabinet, but he records that " O'Connell declined in the handsomest manner to put forward any pretensions on his own part." Reviewing his political career, Russell gave him credit for " a constant and disinterested support." The trouble between O'Connell and the first Whig Government of King William's reign lay really in a clash of personalities. Grey was old, a Whig of " starched traditions," a survival from the eighteenth century; and Edward Stanley, his Irish secretary, who was soon to go over to the Tories, hated everything that O'Connell represented. Saintsbury, in his biography of the future Lord Derby, explains the antipathy : " The great Dan was, in his way, a gentleman : but his way was not that of members of his class in England and it was simply impossible that Stanley and he could get on together." " Scorpion Stanley " was O'Connell's customary expression when referring to him outside the House of Commons; and Grey became " the wretched old man who is at the head of the ministry." When during the discussion on the Coercion Bill a speaker made flattering references to him, O'Connell cried out : " No, no ! Blood, blood ! "

In due course, when Grey had retired, Stanley gone

Torywards, and Melbourne became Prime Minister and governed Ireland—not according to O'Connell's directions, but with an eye to his wishes—the result was five years of content, a St. Martin's summer in the long winter of the Union. Grey could have produced the same peace had he chosen to give good instead of oppressive government. O'Connell was more than ready to help. There is no excuse for Grey; O'Connell's ability to keep Ireland law-abiding was well known. Peel referred to the " fearful exhibition of sobered and desperate enthusiasm " at the Clare election : and Grey had once written to the King to say that a mob which gathered to meet O'Connell dispersed in an orderly fashion at the moment he gave them the word—news which was by no means pleasing to the King. He would prefer that the crowd had not " dispersed in an orderly fashion at *his* bidding."

When Melbourne came to power O'Connell had hopes that he would now be Attorney-General, the one post he coveted. It was not to be. He could have been Master of the Rolls but he did not wish to share the fate of Curran. His refusal was not known and it was generally believed at the time that he was disappointed. Finance, always a trouble, was at this time notoriously an acute one. It was therefore assumed that the security of the Bench was his sole aim. In this the English failed entirely to understand him and it might be said that the unanimity with which they credited him with mean motives reflected no credit on themselves. Stanley said of him that " his trade was agitation ; his sole object personal ambition ; and his end the separation of the two countries." Vanity was his besetting sin, according to Brougham, himself the vainest of men. That the pursuit of private aims was his one concern, De Quincey thought. Greville discussed his character at some length : " He has chalked out to himself a course of ambition which, though not of the highest kind, has everything in it that can charm a somewhat vulgar but highly active, restless and imaginative being." Grey called him " an unprincipled ruffian " whose conduct was beyond any example except that of the worst men at the time of the French revolution."

Grey was rather a prig, but in the matter of abuse was a good deal in O'Connell's debt. In an open letter to the electors of Wexford, O'Connell confessed that he had detected insanity in the old gentleman as far back as 1825 and that his two main preoccupations were hatred of Ireland and securing for his family and friends " the greatest possible quantity of the public spoil."

When in 1838 Melbourne again offered " The Rolls " to O'Connell and he again refused it, Lord Tavistock told Greville that the whole party gave him credit for sincerity and purity of motive—a sentiment with which Greville was inclined to agree but, he reflected, it might well be due to a long-sighted motive. " His present act of self-denial will be ' reculer pour mieux sauter ' and find its reward in the Chief Justiceship."

The vow against duelling won O'Connell a reputation as a coward. We have seen that Villiers questioned his courage ; Lord Anglesey, writing to Peel from Ireland in 1828, gives his opinion that " the hope and indeed the probability of present tranquility rests upon the forbearance and the not very determined courage of O'Connell." Three years later Lord Holland writes to Russell : " Ireland looks better. O'Connell shews a white feather," and when the cholera raged in 1838 Greville hears that O'Connell is supposed to be " horribly afraid."

The charge of self-interest may well have originated in the " Rent." Gladstone in after years was to quote with approval Greville's fine definition of this tribute as " an income nobly given and nobly earned " but there was to many something genuinely distasteful in this annual collection of pennies from the poor, more particularly during hard times and famine years. Many of the Young Irelanders shared this antipathy and found it galling to see the most representative Irishman described as " the big beggarman " and to know there lay even an appearance of truth behind the taunt. " He devoted herculean energies to the acquisition of the Tribute from his starving countrymen and bestowed upon his descendants the remnants of a mendicant revenue when he might have bequeathed them

an honourable name." This was the manner in which
The Times dealt with the Rent in its obituary notice of
O'Connell. He had given his own explanation when he
wrote to the Catholic Lord Shrewsbury, who had also
objected to the Rent. "Who," he wrote, "shall repay me
for the years of buoyant youth and cheerful manhood?
Who shall repay me for the best opportunities of acquiring
professional celebrity or for the wealth which such distinction would ensure?"

Admirers of O'Connell must regret the "Rent," but are
hard pressed to suggest what would have been a better
alternative. Economy was not possible. In this as in
everything O'Connell was larger than life. To have
endeavoured to continue at the Bar was to ensure the failure
which divided attention was later to bring upon Isaac
Butt, and the "Rent," it must be remembered, paid for
party elections and the crushing expense of election petitions,
as well as the mediaeval hospitality of Darrynane.

The coarse invective, the vow against duelling and the
"Rent"—these combined to keep O'Connell partially
ostracised in English Society. Even the more aristocratic
Catholics shunned him. A majority secured his black-
beaning for the exclusive Cis-Alpine Club, a rebuff which
he took good-humouredly. "It was a comical testimonial
of my services in emancipating them," he wrote to Sugrue.
"It would be well, perhaps, if I could unemancipate some
of them." On the continent O'Connell was a wonder of
the world; it came as a surprise to foreign visitors to London
to find that he was not a social lion. He was not to be met
at Holland House or at Lord Lansdowne's, or at the dinners
of the Whig leaders. When Guizot came to London as
Ambassador and expressed his surprise and disappointment
at the continued absence of O'Connell from these gatherings,
Lady Stanley of Alderley offered to arrange a meeting. A
dinner was given to which O'Connell was invited and the
French ambassador noticed in the Irishman "an air of
strength and shrewdness, strength everywhere, shrewdness
in his quick glance, slightly indirect, although not indicating
duplicity; he was neither elegant nor vulgar, his manner

a little embarrassed yet firm with even a tincture of suppressed arrogance." In his politeness towards " the English men of condition " at the party Guizot noticed an attitude of " humility and pride." After dinner more guests came and " a fit of social modesty seized Mr. O'Connell " who made excuses for leaving but he was prevailed upon to stay and when the French ambassador took his leave, O'Connell was " surrounded by four Cabinet Ministers and five or six ladies of rank who listened to him with a mixture, somewhat comic, of curiosity and pride, of deference and disdain."

There are conflicting accounts of the impression which O'Connell made on the rare occasions when he entered society. Lord Broughton described him as " not what is called a man of the world, or with the airs of a town-bred gentleman." Disraeli found him very communicative when they met at dinner; they talked for three hours and O'Connell told him that " from being the son of a gentleman farmer he had raised himself to be une des puissances du monde." A few months later Disraeli, in a letter which he sent to the Press, told O'Connell that at this meeting " I thought you a very amusing, a very interesting, but a somewhat overrated man." Gladstone, who was not the man to object to a brogue, or to care—perhaps to know—whether or not he were a man of the world, paid tribute to O'Connell's " kindly and winning manners." As a young member of Parliament, Gladstone was appointed to a committee of which he was also a member. In a party of four they drove from daybreak to nightfall in a coach to take the evidence of a witness who was unable to come to London. The journey was " an enormous effort " for so busy a man and one " which he could have no motive for undertaking except an overpowering belief that justice to an individual demanded it." In later years an incessant talker, Gladstone on that occasion had to yield to O'Connell the privilege of monopolising the conversation—one of the very few comforts of advancing age. But he remembered the occasion pleasantly and was quite won over by the " frank and kindly conversation of this most remarkable man."

An incident somewhat similar is recorded in the memoirs

of Sir William Gregory. Returning by boat to England after defeating Lord Morpeth in a Dublin election he encountered O'Connell on deck. He had come to Ireland to support Gregory's opponent but he did not allow the defeat to embitter him. Gregory spoke of O'Connell's conversation in almost the same terms as Gladstone and despite political differences they remained ever afterwards on friendly terms. Peel " for whom he had a profound dislike and whom he never spared," was the only stumbling block. " On this subject," Gregory found, " he was un-approachable." It is evidence of a pleasant side to O'Connell's character that these two young men, brought up to regard him as antichrist, should on their first meeting conceive a life-long affection and regard for him.

When O'Connell arrived at a tacit understanding with Melbourne and by his support kept the Whigs in power for five years, he brought upon himself a measure of abuse far exceeding anything that he encountered over Catholic Emancipation or his quarrel with Lord Grey's administration. And the fact that in the meantime he had involved himself in a war with *The Times*, which proved to be life-long, did not help matters. O'Connell had complained of the way in which he was reported, denounced the reporters and, when they refused to report any more of his speeches, made use of the " spying strangers " rule to have them removed from the press gallery. O'Connell won that encounter but *The Times* vowed vengeance and pursued it relentlessly. O'Connell referred to the paper as the " venal lady of the Strand " and *The Times* in reply published three hundred leading articles, all intended to discredit and ruin him. If one were to turn at random to a copy of *The Times* for any day between the years 1835 and 1840 one will find almost for certain an article or paragraph abusing O'Connell.

"As a young and insignificant member of parliament I never (so far as my memory goes) indulged in the safe impertinence of attacks which it would have been beneath him to notice," wrote Gladstone in later years when describing his relations with O'Connell. It is possible that Disraeli came to regret that he could not make the same claim. He

was pleased when of later years he was always greeted with
a deep bow when their paths crossed ; he was proud that
from his death-bed O'Connell sent him a message of reconciliation : and he wrote in delight to his sister when
O'Connell praised an early speech of his in Parliament. It
is significant that he never acknowledged his authorship of
the Runnymede letters, in which O'Connell received
scandalous treatment, although it was a fact which was
widely known. In 1835 Disraeli was not yet in parliament.
With some reputation as a novelist he was without wealth
or family or influence save what he was able by his own
personality to acquire. His only asset was genius. Having
failed as a Radical he was now a whole-blooded Tory and
these letters which are so violent against " that wretched
anti-nation faction " (the Whigs) " the vagabond delegate
of a foreign priesthood " and the " Brutilitarians " are
equally excessive in praise of Wellington, Peel, Lyndhurst
and Stanley. In later years Disraeli spoke of laying flattery
on with a trowel when dealing with Royalty ; his prentice
hand was lavish enough when he beslobbered the Tory
captains with his adulation.

In 1835 the Runnymede letters appeared in *The Times*.
They tilted at the Whigs and castigated O'Connell in
language which Barnes, the editor, described as showing
" a most surprising disdain for the law of libel." Palmerston
is " the Lord Fanny of diplomacy " of whom " the leader of
the Whig opposition was wont to say that your lordship
reminded him of a favourite footman on easy terms with
his mistress " while Melbourne, " this old hack, this most
unprincipled of public men, even of Whigs, . . . is saunter-
ing over the destinies of a nation and lounging away the
glory of an Empire."

These are mere aperitifs to the draught which the author
pours out for O'Connell—" demoralised in character,
desperate in fortunes, infinitely over-estimated in talents."
Every source of hatred is tapped for his benefit. First, the
old no-popery reservoir. O'Connell is the " fee'd advocate
of the Irish priesthood " and " the hired instrument of
the Papacy " who humbles himself in the mud before a

simple priest and presses to his lips " those sacred robes,
reeking with whiskey and redolent of incense." He is not
a great man though the hired writers seek to prove the
contrary. He is " shrewd, vigorous, versatile . . . energetic
from the strong stimulus of his provisional remuneration
. . . a *nisi prius* lawyer with the soul of a demagogue."
His oratory is without " a single flash of genius, or tinctured
with the slightest evidence of taste, or thought, or study.
Learning he has none ; little reading. His style of speaking
as in writing is ragged, bald, halting, disjointed." Many
years later Gladstone was to remember how " he poured
out his wit, his pathos and his earnestness in the cause of
negro emancipation." *Runnymede* will not grant O'Connell
wit ; he has only a large share of " that Milesian humour
which everyone inherits who bears a hod " and his pathos
" is the stage sentiment of a barn."

Having represented him as a popish envoy of mean
abilities, it only remained to divest him of any moral pretensions and this the writer did not hesitate to attempt.
There is not much reputation left to one " who is a
systematic liar and a beggarly cheat, a swindler, and a
poltroon. . . . His public and private life are equally
profligate ; he has committed every crime that does not
require courage : the man who plunders the peasant can
also starve his child."

Notoriety was not the only purpose for which this outrageous attack was made ; a few months earlier O'Connell
had not found it beneath him to notice the account of an
election speech of Disraeli's in which he was reputed to have
described him as an incendiary and a traitor. In reply
O'Connell traced the origin of the Disraeli family to the
impenitent thief. Disraeli challenged Morgan O'Connell
to a duel which he declined, having recently taken the field
on behalf of his father who had called Lord Alvanley a
bloated buffoon. It was rather soon to have to expose
himself again on account of his father's verbal exuberance.
A few days afterwards there appeared in the papers a
savage reply ending with the phrase " I will seize the first
opportunity of inflicting upon you a castigation which

will make you at the same time remember and repent the insults that you have lavished upon Benjamin Disraeli." *The Letters of Runnymede* were the first opportunity.

If love is blind, hate is often preternaturally keen-sighted and in the excesses of Disraeli's attack are to be found many shafts of unhappy illumination. To a stylist—and Disraeli had style—O'Connell was very homespun in texture. He spoke without previous preparation and it needed the stimulus of emotion to work him up to his passionate best. He was often slipshod and humdrum and, as a writer, he had no pretensions to merit. His one book was a sad failure. There is, therefore, a cruel summary of O'Connell at his worst in the phrase : " What ragged ribaldry are his public addresses whether they emanate from his brazen mouth or from his leaden pen."

It was hoped by the Tories that some overwhelming scandal would drive O'Connell out of public life and a dispute over the application of a Carlow election fund seemed to promise favourably. A parliamentary committee sat to examine the charges which, if they had been substantiated, would have ruined O'Connell's reputation. Day after day *The Times* referred to the coming exposure and Disraeli's letter was in anticipation of the expected triumph. When the findings of the Committee were published O'Connell was completely cleared of any suspicion of malversation. This came as a great disappointment to his gallant foes who had so long and so confidently regaled the public with details of the coming exposure. Greville expresses relief when the findings of the committee were made public. " *The Times* have rung the changes on this O'Connell cry till they can do no more, and it has failed them entirely. . . . The subject is worn threadbare . . . and in spite of mistakes O'Connell has made, the anti-popery prejudices which prevail and the blots upon his personal character, I doubt if he is as much hated in England as the Tories would have him."

It was partly because of his influence over working-class crowds that the Tories wished to check O'Connell's career. When the House of Lords threw out a Bill to settle the old

difficulty of Irish tithes, O'Connell set out on a tour of the
north to agitate against the Upper House. He was delighted
with the reception that he received and wrote home to say
" It is only now that the people of England are beginning
to understand me." His nature, as Gladstone remarked,
was sanguine " in a degree almost ludicrous " and the cheers
of the crowds in Glasgow and Manchester raised in his
heart a certainty that he would be in the next Cabinet.
In reckless good spirits he assailed the Peers—" pigs with
soaped tails "—and all the Opposition leaders. As usual
he passed the bounds of taste and good sense. Wellington
is described as " the chance victor of Waterloo," " a stunted
corporal," and his colleague as " spinning-jenny Peel."
O'Connell speeches on this tour were fully reported in the
press. When, speaking at Hull, he expressed sympathy with
the cause of Poland, *The Times* condoled with " those poor
Poles. . . . But let them take courage. They have survived
the vengeance of a heartless despot, and there is reason to
hope, therefore, that the sympathy of a sordid demagogue,
though harder to bear, will do them no permanent harm."

This tour, it was hoped, would be the last. The Carlow
scandal would make that certain.

> " Only give him length of string
> He'll contrive himself to swing."

So end the lines of furious doggerel which, headed " The
Whig Missionary of 1835," appeared in *The Times* and
begin

> " Scum condensed of Irish Bog !
> Ruffian, coward, demagogue."

and continuing in the same vein see him—

> " mounted on a Premier's back,
> Lash the ministerial pack."

and

> " By their leave pursue thy calling,
> Rend thy patriot lungs with bawling ;
> Spout thy filth, effuse thy slime,
> Slander is to thee no crime."

Disraeli, under the moderating influence of prose, is satisfied to say that " the mighty dragon is again abroad. . . . To-day he gorges in Liverpool, to-morrow he riots at Birmingham."

Unfortunately for O'Connell, just before the acquittal on this charge another scandal of a different kind gave his enemies an opportunity of which they took the fullest advantage. *The Letters of Runnymede* contained the sentence, " the man who plunders the peasant can also starve his own child." Disraeli referred to an allegation made during the hearing of a police court summons against John O'Connell, who had beaten a boy with an umbrella for annoying his father by dogging his footsteps in London. At the hearing of the case the boy stated that he was a natural son of O'Connell and his mother complained that she and her son were starving and destitute.

The Times made the incident the subject of a leading article and treated it with heavy irony. The boy was " well off in not having the old gentleman set upon him too, after the true, low Irish fashion which is never to fight fairly but to beat by whatever means. . . . If anyone is to exclaim against the indecency of members of Parliament making a scene of this description on a Sunday morning, we must excuse the old gentleman on the ground that he had just come from chapel." The complainant " is the only one of the O'Connell's, we believe, not in Parliament " and a son by " a sort of left-handed union which the learned gentleman could repeal and therefore did."

It is probably on this one incident that O'Connell's reputation as a libertine is based. His " domestic relations," wrote Gladstone, " were broadly distinguished from those of common men by the vehement and ever-flowing tide of emotion that coursed through them." To his wife he wrote almost daily, and if in this, as in all matters, his manner is over-fulsome no one could deny the obvious affection which permeates these letters. The adoration with which his wife regarded him breathes in every line she wrote to him. To give the lie to her husband's enemies, who tried to use this scandal as a means of spoiling his public appearances, Mrs. O'Connell, though mortally ill, came over to England and accompanied him everywhere. Nevertheless, his next tour of England was a failure and he retired before he had completed his itinerary.

Melbourne and Palmerston had both to suffer the gaze of the public on their private lives and it is satisfactory to find that no excessive hypocrisy kept O'Connell's scandal alive. In 1838 we find Queen Victoria writing to her uncle to say that he had attended her levée and had been greeted " with a very smiling face " for he was behaving very well and it was " a great treat " to see him. And in her diary she makes a note that he had " a remarkably good-humoured countenance." " My good Lord Melbourne," who had also noticed O'Connell at the levée and thought " he looked very smug and very cunning," had the idea of again offering him " the Rolls," but without much confidence that it would be accepted. Twice the Prime Minister asked the Queen if she had " any particular feeling " about it. She had none whatever. Melbourne told the Queen that he hoped, if faintly, by offering the judgeship to prevent O'Connell from beginning a fresh agitation. This was at the time when they were supposed to be in a close alliance.

The Melbourne-O'Connell pact never in fact existed.[1] The Duke of Wellington discussed the subject once with Greville and referred to it as one of those false statements history hands down and which are believed to the end of time. It was in the interest of the Tories to pretend that O'Connell had great influence with the Government; it suited him to let this be believed and " it was vain for the Whigs to deny what facts appeared to prove." On one occasion in the House of Lords, Lord Mulgrave repudiated the charge that O'Connell controlled the patronage of Ireland. " The applications of Mr. O'Connell," said the Irish Viceroy, " have been fewer than those of any other member of Parliament . . . the taunt against me is that I have treated Mr. O'Connell in the same way as I would

[1] See, however, p. 164 above, and R. Barry O'Brien, *Irish Wrongs and English Remedies*, pp. 73-95.—ED.

treat any other member of parliament. So I have, my lords, and so I will always continue to do." Mulgrave on one occasion invited O'Connell to dinner at the Vice-regal lodge and created thereby a political sensation. The King was furious and wrote to Lord Russell to say so. *The Times* pictured O'Connell with " the fumes of Lord Mulgrave's wine still exhaling from his lips " and Disraeli, not yet in Parliament, calls the Viceroy to order for incurring " the strongly-expressed disapprobation of your sovereign." Even Lord Melbourne regarded this hospitality as a daring move by the Viceroy although he approved of it. No one thought the matter too trivial for comment.

The approaching end of the Melbourne administration and the return of Peel to office had the usual effect on O'Connell. He began to agitate once more for the repeal of the Act of Union and centred his activities in Dublin. It was then that he acquired regular assembly rooms (nick-named Conciliation Hall) in the building which is now the offices of the *Irish Press* and was formerly the site of the *Tivoli* music hall.

A letter from Palmerston to Russell written in 1841 lets in some light on O'Connell's position in relation to the English political parties. With the Tories he is always at war. With the Whigs he was ready to come to an under-standing. But the Whig leaders had no partiality for O'Connell, they found him useful and they conciliated him, that was all. Russell acknowledged in his *Memoirs* that he had never found cause " to complain of O'Connell's con-duct. He confined his opposition fairly to Irish measures." But Palmerston exposes the attitude of the party leaders when, writing to Russell in 1841, he says : " What you say of O'Connell is true. He will be a great difficulty for us. To act with him will often be impossible ; to break openly with him would be hurtful." It was with the Radicals only that O'Connell was on anything like terms of association. The emancipation of slaves, universal manhood suffrage, voting by ballot and other Radical reforms, were warmly supported by O'Connell, while the Radicals gave their assistance in attacking the stringent Crimes Acts

which every Government, save Melbourne's, imposed upon
Ireland.

It was by the Radicals in all parts of England and Scotland
that public honours were paid to O'Connell and in their
press only that he was extolled. *Punch*, although anti-papist,
was rather advanced politically and O'Connell was not
harshly treated in its pages. He is the subject of many
cartoons, but none of them are particularly savage and
many are playful. In the nineteenth century it was almost
impossible for a cartoonist to resist the current belief that
the Irish character is largely composed of buffoonery. But,
to the end, he was hated by the real sources of power in
England—Royalty, aristocracy and the upper middle classes
as a whole. "His policy and his success crossed their
religious prejudices, their imperial instincts, their *amour
propre* at every turn. . . . He had humiliated their Government." These are among the reasons given by Shaw
Lefevre for O'Connell's unpopularity with the ruling classes
in England. A remark which bears out the truth of Gladstone's theory that a very small part of the aversion to
O'Connell "may have been due to faults of his own ; but
in the main, I fear that, taking him as the symbol of his
country, it exhibited the hatred which nations, or the
governing and representative parts of nations, are apt to
feel towards those whom they have injured."

When the Repeal campaign of 1843 reached its climax
Peel moved suddenly and resolutely and by banning
O'Connell's great meeting at Clontarf challenged the Irish
leader to a show of strength. O'Connell's capitulation was
a triumph for Peel and the end of O'Connell as a serious
force in politics. The success of his campaign would have
been regarded as a tragedy for England by Whig and Tory
alike, but when Peel and Wellington reduced the movement
to fatuity and the Imperial danger was past, the trial
of O'Connell became a mere matter of party politics.
O'Connell's acquittal would be little more than a reverse
for the Tories. Palmerston in his letter to which we have
already referred suggests that he would like O'Connell to fail,
that the Repeal movement was begun for "pecuniary and

political purposes," and the more moderate demands made by O'Connell since his arrest, for a parliament for local and domestic purposes " did not show much game." Palmerston made an unconscious prophecy in this letter, for he tells Russell that if O'Connell's modest doctrine succeeded it would lead " not to parliament for the whole of Ireland but to one for the Catholics and another for the Protestant part of the nation." And this bears out, as experience has proved, the truth of Lord Clarendon's remark to Russell in the following year : " O'Connell asks too much and in a disagreeable manner, but I am not disposed to blame him greatly for that as it is only through intimidation and exaggerated demands that justice by driblets has ever been extracted from England."

O'Connell's trial in Dublin was eagerly watched in England. To Greville " a trial of O'Connell in Ireland " seemed a desperate measure, and he referred to it as an " unhappy trial . . . one continual cause of blunders." Lord John Russell condemned the whole conduct of the proceedings, including the manner in which the jury was packed to try to ensure a conviction. In a letter, Queen Victoria refers to O'Connell's arrest as " the great event of the day " and reports that " the case against him is very strong the lawyers say." In his excitement Chief Justice Pennefather referred to the defendants (some of O'Connell's supporters were tried with him) as " the other side " and when the jury brought in a verdict of " guilty," " Nothing," wrote Greville, " could exceed the satisfaction of the Government at the result of this trial . . . which after all the blunders and accidents ended very well indeed for them, and far better than they ever expected." He thought the charge of the Chief Justice to the jury " more like an advocate's speech " but considered that most people regarded the result with satisfaction and " think it will do a world of good."

There followed the months of festive imprisonment in Richmond Penitentiary and *Punch* had a cartoon of O'Connell " contented and enormous " as the result of the " turbot and turtle, venison and champagne, embroidered

chairs and turgid addresses, monster cakes and long-winded
condolences " with which he beguiled the tedium of con-
finement. Then came the grand anti-climax when the
judicial committee of the House of Lord upset the verdict.
It is amusing to read *The Times* of the day after the reversal
of the Dublin sentence was announced. An article is
devoted to the subject but it conveys somehow an impression
of stunned silence. The usual vituperation is absent and
there is a lame suggestion that henceforth O'Connell should
alter his view of English injustice. A sermon in Dublin
by a Father Miley in which he attributed the decision of
the Law Lords to the intercession of the Blessed Virgin
brought *The Times* back to its usual form. A leading article
casts doubts on the necessity for supernatural intervention
when " two ministerial Lords and three opposition Lords
met to decide pro or con on a matter in which the decision
was of powerful interest to each side." O'Connell in his
first public speech to tumultuous crowds in Dublin, while
claiming Divine interposition in his affairs, nevertheless,
made " an atonement to a class of public men whom I have
often assailed and who certainly in some things deserved
to be assailed—namely the Whigs."

Superficially this mortifying and calamitous blow to the
Government gave O'Connell a miraculous opportunity of
regaining lost ground in his Repeal agitation. But he
became wild and inconsistent in his pronouncements,
refuting one day the propositions he had put forward on the
day before, and it was quickly sensed that he was no longer
an Imperial danger. It is said that he entered into negotiations with the Whigs who were prepared, if they returned
to office, to make an offer to Ireland of a federal parliament.
If so, nothing came of it and a hasty espousal of the federal
plan was disowned by him as soon as Gavan Duffy attacked
it in the *Nation*. The Whigs when they returned to power
did not need O'Connell's help but they were still in opposition and prepared to bargain and *The Times* saw the
possibility of a plot to make Ireland a nation, for some
among the Whigs "were capable of anything. But the
party still counts honourable names in its list."

From now on O'Connell's career is no cause of pride to his fellow-countrymen. He was a sick man who should have resigned from politics. Carlyle heard him speaking in Conciliation Hall in 1846, the year before he died, and gives a typically splenetic account of the proceeding :

> "I saw Conciliation Hall and the last glimpse of O'Connell, chief quack of the world ; first time I had ever heard the lying scoundrel speak—a most melancholy scene to me altogether ; Conciliation Hall something like a decent Methodist Chapel, but its audience very sparse, very bad and blackguard-looking ; brazen faces like tapsters, tavern-keepers, miscellaneous hucksters and quarrelsome male or female nondescripts the prevailing type ; not one that you would have called a gentleman, much less a man of culture ; and discontent visible among them. The speech, on potato rot, most serious of topics, had not one word of sincerity, not to speak of wisdom in it. Every sentence seemed to you a lie, and even to know that it was a detected lie. I was standing in the area in a small group of non-members and transitory people, quite near this Demosthenes of blarney, when a low voice whispered in high accent, ' Did you ever hear such damned nonsense in all your life ? '
>
> "Beggarly O'Connell made out of Ireland straight away and never returned—crept under the Pope's petticoat to die (and be ' saved ' from what he had merited), the eminently despicable and eminently poisonous professor of blarney that he was."

But on the whole the flames of passion died on both sides. Disraeli, who had so bitterly assailed him, gives a sympathetic and touching picture of the old man in the House of Commons pleading for help to fight the famine. The organ tones of his voice had shrunk to a cracked whisper and the bent and tottering figure bore a sad contrast to the self-confident stance of former years, head back, arms crossed—an attitude of " contempt and utter defiance."

Almost to the end *The Times* kept up the old vendetta.

Two years before O'Connell died a special reporter was sent to Ireland to inspect the condition of his tenantry and when that resulted in a description of abject misery and cabins without a pane of glass in their windows, O'Connell thundered indignantly his wish that the reporter had as many pains in his belly as there were panes in the windows at Darrynane Beg. And when their old enemy died, a page was devoted to his disparagement. From that obituary we have used extracts throughout this essay. Unlike the attacks made upon him in his lifetime this was more poisonous by insinuation than direct attack. Thus Mrs. O'Connell enjoyed " a large share of her husband's affection," and O'Connell's " most loyal valour," in joining the Crown forces during the Rebellion of 1798 was a wise anticipation of the probable fate of those United Irishmen who escaped from the field. Together with these suggestions and hints there are many epigrammatic thrusts. "Alike incapable of manly struggle or a dignified retreat " is the phrase that is used to describe him as a political adversary and " in parliament he seemed to be only the debris of an extinguished demagogue." His student days in London were devoted " to numerous liaisons " and praise of his capacities is always coupled with regret for the wretched purposes for which they were exercised. Having left no shred of credit to his reputation the obituarist heightens the effect of his detraction by suggesting that the tone of his narrative has been indulgent to " one who in his long lifetime seldom spared a fallen adversary." O'Connell's brutalities of speech were at the expense of living adversaries. *The Times* need not have wept over his bier : but did consistency demand that it should spit into his grave ?

For a year or more before his death O'Connell had taken very little part in the proceedings of parliament and when he died there was very little notice taken of his death. This the Prince Consort, in a letter to Stockmar, attributed to the fact that he was not " a man of true worth " but Albert admitted that two years earlier " he had stood before the world like a Colossus." And Greville remarks that his death which not long before " would have filled the world with political speculations was heard almost with unconcern." It is the fate of most men who live long to lose by degrees their influence and power. What made O'Connell's case remarkable was the way in which he fell from a position of great and long-sustained importance into sudden oblivion. Nevertheless, Greville admits in his last short survey of O'Connell's life that History would speak of him as one of the most remarkable men who ever existed, and he makes an illuminating comment upon O'Connell's career.—It was not uncommon for men to rise from humble situation " to the height of Empire " ; history contains many usurpers and adventurers, " but there never was a man who, without altering his social position in the slightest degree, without obtaining any office of station whatever, raised himself to a height of political power which gave him an enormous capacity for good or evil and made him the most important and most conspicuous man of his time and country."

Forty-two years after O'Connell died a great English statesman attempted what he described as " a small effort at historical justice." The essay by Gladstone which appeared in *The Nineteenth Century*, written when he was eighty years of age, is by no means a product of dotage. He was to be Prime Minister again and to introduce another Home Rule Bill and to live for nine more years. It might be true to say that his feelings on the Irish question were partisan and that he felt for the memory of O'Connell a peculiar warmth. He confesses that in early life he shared the prejudices against him but he was never " blind to his greatness. Almost from the opening of my parliamentary life, I felt that he was the greatest popular leader whom the world has ever seen." If Gladstone could find praise for O'Connell's book, to which his warmest admirers prefer to extend the charity of silence, he was not blind to the personal faults of " this great child of nature " and his gravest he considered to be " too ready and rash indulgence in violent language."

A reference in Parliament to a dead child of Brougham's is one of the worst examples of this and a similar lapse caused one of the most violent scenes that were ever witnessed in the House of Commons. During the debate on the Irish Registration Bill which was introduced by Stanley, O'Connell rebuked him for leaving the death-bed of his mother-in-law in order to indulge his hatred of the Irish. The approaching death of a mother-in-law is not generally considered to be the most poignant of sorrows but the introduction of such a topic in public business was unpardonable. "A most blackguard speech" was Greville's comment. " One of the worst of those disgraceful and stupid brutalities which will obliterate (if possible) the fame of the great things O'Connell has done in the course of his career." Macaulay, who was also a witness of the scene, while regretting O'Connell's violence—" he raged like a mad bull "—was far more censorious of the behaviour of other members. " Lord Norreys was whistling and making all sorts of noises. Lord Maidstone was so ill-mannered that I hope he was drunk." When that nobleman asked O'Connell to withdraw he replied : " I advise the noble lord to carry his liquor meekly."

An Irish reporter gives a vivid picture of O'Connell, his head back, arms folded, cloak swathed around him, glaring in defiance at the red faces of the angry squires who yelled, booed and whistled to relieve their outraged sense of delicacy.

He was vain, Gladstone thought, but with " an innocuous and sporting vanity." A trait which he may seem to have revealed when, in reply to the question " who was the greatest Irishman that ever lived ? " he said " Next to myself, I think old Harry Grattan was," but it was a reply with which Gladstone would not have quarrelled for " there cannot but be many," he wrote, " in whose eyes O'Connell stands as clearly the greatest Irishman that ever lived." He had encountered the " victor of the Peninsula and of Waterloo on the battle ground of the higher politics . . . and had obtained from his own lips the avowal of his defeat." Beside him Kossuth and Mazzini were small ; he was " more nearly level to the great Cavour." When he died a great man passed " from the millstream of politics into the domain of history."

It is not difficult after a lapse of time to say of an artist or a writer that he is truly great. How are we to predicate this of a public man? Why does O'Connell live in history while his contemporary Brougham, " his superior in parliamentary eloquence and in general attainments," lies embalmed in her pages? It is not a question of virtue. It has probably a great deal to do with chance. Did Waterloo owe so much to Wellington as Wellington to Waterloo? Catholic Emancipation would have come in time. It came when it did because of the moral force of one man. There is no question about that.

There is the fame of noble achievement and the fame of romantic failure. In Ireland Robert Emmet is probably a greater name than O'Connell although he accomplished only an unsuccessful street rising and death in the hangman's noose. England's happy history has allowed her to dispense with martyrdom as a passport to immortality and Gladstone in estimating O'Connell's genius could overlook the fact that he died in his bed. It is clear that for him the secret of O'Connell's greatness lay in the complete integration of his personality, his single mind and dedicated heart. " If he ever seemed to wander into violence, these were the wanderings of a moment, his boomerang soon came home."

He could have turned his gifts at any time to his own advantage in the way that ordinary men and women do. By not doing this, he lived a life of strain and financial embarrassment, he encountered the most deadly hatred that any man has ever had to face in the public life of England. " He was all along the missionary of an idea—the restoration of the public life of his country. . . . It lay in his heart's core from the dawn of his opening manhood; from the commencement of his full political career it became the mainspring of his acts, his words, his movements, the absolute mistress of his time, of his purse, and of whatever additions his credit could make to his pecuniary resources." His faults were great, for " nothing in him was little," but " in the assemblage of all his properties and powers he was one, indivisible and deeply cut."

CONTINENTAL OPINION

John Hennig

" An Irishman on a visit to Heidelberg asked a postillion whether he had ever heard of Daniel O'Connell. ' Yes,' replied the German, ' he is the man who discovered Ireland.' "

STARTING his biography of O'Connell with this " pregnant and decisive " summary of " the achievements of the Irish Tribune," Michael MacDonagh described it as " an inspiration of ignorance." He was well aware though that the reply by which the German postillion pulled the Irish quizzer's leg might also be interpreted as a ramification of the intense interest which the Continent had taken in O'Connell during his lifetime. In the course of his work, MacDonagh mentioned the request for an autograph which King Louis of Bavaria addressed to O'Connell. He recalled the tribute which Montalembert paid the Liberator on his last sad journey, and he quoted from the funeral sermons delivered by Father Ventura. In these instances he drew on McCabe's still invaluable *Last Days of O'Connell* (1847), the first summary published in these countries of Continental opinion on O'Connell. C. M. O'Keeffe, in the most extensive biography of O'Connell ever published (Dublin, 1864), quoted a description by " a German traveller " (Venedy) of one of the monster meetings. MacDonagh followed up this track, stating that

" there is hardly a book about travels in Ireland between 1829 and 1847 that does not contain a description of a visit to Iveragh."

None of the books on Ireland published during that period by Continental writers could fail to speak of O'Connell, and during that period far more books on Ireland were published on the Continent than during any other period of the same length, in fact, more than during the remaining eighty-two years of the nineteenth century.

235

We may take as the motto of this study what Macaulay said with reference to O'Connell on 13th February, 1844, in the Commons :

"You are mistaken if you imagine that the interest with which he is regarded is confined only to these islands. Go where you will on the Continent, visit any coffee-house, dine at any public table, embark upon any steamboat, enter any conveyance—from the moment your accent shows you to be an Englishman, the very first question you are asked by your companions, be they what they may—advocates, merchants, manufacturers, physicians or peasants like our yeomen, is : 'What will be done with O'Connell ? ' (Cheers, and cries of ' Oh ! Oh ! ')."

The trial of O'Connell, at that moment, marked the climax of Continental interest in Ireland. The study of the development of this interest and of Continental knowledge of Ireland, in fact the mere appreciation of the importance of this subject, is still in its infantile stage. In Continental interest in O'Connell the various earlier and perhaps deeper strata of Continental interest in Ireland came to a point. When O'Connell died he was recognised as the most outstanding man of the first half of his century, surpassing even Napoleon Bonaparte.[1] In this opinion the Continent was virtually unanimous ; Liberals and Conservatives, Romantics and Socialists acclaimed him. A study of the historical background of Continental opinion on O'Connell may perhaps contribute towards a new realisation of his significance in the history of Ireland.

At no period of history has the Continent taken a more sustained interest in Ireland than it did during the period from 1829 to 1847. This interest followed exactly the rise of O'Connell's activities, and rapidly declined after his death. Through O'Connell, Ireland, for the first time in the history of European politics, became an agent, stirring the Continent by her activities, rather than being the victim of activities radiating from the Continent.

[1] McDonagh, op. cit., p. 77, speaks of " a foreign visitor in 1815 " who compared O'Connell to Napoleon.

The first mention of the name of Ireland in any modern Continental language was made by Adam von Bremen in one of the numerous references occurring in tenth-century Continental literature to the Danish invasions. The first mention of the name of Dublin in any work of Continental vernacular literature was made by Gottfried von Strassburg in his *Tristan*, which, written in the early thirteenth century, was the first Continental account of cultural and social conditions in the Norman settlements in Ireland. The first books in Dutch, French and German to deal exclusively with Ireland were written in connection with accounts of the Siege of Derry, the Battle of the Boyne and the Treaty of Limerick. Thus the milestones of Continental interest in Ireland were fixed by the chief phases of what Ranke called the " Teutonic invasions " of Ireland.

Continental knowledge of the geography of Ireland was shaped during the Middle Ages mainly through the classical accounts by Solinus and Orosius embodied in hagiographical and cosmographical works. We have early German prints of the works of Giraldus and Camden, and the English conception of Ireland in general prevailed in Continental *Irlandkunde* right down to the late eighteenth century, when Ossianic enthusiasm for the first time induced Continental writers to try to obtain an independent view of Ireland and to be interested in Ireland for her own sake rather than as a field of Continental activities.

The first Continental writer to devote a book exclusively to an account of his travels in Ireland was Karl Gottlieb Küttner, who while staying in this country in 1783 and 1784 in his capacity of tutor to the sons of Lord Tyrone, the brother of John Beresford, gained an insight into the political situation of Ireland which was never again reached by any Continental observer. Küttner said that the traditional neglect of Ireland in Continental literature was mainly due to the fact that she was regarded as the least important of England's *Nebenländer*. The earliest travel-book on Ireland published in France was the account given in 1800 by Baert-Duholand of his journey in 1787, entitled *Tableau de la Grande Bretagne, de l'Irlande et des possessions Anglaises,*

Next came the account given in 1792 by Pierre Nicholas Chantreau of his short sojourn in the North-Eastern parts of Ireland, embodied in his *Voyage dans les Trois Royaumes en 1788 et 1789;* at the same time, the Italian Chevalier Angliolini could write his *Lettere sopra l'Inghilterra, Scozia ed—Ollanda!*

In Ireland the hostile reaction against the French Revolution (by which reaction O'Connell was so decisively influenced) for the first time established a common front of Protestants and Catholics. The French Revolution terminated not only young O'Connell's Continental education, but the whole period during which Irish refugees, both clerical and military, had endeavoured to convey to the Continent their view of Ireland. These refugees were naturally royalist in their outlook. Also the first French travel-book exclusively dealing with Ireland was written by a French royalist refugee, who regarded Irish antipathy against England as " un étrange préjugé "; both the original edition and the English translation of his work (" by an Irishman ") appeared at Dublin.[1] Right up to the thirties of the nineteenth century, conservative and Catholic circles on the Continent took a detached and theoretical view of Ireland. The practical interest which revolutionary France took in Ireland produced a considerable literature. To be sure, after the various memoirs published by French soldiers who took part in Hoche's landing, there is no Continental travel-book dealing with Ireland until 1825.[2] In 1799, however, in the appendix to his translations of Twiss's and Young's books on Ireland, Charles Millon published the first comprehensive studies written on modern Ireland by a Frenchman in France. Millon says that the aim of these studies was " de faire connaître une des nations des plus anciennes de l'Europe." Like Küttner he was deeply impressed by the theories on ancient Ireland propagated by Vallancey. Millon also published the most detailed map of Ireland up to that time

---

[1] Chevalier de la Tocnaye. For most of the French travel-books quoted in this article see Marie-Hélène Pauly, *Les Voyageurs Français en Irlande au temps du Romantisme* (Paris, 1939).

[2] A French translation of John Carr's *Stranger in Ireland* appeared in 1809.

found in a Continental book. This map was provided by the greatest French cartographers of the time ; giving longitudes from the Isle de Fer and in French measurements, it is a record of the practical interest which official circles took in Ireland.

When in 1802 Christian August Goede published his work entitled *England, Wales, Irland und Schottland* (the order in which England's *Nebenländer* are enumerated is interesting), the title was misleading, as Goede was unable to write on, and perhaps even to come over to, Ireland. At the same time, Heinrich E. G. Paulus, the Rationalist theologian, Goede's colleague at Jena, published a translation of George Cooper's *Letters on the Irish Nation written during a visit to that kingdom in the autumn of the year* 1799. It is significant that Paulus rendered this title by " Cooper's Letters on the present state of Ireland, with an apologetic account of Catholicism in England." In his introduction, Paulus said that he became interested in these letters on " undeservedly neglected Hibernia " because " I have always espoused the cause of that party whom I thought to be oppressed." These words are an early summary of the moral basis of Continental Liberal interest in Ireland during the subsequent fifty years. The same words were used twenty-five years later by Isidore Nachet in the introduction to his translation of Moore's *Memoirs of Captain Rock*. Nachet originated a literary tradition by his comparison of the Penal Laws in Ireland with the anti-Protestant legislation of the *ancien régime*.[1]

But for O'Connell, Catholic circles on the Continent would not have been induced to take a practical and sympathetic interest in Ireland's attempt to achieve redress of her grievances by means of peaceful revolution, nor would non-Catholic and anti-clerical circles have proceeded seriously to apply their Liberal principles to Catholic Ireland. In 1806, the first *Survey of Irish History* ever published in a separate book by a Continental scholar,

[1] It will be remembered that in his defence of Magee, O'Connell stated that " every religion is good, every religion is true." See also Seán O'Faolain, *The Story of Ireland* (1943), p. 33.

Professor Hegewisch of Kiel, was given the significant sub-title : "for the proper understanding of the remote and direct causes of the rebellion of 1798, the Union with Great Britain in 1801 and the so-called Catholic Emancipation, so far not yet realised."

"Since the word 'Emancipation of the Irish nation' has come into circulation, this subject has been given greater publicity in Germany than it really deserves. With the Act of 1793 all decent-minded Catholics were fully satisfied ; they felt that they had obtained everything they could duly expect."[1]

We may compare with this passage what William Dillon said in his *Life of Mitchel* of the Old O'Connellites, that even in the days of Parnell they still held that "in 1829 Irish Catholics had got all that they could reasonably claim."

Küttner, one of Hegewisch's principal sources, had seen the position much more clearly. In the preface to his letters, Schenk, the recipient and editor of the letters, said :

"If the Irish nation would become again a nation, re-attaining her former fame and the rank she used to occupy among the nations, perhaps even exercising influence on the conditions of other nations, she would be of interest not only to her neighbours, but even to those not directly connected with her in political matters. . . . Since the time when, during the American War, Ireland threw off part of the English yoke, she has become interesting to contemporary spectators."[2]

These two sentences outline the programme of Continental interest in Ireland for the subsequent eighty years. During that period, Ireland's struggle to become "a nation once

[1] Perhaps derived from the statement made by Lord Ellenborough in spring, 1805 in the debates on the petition of the Irish Roman Catholics : "Catholic Emancipation, as it is improperly called, has been fully attained. The only remaining emancipation must be acquired by an act of their own."

[2] Compare Byron's
   "Hereditary bondsmen, know you not
      Who would be free themselves must strike the blow ? "
These words were written on O'Connell's carriage when driving through Ennis after his election.

again " was one of the primary topics of world politics. The study of Continental opinion on O'Connell will show that it was due to him that Ireland did not remain the theoretical subject of Continental sympathy and compassion but actually " exercised influence on the conditions of other nations, even those not directly connected with her." Schenck seems to have foreseen that, however deep the Ossianic and subsequent Romantic interest in Ireland, it would never have attained real and practical significance had Ireland herself not taken action in that sphere in which for the following 150 years the decisive battles of human civilisation were to be fought, the sphere of social politics. In his essay *L'esprit national des Irlandais* (1819), Thierry predicted that the literary interest taken by Romanticism would have to be reinforced by the political interest which Liberalism was bound to take in Ireland. It may be mentioned, however, that also in Romantic interest in Ireland, Ireland herself was the active partner. In a note in his *Moines de l'Occident*,[1] Montalembert rightly remarked that Moore's *Irish Melodies* made " the impression of passionate fidelity to the proscribed faith and an oppressed country," because their popularity could be regarded as " not the least powerful among those pleas which determined the great contest of Catholic Emancipation."

The extent of the new Continental interest in Ireland may be seen from the publication in 1825 by Messrs. Manz at Breslau of a translation of *Memoirs of Captain Rock* and of Whitty's *Tales of Irish Life*.[2] We are taken even further to the East by the German translation by W. A. Gerle of the *Description of the United Kingdom of Great Britain and Ireland* by George Depping, which appeared at Pesth in 1827. In the preface to his work (the French original had appeared four years earlier), Depping stated that while devoting only one-tenth of his work to Ireland, " in describing the causes which have produced the long and violent agitation of that unfortunate Catholic province," he hoped

---

[1] iii, 214 ; English translation, iii, p, 203.

[2] See my articles in *Irish Monthly*, 1947, p. 116, and *The Irish Bookman*, February, 1947, pp. 39ff.

to have "judged the moral, political and religious situation
in an unbiased manner." Depping was a Catholic; his
objectivity contrasts most favourably with the emotional
superficiality of many later Continental writers on Ireland.
Only in one or two instances did he allow his personal
feelings to speak. The appearance of the people in the
West of Ireland " evokes the most vivid pity " ; in spite of
their well-known hospitality, some are unable to entertain
a visitor, " since their distress is too great."

"At the present moment, Ireland counts among her
children the poet Moore, Maria Edgeworth and Lady
Morgan. What a pity, that the Catholic population has
no one to equal these writers ! "

Even more in the traditional encyclopaedic style of
accounts on Ireland (in France still represented by Baert
and Millon) was the *Coup d'Oeil historique et statistique sur
l'Etat passé et présent de l'Irlande sous le rapport de son gourverne-
ment, de sa religion, de son agriculture, de son commerce et de son
industrie* by Charles-Henri Maillard de Chambrune, who a
few years earlier had published *Senna ou la fille du druide*,
apparently inspired by the French translation of Lady
Morgan's *Wild Irish Girl*, which appeared in 1813—the first
work of nineteenth-century Anglo-Irish literature translated
into any Continental language—under the title *Glorvina
ou la jeune Irlandaise*. Maillard de Chambrune had not been
in Ireland, but he recorded what was probably the official
attitude of the Restoration towards O'Connell. At the
moment when he wrote " the question of Catholic Emancipation and the Clare election occupied all minds." He
defended the British, saying that from their historical
experiences they could not be expected to trust Irish
Catholics. Hegewisch had already foreseen that Catholic
Emancipation was merely a step towards what he called
" the Emancipation of the Irish nation." Maillard de
Chambrune warned his contemporaries of the shadow of
political and social revolution rising behind the clamour
for religious emancipation. We shall see that this attitude
was shared by no less a man than Goethe.

The first Continental writers who gave eye-witness accounts of O'Connell and his movement were a French and a German nobleman. Though vastly different in their mental, moral and political attitudes, they arrived at practically the same conclusions. In 1826 Duvergier de Hauranne, a young French journalist, took his friends, the brothers Thayer and the Duc de Montebello, for a tour to Ireland. In the following year he published in *Le Globe*, and subsequently in book-form, his *Lettres sur la situation de l'Irlande*. The young Frenchmen followed O'Connell and Sheil on " their ceaseless campaign from province to province, from meeting to meeting." In October 1826, they attended a meeting of the Association at Ballinasloe, at which the Duc de Montebello made a speech which caused a considerable sensation. Duvergier de Hauranne described his first impression of O'Connell when entering the meeting-hall :

" I saw on the platform a man of about fifty years, standing, his hand on his chest, throwing, with apparent negligence, his opinions at three hundred attentive listeners. He is tall, of imposing *tournure*, his face full of frankness and gentleness, although somewhat boorish. When he talks, his features, as lively as his imagination, express in two minutes twenty different passions. Nothing is studied in either his gestures or his speech. The thought gradually rises in him, develops and seems to take palpable shape. Words, accent and gestures are produced in one and the same effort. He utters threats, and his whole body seems to steady itself in defence. He jokes, and before the joke is on his lips the cheerfulness appears already on his face. I do not know of any other orator who gives so much the impression of deep conviction. Sheil's eloquence is always classical and calculating, O'Connell's is popular and inspired."

The quality of de Hauranne's work is evident from this glowing picture of O'Connell's personality as an orator, although objectively he found much fault with him. He complained bitterly of O'Connell's vanity.

" He is the slave of his own popularity. In some respects he is the Chateaubriand of Ireland, bigoted and intoxicated with his own words, especially with his sentimental romanticism. He weeps at the name of the great Dulachtar, Flabertak and Bryan Borhomhe, the great princes who defended the Emerald Isle against the Danes. One must see him among the people, in a Munster church, with ruffled tie and unbuttoned waist-coat, praising the beauties of Ireland, her hills and dales, the incomparable superiority of her inhabitants. When he refers to ' the children of your bosom ' and ' the wives of your affection ' [these words are in the original in English], he can be sure that his audience is touched."

However, de Hauranne admits, " his ardent love of Ireland has saved him from sacrificing his principles to cheap popularity. Listening to him, one cannot help being moved, for he is not only the mirror of Ireland, but Ireland herself."

Of the early Continental visitors to O'Connell, Count Pückler-Muskau has come to be the best known in these countries, mainly because his work appeared in an excellent English translation. By this translation, Mrs. Austin established her reputation as a congenial interpreter of contemporary German literature. She recognised that Pückler's *Letters of a Deceased* were bound to attain some fame owing to the fact that Goethe had reviewed them for Varnhagen's *Berliner Fahrbücher*. The international success of these letters was chiefly due to the rumour that the noble spendthrift and good-for-nothing undertook his journey " through England, Ireland, Wales and France " in search of a rich heiress who would marry him after he should have divorced his first wife, the daughter of the Prussian State Minister, Hardenberg. "Adorable Lucy," to whom these letters were addressed, was said to have consented to this scheme on condition that she should receive a fair share in her successor's dowry. It is interesting to compare Goethe's attitude to the corrupted aristocracy of his age with O'Connell's. Goethe said in his review :

" England, Wales, and especially Ireland are described

in a masterly manner. It is only through his pictorial talent that the ruined abbeys and castles, the bare rocks and scarcely pervious bogs of Ireland become remarkable and endurable. Poverty and careless gaiety, opulence and absurdity would repel us at every stage but for him. We can endure the recital of an endless series of dull social entertainments, because He [capital in the original] endured them."

Then follows the only passage in which the name of O'Connell occurs in Goethe's works :

"He introduces us into distinguished society. He visits the famous O'Connell in his remote and scarcely accessible residence, and works out the picture which we have formed to ourselves from earlier descriptions of this wonderful man. Next he attends popular meetings, and hears speeches from O'Connell, Sheil and other quaint persons. He takes the interest of a man of humanity and sense in the great question which agitates Ireland, but has too clear an insight into all the implications it involves to be carried away by exaggerated hopes."

In December, 1829, Goethe wrote to Carlyle : " It is well known indeed that the inhabitants of the three kingdoms are not living in the best possible agreement." Up to that time, Goethe's interest in Ireland had been literary, personal and scientific. The earliest indication of his political interest was his acceptance, in May 1827, of a map of Ireland. Towards the end of 1829 Goethe drew up a sketch for a comparative study of political events in Europe during the previous two years. Exemplifying his theory that a number of " Krisen " beginning in 1828 were partly solved, partly absorbed by 1829, he stated :

" 1828 : the crisis of the Irish question,—1829 : decided in favour of the Catholics,—new demands : Protestant Church endowment threatened . . ."

Early in April 1829, Eckermann[1] reports, his conversation

---

[1] It may be mentioned that the best English translation of Eckermann's Conversations with Goethe was made by John Oxenford, the author of *The Lily of Killarney*. See also my article on " Goethe's personal relations with Ireland " in *The Dublin Magazine*, January–March, 1943.

with Goethe "turned from the Jesuits and their wealth upon Catholic and Irish emancipation." A friend of Goethe's said on this occasion :

"Emancipation will be granted, but the British Parliament will surround it by so many stipulations that it cannot become dangerous to England."

Goethe whole-heartedly agreed with this view of British policy :

"With the Catholics one cannot be cautious enough. If I were a member of Parliament, I would not prevent Emancipation, but I would ask them to think of my warnings when the first important Protestant would be beheaded."

Four days later, the topic of Goethe's conversation was again "the Emancipation of the Irish" :

"The instructive point for us is that on this occasion things are coming to light of which no one had thought. It is hard to obtain a clear view of conditions in Ireland ; the matter is too involved. So much however seems to be evident. The country suffers from many evils that cannot be cured and will certainly not be relieved by Emancipation. Up to now, it was a misfortune that Ireland had to bear her evil alone ; now it becomes a misfortune that England is being dragged into it. That's what it is. Catholics cannot be trusted. We see with what difficulty the two million Protestants of Ireland have kept their ground hitherto against the preponderant five millions of Catholics. Poor Protestant tenants are oppressed and tormented by their Catholic neighbours. The Catholics do not agree among themselves, but stick together against the Protestants. They are like a pack of hounds who bite each other, but when a stag comes in view, they all unite immediately to run him down."

It is obvious, on the one hand, how dependent Goethe was on the picture of Irish conditions which he had been given by the numerous Irish visitors to Weimar, all of whom were members of the ascendancy. On the other hand, Goethe realised how little was to be expected from Catholic Emancipation. He tried to obtain an insight into the historical background of the " involved affairs of Ireland " by studying " in the *Revue Française* the ancient history of Ireland " (12th August, 1830). However, when a year later he was visited by Crabb Robinson, he said :[1]

" ' My daughter-in-law will be delighted to speak with you on Catholic Emancipation. I take little interest in such matters.'

He enquired, however, about O'Connell and praised the speech of Sheil in which he urged the Catholics not to triumph. 'It was skilfully done,' said Goethe. 'Really insulting, but no one can complain.' " At the same time, he was induced by his daughter-in-law to read a few pages in Moore's *Fitzgerald*. However, we do not know whether he read the preface in which Moore stated that

" of the two great measures, Emancipation and Reform, one has already been granted, while the other is now in triumphant progress."

Goethe's casual and conservative, yet intelligent and sympathetic interest in O'Connell's activities may be taken as a typical example of the attitude of official circles in Europe prior to the revolution of 1830.

When we consider what Goethe made of the slender knowledge he had of Ireland, the inferiority of Prince Pückler will be fully realised. On 29th August, 1828, Pückler went to a meeting of the Catholic Association at Dublin.

" but neither O'Connell nor Sheil were present. Heat and bad smell [car l'humanité Catholique pue autant qu'une autre] drove me out in a few minutes."

The major part of the description of his journey to Darrynane is taken up by a minute account of his sufferings on the road.

"A tall handsome man, of cheerful and agreeable aspect, rose to receive me, apologised for having given

[1] Normand in *Public. English Goethe Soc.* N.S. viii (1931), p. 3.

me up in consequence of the lateness of the hour, regretted that I had made such a journey in such terrible weather, presented me in a cursory manner to his family, and then conducted me to my bedroom. This was the great O'Connell."

Pückler's account of his conversations with O'Connell is on the same level :

"After dinner, he drew his seat near me, and Ireland was of course the subject of our conversation. He asked me if I had yet seen any of the curiosities of Ireland ? Whether I had been at the Giant's Causeway ?— ' No,' replied I laughingly, ' before I visit the Giant's Causeway, I wished to see Ireland's Giant. Daniel O'Connell is indeed no common man, though a man of the commonality. His power is so great that at this moment it only depends on him to raise the standard of rebellion from one end of the island to the other. He is, however, too sharp-sighted, and much too sure of attaining his end by soft means, to wish to bring on any such violent crisis. He has certainly shown great dexterity in availing himself of the temper of the country at this moment, legally, openly, in the face of the government, to acquire a power scarcely inferior to that of the sovereign, indeed in some instances far superior to it. For how would it have been possible for H. M. George IV to withhold 40,000 of his faithful Irishmen for three days from whisky-drinking, which O'Connell actually accomplished in the memorable Clare elections."

O'Connell had rightly predicted to his Clare electors that " the discussions on the attempt to exclude your representative from the House of Commons must excite, will excite, sensation all over Europe . . . and a burst of contemptuous indignation in every enlightened country in the world. The universal shout of the nations of the earth will overpower every opposition." The effect of these elections and the subsequent events may be traced, for instance, in Dufau's introduction to his translation of Croker's *Fairy Legends of the South of Ireland,* which

eventually appeared in the autumn of 1829 under the title
Contes Irlandaises.[1]

" In this country [France] where even the slightest
shadow of religious persecution is abhorred, we have
taken a lively interest in the affairs of Ireland, and at
present we are accompanying with ardent wishes the
work of the [British] Government, who have at length
decided to change the fate of that unhappy island and
to close the wound so shameful for England. It is a wise
decision, after all, for the time of splendid isolation has
gone, and it would be indeed inconsistent to emancipate
Greece but to leave the system in Ireland unchanged. A
lively sentiment of pity in favour of the distressed peasantry
of Ireland has been moving the whole Continent."

It was not until the July Revolution that O'Connell realised
that there were dangers looming behind this one-sided
interest which Liberal Europe had begun to take in his
advance.

The part played by O'Connell in this change of Continental interest in Ireland is illustrated by a comparison
between the 1827 and the 1833 edition of Brockhaus's
Conversations-Lexikon. In the 1827 edition the article
" Irland " occupied three columns, concluding with a short
summary of John O'Driscoll's *Views of Ireland*, which may
have been the source of Goethe's opinion

" that the *Catholic question* or *Emancipation* (once again
rejected, by a majority of four, in the British Parliament
in February 1827) will have little influence on the wretched
state of the Irish."

Pückler had given a brief description of O'Connell's
qualities as an orator :

" He has perhaps more of persuasiveness than of genuine,
large and lofty eloquence ; one frequently perceives too
much design and manner in his words. Nevertheless it
is impossible not to follow his powerful arguments with
interest. . . ."

[1] See my article on this book in *Modern Language Review*, xlii (1947), pp. 237 ff.

The anonymous writer in the 1833 edition of the *Conversations-Lexikon*, however, at the end of an article of nine pages on O'Connell gives a far more detailed account :

" The style of his speeches is vigorous but incorrect and lacking in conciseness. Only when seized by some vivid emotion does he make an impression. He knows the principles of art, but the distractions of his public life have prevented him from learning how to exercise them. Therefore, only few of his speeches can be regarded as masterpieces of political eloquence. His appearance corresponds to this character of his speeches. He is sturdy, but his features are lively, his eyes bright. His slight Irish accent is not unpleasant, with his clear and flexible voice which is audible even in the remotest corner of the House, although he speaks less loudly than most others. O'Connell in the House is quite different from O'Connell in a popular meeting in Ireland. In the Commons he restrains the flight of his eloquence. At the meetings he uses every means to whip up public passion."

Pückler had said :

" His desire for celebrity seemed to me boundless ; and if he should succeed in obtaining Emancipation (of which I have no doubt), his course, so far from being closed, will, I think, only then properly begin."

Brockhaus's article seems to follow up this prediction, saying :

"After reaching the goal for which he had striven so long, by obtaining a seat in Parliament, he had to face many difficulties. He made his appearance there at an age when others have already firmly established themselves. He forced his presence upon an assembly the majority of whom detested him. At first he made no impression, but he has gradually refined his oratorical gifts, and while his own confidence in his powers increases, he has made others conscious of his superiority. Only occasionally does he fall back into his old mistake : to cling to these aspects of a question which have been thrashed out. On the whole, he has learnt, like a good lawyer, to obtain a full view of the very essence of the matter he has to deal with."

Before we take leave of Pückler we may mention that he was the first to compare O'Connell with Napoleon. I do not know whether Balzac knew of this comparison when he stated that O'Connell was greater than Napoleon, because he incarnated a whole nation, a statement expressive not so much of Balzac's high opinion of the Liberator as of his hatred of the Bonapartists.

After de Hauranne and von Pückler, Montalembert was the next Continental visitor to Ireland to give an account of O'Connell. By his visit to this country in 1830, Montalembert realised a dream he had cherished from childhood days. For the first nine years of his life he had been educated by his grandfather, James Forbes, who belonged to the Irish branch of a family the heads of which had been, since Charles II, Earls of Granard. Old Forbes kindled in the boy interest in Ireland, reading to him the speeches of Burke and Grattan ; at school at St. Barbe, Montalembert recited long passages from these speeches. His mother was converted from Anglicanism by an Irish priest, who at that time preached in the chapel of the Tuileries before the royal family.

Montalembert stands for that type of Liberal Catholicism to which Ireland was a focal point of interest. He was the first to undertake a pilgrimage to Ireland as the country of O'Connell. Even before setting out for his journey, he used to pray for O'Connell's success ; he regarded his cause as a holy one. In fact, he dreamt of taking an active part in " the great work of emancipating a nation and of evoking in its favour the sympathies of France." In June, 1829, he wrote to a friend, he had conceived " le projet adorable " of making known to the world the extent of the sufferings of Ireland.

A few months earlier he had begun to collect materials for a history of Ireland from 1688, and eventually it was only the publication of Moore's *History of Ireland* that made him abandon this plan. It may be mentioned at this point that much as Moore's work has been abused by modern critics, its value at its time was great. This may be gauged from the fact that within a year of the publication of its first volume, there were no less than three French translations. I have quoted already some instances to show how introductions to contemporary French translations of works of Anglo-Irish literature give valuable information on Continental opinion on Irish affairs. Bion-Marlavange, one of the translators of Moore's *History*, said for example that this work had appeared under most favourable conditions :

" Indeed the whole world is looking upon Ireland and listening to the dull sound of the last chain falling from the arms of that unfortunate people. At present more than ever Mr. Moore's history is bound to find readers. O'Connell's election was greeted by most Frenchmen as a personal victory."

On 29th September, 1830, Montalembert called at Connell's home.

" I had not even a letter of introduction when I visited the great Liberator, the man of the people, in his retreat at Darrynane. I found 100 to 150 peasants waiting at his door for his advice. I handed him my card, and he received me most graciously and affably. While he finished his meal, I was conducted into the drawing-room, where I found Mrs. O'Connell and young people of both sexes. I was embarrassed in the midst of this large family, of whom I saw successively 34 members. At table we were 25 ; the food was all home-grown. I was sitting between his wife and his eldest daughter. During dinner I talked to him, but at the end we had Irish music. He spent all evening reading the papers, while I talked to Captain Morgan, his second son. O'Connell is a tall heavy man, of reddish complexion, with a clear gentle voice, intelligent and lively eyes, but except for some moments during the conversation, one would not have felt himself in the presence of a great man. He wore a wig. He treats his wife with the greatest affection and loves his estate.

Our conversation treated of the fate of France and of the Catholics. He confirmed to me the opinions laid down in his excellent letter to the Dublin meeting, and spoke extensively of the present state of Ireland, of the untrustworthiness of the Duke of Wellington, and of the monstrosity of the established Church, of which he gave several examples. On the following morning after breakfast I had a long conversation with the Liberator. He is really great, without any affectation, but I think also with particularly high ideas. *Ce n'est pas un homme complet, mais c'est un homme enthousiaste et simple ; dans nos jours c'est déjà bien assez.*"

Montalembert then attended a meeting at Killarney, but was disappointed at O'Connell's speech. O'Connell, on the other hand, was not particularly impressed by the young Frenchman, enthusiastic, but then still unknown. In 1831 Montalembert published in *L'Avenir* his *Lettres sur le catholicisme en Irlande* which were reprinted in *Mélanges Catholiques* and sold by the "Association for Religious Freedom " for the benefit of Ireland. Montalembert stated that an English translation of them appeared in Ireland. In 1854 George Henry Moore of Moore Hall, Co. Mayo, published at Dublin his reply to Montalembert " in which the grievances of the Catholics of Ireland are exposed."

In 1830 *L'Avenir* had published an introduction to Mrs. Belloc's translation of Sheil's *Popular Scenes of Ireland*, which Goethe praised for its " inestimable clearness of presentation and style." *L'Avenir* was only one of the numerous French periodicals which contributed to the spreading of Continental interest in Ireland and O'Connell. Thierry's articles on the national spirit of the Irish (see above p. 241) appeared in *Le Censeur Européen*. In 1824, 1827 and 1829 Baron d'Eckstein, a convert from Judaism, wrote articles on the antiquities and poetry of Ireland. In June, 1829, Thomas Charles Morgan contributed to *Revue Encyclopédique* an article entitled " De l'Emancipation des Catholiques en

Angleterre," in which he said that " the friends of justice and of legal order were in favour of Emancipation," but did not mention the name of O'Connell.

Right up to the eighteenth century, Continental knowledge of Ireland cannot be traced in actual books on Ireland, but is to be gauged from the chapters on Ireland in encyclopedias, chiefly cosmographical works (see above p. 237). In the early nineteenth century, the extensive production of Continental books exclusively dealing with Ireland is only one source of our information on foreign interest in this country. A more spontaneous expression of this interest is found in periodicals. Goethe had been one of the first to recognise that cultural magazines, such as then produced in all parts of Europe in imitation of the great British reviews, were an important means of international information. The importance of reviews for the study of Continental opinion of O'Connell may be illustrated by just one year of *La Revue des Deux Mondes*. In the May issue of 1843 an article by R.S. on Moore said that " O'Connell, O'Gorman Mahon, Sheil, Curran and Grattan, all these brave and noble defenders of Erin " were among the admirers of *Irish Melodies*. The June issue had an article entitled " Les Affaires de l'Irlande," a continuation of an earlier article on this subject, stating that O'Connell had

> brought Ireland into a difficult position : She claims self-government though she is unable to rule herself. O'Connell is the representative, the soldier and the avenger of an oppressed race, of a proscribed religion and of a conquered country. We in France have nothing that could be compared to him. We have only mediocrity."

The author of this article, like Montalembert, admired the great man as such ; Continental enthusiasm for O'Connell was largely expressive of the democratic " cry for the leader." In July *La Revue des Deux Mondes* had an historical article on the position of the Church in Ireland, which contained the statement :

> " Ce n'est pas O'Connell qui a créé l'agitation, c'est l'agitation qui a créé O'Connell."

We shall see that O'Connell was the first to supply nine-teenth-century philosophy of history with a living illustration of one of its favourite problems, viz. whether it is the great individual that makes history, or whether the great indivi-dual is merely a product of mass movements. Finally, in the autumn of the same year, *La Revue des Deux Mondes* stated :

> " Ireland has completely absorbed public interest. Her affairs are occupying public opinion just as much as if we were concerned with the Vendée. This pre-occupation has doubled since O'Connell has thought fit to embark on French politics.[1] He has not met with much success, because though France has always sym-pathised with Ireland, she felt that he had gone too far and was pushing his country to actions of despair and folly. He insulted the French Government when he offered the Legitimists an Irish brigade to instal Henry V on the throne of his fathers. France continues to be sympathetic to Ireland, but the British Government has rendered a good service to O'Connell by arresting him. He no longer knew where to stop. His popularity had grown into tyranny."

Montalembert was the first Continental writer to give us a definitely Catholic view of O'Connell. In this respect his counterpart in Germany is the anonymous author of "Account of the present state of Ireland by an Observer who stayed several years in that country " which appeared in 1835 at Stuttgart. This curious book was published by Messrs. Cotta, then the leading German publishing firm. Among German Catholics, Liberalism did not make as easy headway as it did in France. Liberalism expressed itself in theological movements such as Hermesianism, Güntherianism and Ronge's " German Catholicism." Poli-tically, German Catholicism remained conservative right up to the revolution of 1848, and it was only through his trial and imprisonment that O'Connell became acceptable

[1] O'Connell's interest in Continental politics is a subject worthy of special investigation. See e.g. McDonagh, p. 335. On O'Connell and Ledru Rollin (see also Venedy, *Irland* below).

to the German Catholic public. "Observer" gives us a fair summary of early German Catholic opinion on O'Connell when he says :

"As a Catholic I cannot agree with the oppression of my co-religionists, but I cannot agree either with the association of Catholics with the revolutionaries. I must condemn the revolutionary and radical tendency, expressing itself in the activities of O'Connell and his adherents."

O'Connell's name, "Observer" says in his chapter on Irish factions,

"is closely interwoven with present-day Irish history ; his influence on his nation is omnipotent, and even on England it is important. In his work he is the organ or rather the substance of his party."

From his conservative standpoint, "Observer" takes a rather contemptuous view of a great man who is produced by, rather than leads, the masses. The more important is the characteristic he gives of O'Connell's personality :

"Penetrating intelligence, exceptional power of combination, extraordinary memory, extensive knowledge of Irish history, of the Acts of Parliament, of laws and general conditions—in all this he is unsurpassed by any politician in the three kingdoms. His private life is admitted by his adversaries to be strictly moral and Catholic. He receives the Sacrament every Sunday and obeys the laws of the Church. In his public life he shows extraordinary agility and certainly relentless effort. He is an excellent orator, clear, pertinent and vivid, often sarcastic and witty, with a full vigorous voice, audible to hundreds of thousands. His vivacity often becomes fierce passion. He is not ashamed of getting at times rude or even low. He speaks English and also Irish very well, and is acquainted with popular sayings, proverbs and bon-mots ; commanding a large stock of jokes and funny stories, he can speak extempore for hours on the driest subject without tiring his audience. He is not an orator like Cicero, but speaks in a popular, conversational way. Therefore his speeches are popular even in England.

I was present when he presided for the first time at a radical meeting in London : Every word of his was applauded, there was no end of acclamation and merriment. No British monarch has ever wielded in Ireland as great an influence as O'Connell does."

" Observer " accused O'Connell of " frustrating all measures aiming at the appeasement of Ireland," and of deliberately sabotaging measures to relieve the conditions of the poor by granting security of tenure, a comprehensive poor law and settlement of poor tenants and by promoting native industries such as mining. Revolution seems to " Observer " to be the ultimate object of his agitation, which therefore is as objectionable as open rebellion. At this point, " Observer " refers to O'Connell's opinions on Continental politics. He does not mention his sympathy with the brave peasants of Innsbruck (who in spite of their weak Emperor defended themselves against combined French and Bavarian aggression),[1] but does refer to his sympathy with revolutionary France and Belgium in 1830, with the Polish insurgents and the Italian *Carbonari*, his defence of " the base cause of the ex-Emperor of Brazil," and his accusation of legal monarchs as despots, tyrants and ogres.

" In alliance with those who, as spokesmen of sovereignty of the people and of the rights of man, endeavour to destroy every order, he has challenged the British aristocracy and even the Crown, and put up a staunch opposition to the Established Church together with those who, while making it equal to the other Churches, despise all religions. But like all revolutionaries, in order to make Ireland great and happy, he ruins her, and, in order to make the Catholic Church the ruling one, he robs her of her adherents. His zeal for the Catholic Church is praiseworthy, but his means are objectionable. At present, the Catholic Church in Ireland enjoys a freedom which she does not enjoy in

---

[1] See McDonagh, p. 335 ; a poem on Andreas Hofer appeared in an English translation in *The Nation*.

countries where she is said to be the official Church. She is poor, but greater wealth would not improve her internal position, and certainly the Catholic Church cannot be enriched at the risk of open war. Let the odium rest with the Anglicans ! Laymen are generally more zealous to enrich the Church than are the clergy. There is but one way to improve the conditions of Catholic Ireland, that is, ceaseless work by doctrine and good example. Let there be pious Christians, loyal subjects, peaceful citizens, honest neighbours, just judges, true witnesses, let there be defence against any assault, but do not draw the sword of force. O'Connell, however, where the axe of justice does not avail, uses the crow-bar of power, which he borrows from atheists and indifferentists."

I have given so much space to this account, first because it seems to be little known and not easily accessible, secondly because it is one of the most extensive and original Continental accounts of O'Connell. How far this anonymous German anticipated later Continental fascination with O'Connell, one may realise by a study of Michelet's diary of his tour in Ireland at the same time. It does not mention O'Connell's name.

The year 1835, however, saw the first[1] publication on the Continent of a work by O'Connell. This was the re-publication in book-form of two speeches made by him in Manchester and Edinburgh " en faveur de l'Irlande et contre Robert Peel," which had first appeared in the previous year in *Le National*. The year 1843 (which, we shall see, marked the climax of O'Connell's fame on the Continent) saw the publication of two French translations of his *Memoir on Ireland*, one by Octave Fournier, the other by G. de Courtaud. As late as 1892 extracts from the latter work appeared in *O'Connell, le martyre d'un Peuple*, edited by Charles Simond, together with *Les Griefs de l'Irlande* (*discours par O'Connell, 25 février 1833*).

---

[1] McDonagh, p. 61, however, says that " O'Connell's defence of Magee was translated into French and circulated in France. A copy of the Spanish translation was presented to every member of the Cortes."

The steep rise in Continental interest in O'Connell started in 1839. In that year Timon in his *Études sur les Orateurs Parlementaires* admitted :

" I am not an Irishman ; I have never seen O'Connell ; I do not know his language, but I have been more moved by his speeches,—badly translated, discoloured, maimed, stripped of all the ornaments of style, gesture and voice though they were—than by all those I heard in my own country. They are pervaded by true passion. His soul utters cries that ravish mine. Under the impression of his mighty eloquence, I abhor and detest with a furious hatred the tyrants of that unfortunate country,[1] as if I were a countryman of O'Connell, and I take to loving *la Verte Irlande* as much as if she was my own country."

Gustave de Beaumont's *L'Irlande sociale, politique et religieuse,* which appeared in the same year, is remarkable chiefly for two reasons. It was the first Continental book on Ireland to be translated at once by an Irishman, William Cooke Taylor of Youghal, a Trinity man ; it was the most popular of nineteenth-century Continental books on Ireland,[2] permitting us to trace through its various editions the development of knowledge of Ireland on the Continent. The preface to the 7th edition, published in 1863, begins with a reference to the collection then begun for O'Connell's monument in Dublin. There follows an important account of the Famine. While the first edition said that Thierry's *Histoire de la conquête de l'Angleterre par les Normands* and Duvergier de Hauranne's *Lettres* were the only French books in which Ireland was the chief subject, the 7th edition gives an impressive list of accessions to French literature on Ireland : an article by Lemoinne on " Robert Peel and Ireland " and two articles by Jules de Lasteyrie, the grandson of Lafayette, in *La Revue des Deux Mondes* 1843, 1853

---

[1] In *Les Feuilles d'Automne* (1831), Victor Hugo had written :
  " Je hais l'oppresseur d'une haine profonde,
     Quand l'Irlande saignante expire sur la croix."
Freiligrath's poems on Ireland were inspired by similar feelings.

[2] Quoted already in O'Keeffe's *O'Connell,* i, pp. 501f.

and 1860 respectively; a book on Robert Emmet published by the grand-daughter of Mme. de Stael; the books by Pichot and Perraud (which were published after O'Connell's death). In his article in 1853, de Lasteyrie had said that de Beaumont's book was not yet out of date, and associated himself with the author's conservative attitude.

In the preface to his first edition de Beaumont gives what may be described as a summary of contemporary Continental opinion on Ireland,

> " Ireland is a small country on whose soil a battle is in progress on the greatest problems of politics, morals and humanity."

In the preface to his translation, Taylor remarked on this statement :

> " The political supremacy of the British Empire rests so much on public opinion for its support that nothing by which that opinion may be changed or modified can be neglected with impunity."

De Beaumont was the first Continental writer to study O'Connell as the logical product of Irish history since Henry II. Like Montalembert, he admires in him one of the rare really great men of his age, and like the German " Observer " he is fascinated by the spectacle of a nation, tending to become free, yet surrendering apparently all her freedom to one individual. The fact that O'Connell wields even greater power than did Caesar or Napoleon can be explained only as the result of a unique historical situation.

> " O'Connell came at exactly the right moment. Fifty years earlier he would have perished on the scaffold, and fifty years later, he would not have been listened to in a country that had become more free and more prosperous. O'Connell did not make Ireland free, but without him she would never have become free."

De Beaumont's delight in O'Connell is aesthetic rather than political. I quote the decisive passage in its untranslatable beauty :

"Il est doux de penser que la résistance à l'iniquité
soit une si belle source de la gloire. Quel chef ! quel
zèle ! quelle prudence ! quelle sagesse impètueuse !
quelle fécondite d'expédients ! quelle variété des
moyens ! "

Is this almost theatrical interpretation of O'Connell totally
inadequate, or does it rather point to the fundamental
weakness in the personality and the work of the Liberator ?

The earliest works of O'Connell's to be published on the
Continent were his speeches. These and Parliamentary
Reports in general were also among de Beaumont's sources.
However, de Beaumont tapped still another source of
information, without which neither O'Connell's work nor
his Continental fame would have been possible : the daily
press. In his first edition de Beaumont quotes for example
the *Dublin Evening Post* of 1837. In the same year O'Connell
learnt through Continental newspapers that he was accused
of having spoken with little respect of the Spanish clergy.
Seven years later Macaulay, in the speech quoted in the
beginning of this article, said :

"Let those who deny this assertion [that O'Connell
is the chief topic on the Continent] turn over the French
journals, and they will see what a space he occupies in
the eyes of the French people."

In this respect the fragmentary character of the present
study is most obvious. I have referred to the important
part played by magazines in the promotion of Continental
interest in O'Connell. But few of these periodicals are
available in this country ; of Continental newspapers of
that time there are none at all accessible, and it is only
from occasional references in other sources that we can
gauge the extent to which they were instrumental in spreading the fame of O'Connell. It was chiefly due to its journalistic foundation that Continental interest in O'Connell
proved so frail. O'Connell himself and his adversaries
however realised that at the time public opinion was mainly
represented by the press. This first democratic leader in
the modern sense of the word was also the first outstanding

figure in world history whom posterity has to study chiefly from newspaper-sources.

This can be shown most clearly with regard to O'Connell's trial. In 1843 Regnault published his *Procès d'O'Connell et ses co-accusés*, while in Germany one G. wrote " England versus O'Connell or the World Trial," and Messrs Funcke in Crefeld, popular Catholic publishers, produced an "Account of O'Connell's Trial from the sources." The preface to this latter publication states that

> "newspapers were not for a long time so interesting to German readers as they were when their columns were filled with reports of the 25 sessions at Dublin, on the attitude of O'Connell, of Ireland and of the Crown. It was generally admitted that we were witnessing something extraordinary, important for all nations. As this trial was of international and historical significance, we have summarised in this booklet what would otherwise be lost in the dailies. What we have read there with tensest curiosity, we can now study at greater leisure."

At page 121 this account adds extracts from the *Freeman's Journal* and the *Evening Freeman*, and finally some reprints from the reports on the trial given by the *Kölnische Zeitung*. I assume that the author of these reports was George Weerth, then the London correspondent of that newspaper. In 1846 Weerth wrote a poem entitled "An Irishman's Prayer,"[1] in which " Poor Paddy " invokes St. Patrick to protect him from the night (of death from hunger) " that blows so cold over here from England " or to turn him into a tiger " that can tear rich tyrants with his claws." St. Patrick, however, remains deaf to Paddy's prayer, and the poem concludes pathetically :

> " Everything will remain as it was, and the night is cold,
> And Daniel O'Connell becomes fat and old."

Even such popular accounts of topical events as Regnault's and Messrs. Francke's summaries of O'Connell's trial follow

---

[1] I owe a copy of this poem to Prof. Georg Kayser, Berlin. On Weerth see Kosch's *Deutsches Literatur-Lexikon*.

the lead given by Beaumont in investigating the historical background of O'Connell. The Crefeld account goes back as far as Henry II, while Regnault confines himself to the post-Union period, tracing in particular the whole development of the Repeal Movement, a subject to which later editions of Beaumont's work devoted a special chapter. While this type of study represents O'Connell as a mere product of historical circumstances and of mass-aspirations, the need was also felt to obtain a fuller view of the biographical background of the Liberator. We have seen that the 1833 edition of Brockhaus's *Conversations-Lexikon* had a new and extensive article on O'Connell. When in 1844 the supplement to *Biographie Universelle* was published, vol. lxxxvi referred only to Count O'Connell, the general, adding that he was " of the same family as the illustrious orator." It was not until 1862, in the 38th volume of *Nouvelle Biographie Générale*, that a French dictionary devoted to Daniel O'Connell an article comparable to Brockhaus's. The earliest biography of O'Connell published on the Continent was written in 1843 by Edward A. Moriarty, a Trinity man,[1] at that time Professor of English literature at the Royal Academy of Commerce in Berlin. This work appeared at Berlin under the title *Leben und Wirken O'Connells* ; it is apparently not available in this country. It may be mentioned that prior to this work, Moriarty had published an English translation of Kugler's standard work on Frederick the Great, while in later years he produced the first German translation of Dickens's *Barnaby Rudge*. Moriarty died in 1847 at London and was buried in the Catholic cemetery of Kensal Green. Also in 1843 T. Fortin d'Ivry wrote *Question d'Irlande : O'Connell*. In 1844 one Ludwig Schipper published a biography of O'Connell which appeared at Soest in Westphalia, while in the following year Jules Gondon wrote the first French

---

[1] In Davis's file of *The Nation*, I, owned by the R.I.A., one of the first articles on French reaction to O'Connell is marked as written by Dr. Moriarty. Lappenberg, in the passage referring to O'Connell in his excellent article on Ireland in Ersch-Gruber's *Real-Encyclopaedie* (1844) was the first German writer to draw on Moriarty's biography of O'Connell. Writing at the time of O'Connell's trial, Lappenberg expressed the opinion that neither O'Connell nor the Crown was really in earnest.

biography of O'Connell, a reprint of which appeared in the French translation of Father Ventura's funeral orations on O'Connell (Louvain, 1847).

Studying the biographical tradition of O'Connell on the Continent, one cannot fail to recognise that O'Connell was only one of three great Irishmen who occupied a prominent place in Continental literature during the second third of the nineteenth century. The first of them is of course Thomas Moore, whose Continental reputation, as Allen Thomas[1] and Henri Jousselin[2] recognised, must be studied chiefly from journalistic sources, sources which actually contain, or at least point to, important materials for O'Connell too. The second, more closely associated with O'Connell is Father Mathew.[3] Apart from the account of O'Connell's trial, published by Messrs. Francke, and the book on *O'Connell's Prozess* by Carl Gustav Nicolaus Rintel (Münster, 1845), the most important expression of German Catholic sympathy with O'Connell was the " Encyclopedia for Catholic Germany " (Regensburg, 1847), to which important articles on Ireland, Father Mathew and O'Connell were contributed partly by Binder, the editor, partly by Brühl, the historian,[4] both having been in England and probably also in Ireland. A few years later, Schroedl followed Binder and Bruehl when presenting the German public, in the famous *Kirchenlexicon* of Wetzer and Welte, with what from that time on has remained the official view of the Liberator among German Catholics :

" He used his bold spirit and his powerful eloquence, all his outstanding gifts and his marvellous activity, against the tyrannical oppression by the English. The Catholicity of his public life is unparalleled in world history."

[1] *Contribution à l'histoire de la fortune des œuvres de T.M. dans la littérature française de* 1819–1830 (Paris, 1911), like O'Donoghue's list of French translations (*Poets of Ireland* (1912) 318) referring only to Moore's poetical works.

[2] *Appendice aux Mémoires Irlandaises* (Paris 1871).

[3] See my articles in *Father Mathew Record*, July and September, 1946, and February, 1947.

[4] In 1843 Brühl wrote " Contributions to the knowledge of the recent history of Ireland and of O'Connell's trial " as a continuation to E. Willmann's translation of O'Connell's *Memoir on Ireland*.

The idea of the partnership of O'Connell and Father Mathew was firmly established in Continental literature through Kohl and Venedy. The works of these are probably the best-known Continental accounts of O'Connell at the height of his glory ; in fact, they have been valuable sources even to Irish historians. Kohl's work on Ireland (1843) appeared at once in an English translation, which was even reprinted. Kohl was one of the most successful travel-writers of his age, and to this day his work is quoted in Continental books on Ireland. He was an " objective " globe-trotter whose Liberal broad-mindedness kept him always in the safe waters of shallowness. He left us, however, quite an interesting account of a Repeal meeting in Dublin, in which he embodied a long speech by O'Connell, obviously from memory, though his reference to O'Connell's catch-words—" Poor Erin," " Emerald Isle," " Blood of the Redeemer "—shows that he listened carefully. Admitting that O'Connell was a typical product of the nineteenth century, " the money century," he says :

> " We must in this respect make great allowances for his conduct. By means and ways hitherto unheard-of, he rose to authority, power and wealth ; without any physical force, without making any concessions, he has opposed, for forty years, the most powerful aristocracy in Europe."

The most interesting point in Kohl's account of the Dublin meeting is that " as a finale, a German was brought forward, who had just arrived from America," bringing greetings from the German-Americans. " He compared O'Connell with Washington and his movement with that of Father Mathew. Tom Steele proposed three cheers for the noble German from America."

Jacob Venedy's *Irland*, published by Brockhaus in 1844, was the first Continental book on Ireland of which an English translation made by an Irishman was published in this country. This was by James Duffy, then, of course, the leading national publisher. William Bernard McCabe, the translator, was a personal friend of Venedy's, though he did not agree with his socialist tendencies. Venedy, like Weerth, belonged to the circle of German democratic exiles in London, where he was one of the sources of Marx's information on Ireland. McCabe's translation—curiously enough not mentioned in the article on him in the *Dictionary of National Biography*—omitted the first (historical) part of Venedy's work. The motto of Venedy's *Irland* was O'Connell's " Within that land was many a malcontent. . . ." His description of the monster meeting at Tara is referred to in most biographies of O'Connell, while his theory that O'Connell's movement was bound—by the laws of historical materialism—to become anti-clerical and socialist has exercised some provocative influence. As to his personal contacts with O'Connell, the most interesting point is that he obtained an introduction for his friend Biernatzki to John O'Connell at that time in Paris.

Venedy admits that he derived valuable information on Ireland from the works of his predecessors, among whom he named, apart from Pückler and Beaumont, J. Gabriel Capo de Feuillide, whose *L'Irlande* (Paris, 1839) also bore a motto by O'Connell : " Justice pour l'Irlande." Diametrically opposed though he was to Venedy's opinions in general, de Feuillide agreed with him that

" realising the immense task of elevating a country from political and social prostration, one asks oneself whether O'Connell was sufficiently gifted, sufficiently strong, sufficiently great to perform it."

However, on the three occasions that de Feuillide heard O'Connell addressing the multitude " from the tribune in Green Street," he was impressed by his sincerity. Referring to O'Connell's failure to co-ordinate his cause with that of other oppressed nations and classes, de Feuillide remarks :

" The Irish are too unfortunate to be able to concern themselves much with the misfortunes of other nations. When one is in Ireland, one cannot be anything but Irish, and O'Connell is nothing and wants to be nothing but Irish."

De Feuillide was the first to notice in O'Connell the gift of simplifying political issues so that even the lowest of his followers can grasp them.

" Perhaps O'Connell has nothing more to say than ' Toryism—Reform—Ireland,' perhaps he is mistaken in assuming that Reform will be the solution, but it is these eternal subjects of O'Connell's that all Europe is re-echoing."

After an excellent description of the personal appearance of O'Connell, de Feuillide makes the prophetical statement :

" If O'Connell dies before having achieved his aim, Ireland will fall back into revolution. He was unable to banish it for ever. It was behind his brows."

The last Continental book on Ireland to be published before O'Connell's death was *Un Tour en Irlande* by Count Joseph d'Avèze, editor of the *Revue Britannique*. In the year of O'Connell's death this work was reprinted and another book by d'Avèze entitled *Ireland in the 19th century* published. Beaumont had given d'Avèze a letter of introduction to O'Connell, which enabled d'Avèze to obtain some interesting information on the development of the Repeal movement. His main interest, however, was literary, and in this respect he is an early representative of the more sentimental type of Continental books on " Erin," in which O'Connell occupies only a minor place. [1] Also in the year of O'Connell's death, Messrs. Cotta at Stuttgart once again published a book on Ireland, v. Killinger's collection of Irish folktales, entitled *Erin*. In a note, among valuable literary and biographical information, the editor refers to the Clare elections, to the title " Liberator " and to Sheil. v. Killinger was the first to realise that the future of Ireland would be shaped by Young Ireland rather than by O'Connell's Old Ireland.

---

[1] K. Jongbohm Clement, *Reisen in Irland* (Kiel, 1845), the first Dane to write a travel-book on Ireland (see my article in *Bealoideas*, 1946), was too interested in the historical, folkloristic and social aspects, to refer at length to O'Connell (p. 240 f).

The first Continental book on Ireland to refer to O'Connell's death was the curious study which Dechy, an officer of the gendarmerie of the arrondissement of Rambouillet, made of the police in famine-stricken Ireland. Of O'Connell he says : " Son immortalité commence." The study of O'Connell's posthumous glory in Continental literature is outside the scope of this article.

Was it perhaps more than a mere coincidence that O'Connell died on the Continent, and that his last journey produced some of the most glowing tributes paid to him by the Continent ? At his arrival at Paris, Montalembert told him that France was beginning to learn from him. At Lyons, Masses were offered for his recovery (as during his imprisonment, it was said, prayers were said in many parts of Europe for his deliverance). The funeral orations by Father Orioli in Genoa and by Father Ventura in Rome were the first Italian books bearing O'Connell's name on the title-page. Lacordaire's sermon on O'Connell's death is to this day a standard text of French literature. Jules Gondon made use of the final climax of European interest in the Liberator by publishing an enlarged version of his biography to which the later Italian, Dutch, Polish, German and French biographies of O'Connell have been indebted.

The present study would have failed to convey an impression of the vastness of its subject, were it to be expected to conclude by a summary of results. I had to confine myself to books primarily dealing with contemporary Ireland, written by Continental writers in O'Connell's lifetime, so far as available in the public libraries at Dublin. Even so, this article may have offered some indication of various aspects of a subject the detailed investigation of which may appear attractive. Such an investigation should proceed from the study of Continental opinion of O'Connell to the study of Continental knowledge of Ireland. During O'Connell's time, Continental study of Celtic languages was placed on a modern scholarly basis. How far and in what respects did O'Connell's achievements exercise actual influence on Continental politics, and how far was British policy influenced by Continental opinion of Irish affairs ?

In one of the appreciations of O'Connell which appeared on the centenary of his death,[1] it was stated that

> " the time has not yet come when the gain and loss to the nation attributable to O'Connell's leadership can be accurately assessed and a balance struck."

Perhaps, to obtain the appropriate historical perspective of a man of O'Connell's calibre, we must take a few steps back not only in time but also in space, and the picture of O'Connell's Ireland drawn by the Continental writers of his age may be regarded as an interesting source for that decisive period of Irish history ?

[1] *The Leader*, 24th May, 1947.

O'CONNELL—THE MAN

John J. Horgan

"And God gave him wisdom and understanding exceeding
much, and largeness of heart."—3 Kings iv, 29.

THE personality and character of Daniel O'Connell were
as remarkable and outstanding as his political achievements.
Indeed it may be truly said that the latter derived from the
former. He achieved greatness because he himself was
inherently great. After a hundred years this man, in blood,
environment and characteristics the most Irish of our
democratic leaders, who initiated a new era in the history
of political agitation, emancipated his people and spent
himself unstintedly in the service of freedom, remains a
figure without parallel in our history. Greville, a hostile
contemporary English chronicler, did not exaggerate when
he wrote that " History will speak of him as one of the
most remarkable men that ever existed ; he will fill a great
space in its pages ; his position was unique ; there never
was before, and there never will be again, anything at all
resembling it."[1]

It was inevitable that such a tremendous figure should
have been the subject of extravagant praise and blame.
" Never perhaps," as has been said, " was there a man so
hated and so loved." It is therefore difficult to disentangle
truth from falsehood and describe him as he really was.
Yet a candid historian, weighing carefully the now complete
evidence, must admit that the greatness of this man who,
without spilling a drop of blood, governed a people more
absolutely than Napoleon, was idealised while he ruled,
and received a " tribute " envied by kings, sprang from his
own generous heart and simple soul, and above all from
the fusion in his character of the spiritual and material
functions of life, without which no man can be called
complete.

[1] *Greville Memoirs*, vol. iii, p. 386.

He was not indeed perfect, nor did he pretend to be so. Chief amongst his faults was his inveterate habit of indulging in outrageous abuse of his opponents. Yet it must be urged in his defence that it was an age when political defamation was a commonplace, and that he himself was violently assailed by an unscrupulous press. He was, however, well aware of this failing and once warned his son to avoid personalities in his speeches as it was an " hereditary defect."[1] But he was devoid of rancour, he did not bear malice, and was always ready to forget and forgive. The Big Beggarman, as they derisively called him, was more magnanimous than his detractors. It must be remembered also that in Greville's words : " Had he never been violent he would not have been the man he is and Ireland would not have been emancipated." In society, however, as Greville also noted, he was " lively, well bred and at his ease."

Like most Irishmen then, and many Irishmen still, he had a stronger attachment to the clan and the family than to the community, and did not hesitate to forward the interests of his relatives in public life. In the first reform parliament he had, as he boasted, a family party of eight which consisted of his three sons, two sons-in-law, brother, first cousin and himself. Great men are notorious for mismanaging their own affairs, partly no doubt through their public preoccupations, and O'Connell was no exception. While still a practising advocate he earned what even now would be considered a large income. In 1814 his fees totalled £3,800, and later £8,000 a year. When he sacrificed his professional career in his country's service the national tribute he received, largely made up of small subscriptions, averaged £13,000 a year. In the first year after Emancipation it actually reached £50,000. But it must be remembered that the Tribute was devoted not only to personal, but to political purposes. It was, in fact, what we should to-day call a party fund and out of it had to come his considerable political expenses. In the years between 1830 and 1837 he had, for instance, to meet the expense of no less than six

[1] *Leaders of Public Opinion in Ireland*, by W. H. Lecky, vol. iii, p. 36.

general elections. It is, therefore, hardly surprising to find that he was never well off and died comparatively poor. From his estates, for he was a landlord as well, he is said by Campbell Forster, a hostile critic, to have received some £3,000 a year. This was, however, probably a gross figure and his real income from this source was, having regard to arrears and outgoings, no doubt small enough. Altogether, after deducting party and estate expenses, his net personal income can hardly have exceeded £5,000 a year. The expense of three establishments, at Darrynane, in Dublin and in London, together with his lavish hospitality, and generous, if sometimes indiscriminate, charity, would have absorbed more than this. What he received with one hand he gave away with the other.

Most landlords at that time were careless, slovenly and negligent in the management of their property and O'Connell was no exception, allowing sub-division to proceed unchecked and doing little to educate or improve the condition of his tenants. Campbell Forster, a special correspondent of his enemy, *The Times*, wrote that his tenants were " the most wretched to be seen in Ireland,"[1] but an independent English observer, W. E. Forster, declared later that this was " most unfair and untrue." " I should say," he wrote, " he is decidedly the best landlord in his district, but owing to his having allowed ejected tenants from other properties to squat on his estate at nominal rents there are, of course, some wretched cabins." In truth the Kerry of O'Connell's day was a sordid, poverty-stricken rural slum where hunger and disease were rampant. For this state of affairs a long train of neglect, ignorance and oppression were responsible. For example, in March, 1834, when the first visitation of Asiatic cholera was ravaging the country, we find O'Connell writing to his land-agent, John Primrose, from London : "As far as I am concerned spare no expense that can possibly alleviate the sufferings of the people. You had better at once get Maurice O'Connor from Tralee, so as to have one medical man in Caherciveen, and another to go to the country villages or single houses, wherever the disorder

---

[1] *Campbell Forster in Ireland*, p. 395.

appears. Do not delay, my dear John. Everybody should live as full as possible, eating meat twice a day. Get meat for the poor as much as possible. . . . Coarse blankets also may be very useful if got for them promptly. Could you not get coals from Dingle ? If not get them from Cork. In short if I could contribute to save one life I would deem it a great blessing at the expense of a year's income. Give me the fullest details ; but above and before all things, be prodigal of relief out of my means—beef, bread, mutton, medicines, physician, everything you can think of. Write off to Father O'Connell to take every previous precaution— a Mass every possible day and getting the people to go to confession and communion, rosaries and other public prayers to avert the Divine Wrath."[1] This letter throws a flood of light on the condition of Kerry and the character of O'Connell. Yet it is only in the previous year that we find him writing to his friend, Fitzpatrick, what amounts to a confession of poverty. " I cannot tell you," he writes, " how annoyed I feel that a bill of mine for £205 will be due on Monday. I am the most stupid scoundrel living on this subject. I can only say you shall have full provision within the week."[2]

O'Connell had many temptations and dangers to face. The morals of his class were loose. Duelling was looked upon as the hall-mark of a gentleman and the young dandies boasted, with as much complacency as an Indian brave counting his scalps, of the men they had disabled or killed. O'Connell himself, on serious provocation be it said, killed D'Esterre in a duel. The latter was an Orangeman who took upon himself as an insult some abuse O'Connell had uttered concerning the Dublin Corporation of which D'Esterre was a member. O'Connell was the most tender-hearted of men, and, apart from his deeply religious nature, he had a genuine horror of bloodshed. The death of D'Esterre therefore filled him with remorse. He offered to pay a handsome annuity to D'Esterre's widow—or rather " to share " as he said " his income with her." This she

---

[1] *Correspondence of Daniel O'Connell*, vol. i, pp. 412, 413.
[2] *Correspondence*, vol. i, p. 387.

declined, but several years after the duel when she was involved in an important law suit he threw up some lucrative briefs in Dublin and posted down to Cork to plead her cause, which he did successfully. He later prevailed upon a daughter of D'Esterre to accept an annuity which was regularly paid until his death.[1] It was noticed by his friends that, long after the duel, whenever he passed the house in which D'Esterre had lived, he lifted his hat and his lips were seen to move in prayer. He also apologised at the time of the duel to the Archbishop of Dublin for the scandal he had given, and when going to Holy Communion afterwards he always wore a glove on his right hand to remind him of his unworthiness. He was challenged on various occasions afterwards, often in words of exasperating nature ; but the Champion of Moral Force, as he now proclaimed himself, kept his resolution even if he did not hold his peace. Charles Phillips well remarked that refusal to fight in the then state of society showed more courage than to take up the glove.

One charge has been made against O'Connell, even in recent times, which must be clearly stated, and, let us hope, finally disposed of. The morals of men of his class in the early part of the last century were such as to make people easily credulous of rumours about the sexual immorality of public men. Like drunkenness, deflection from a pure life was looked upon as the sign and privilege of a gentleman, and was passed over lightly, when not actually condoned. We can thus at once understand how easily the breath of malice succeeded in creating in the public mind an atmosphere of slander in regard to O'Connell.

He himself once wrote of his trials in this respect, " What taunts, what reproaches, what calumnies have I not sustained ? What modes of abuse, what vituperation, what slanders have been exhausted against me, what vials of bitterness have been poured on my head, what coarseness of language has not been used, abused, and worn out in assailing me ? What derogatory appellation has been spared, what treasures of malevolence have not been expended,

[1] *Correspondence*, vol. i, p. 34.

what follies have not been imputed, in fact—what crimes have I not been charged with?"[1]

The suggestions concerning his immorality might be ignored, as Lecky, writing with the gravity of a great historian soon after O'Connell's death, properly ignored them, had they not been revived in our own day by a great Anglo-Irish poet, W. B. Yeats, and a leading Irish Catholic lawyer, Lord Justice Sir James O'Connor. From these distinguished Irishmen one would hardly have expected a renewal of the bitter calumny of which O'Connell justly complained. Their attacks on his reputation must, therefore, be dealt with fully.

Yeats, speaking during the Senate debate on divorce legislation, on 11th June, 1925, said : " I have no doubt whatever that when the iceberg melts it (Ireland) will become an extremely tolerant country. The monuments are on the whole encouraging. I am thinking of O'Connell, Parnell and Nelson. We never had any trouble about O'Connell. It was said about O'Connell in his own day, that you could not throw a stick over a workhouse wall without hitting one of his children, but he believed in the indissolubility of marriage and when he died his heart was very properly preserved in Rome. I am not quite sure whether it was in a bronze or marble urn, but it is there, and I have no doubt the art of that urn was as bad as the other art of that period."[2] He then proceeded to assail the moral character of Parnell and Nelson, with which we are not here concerned. The whole speech, which deserves more notice than it has yet received, is an interesting example of the old " ascendancy " mentality.

It may be doubted whether the records of parliamentary debate contain a more flagrant example of insolent slander than this reference to O'Connell. It is the very embodiment of Anglo-Irish racialism in all its ugly nakedness. It can hardly be said to have been inspired by " religious " bigotry since Yeats was indifferent in such matters. Indeed it may be doubted whether any practising Christian, Catholic or

[1] *Reply to Lord Shrewsbury*, February, 1842.
[2] *Senate Debates*, vol. v, cols. 441-2.

Protestant, would have used such slanderous words without at least making an attempt to prove their truth. They will remain not as proof of O'Connell's immorality but of the depths to which a great poet can sink when blinded by racial arrogance.

The astonishing and vindictive attack on O'Connell by Sir James O'Connor, which is contained in his unfortunate *History of Ireland*, published in 1925, is of a more specific kind and must receive fuller treatment. Writing of O'Connell he states : " He was a man of strong animal passions and seems to have indulged them somewhat promiscuously. *The Times* charged him with the parentage of ' broods ' of illegitimate children in Dublin and Kerry. A story, published in London by a Miss Courtenay, is unpleasant reading. We may safely discount much of it, but the residue that must be accepted goes to show that O'Connell was not prepared to act with much generosity to one partner in his amours."[1]

This statement, couched in semi-judicial language, by a leading Irish Catholic barrister who was also a High Court Judge and must therefore be presumed to have some knowledge of the law of evidence and the claims of natural justice, cannot be lightly brushed aside. On examination, however, it proves to be even more contemptible than the reckless rhodomontade of W. B. Yeats. In the first place, although every other important statement in his book is verified by reference to original sources, these accusations, which none of O'Connell's many previous biographers had ever made, are not supported by a shred of evidence other than the reckless defamation of a violently hostile newspaper and the unsupported statement of a woman who was a confessed blackmailer.

To discount the statement of the *The Times* it is sufficient to recall that no reputable newspaper has ever descended to the depths reached by this journal in its attacks on O'Connell. It once described him as " an unredeemed and unredeemable scoundrel " and, in 1835, even published the following vile doggerel attack on him :

[1] *History of Ireland*, 1798–1924, by Sir James O'Connor, vol. i, p. 251.

" Scum condensed of Irish bog !
Ruffian, coward, demagogue !
Boundless liar, vile detractor !
Nurse of murders, treason's factor ! "[1]

and much more of like kind. Such language, almost
incredible to-day, is sufficient to dispose of any criticism
of O'Connell by *The Times*. It remained for another Irish
leader to teach its anonymous assassins that they could not
slander him with like impunity. Unfortunately O'Connell
could not have hoped for equal justice. He had to leave his
reputation in the hands of his fellow-countrymen !

What of the charges made by Ellen Courtenay in her
pamphlet ?[2] Let us see if they can be accepted as trustworthy evidence of O'Connell's promiscuity and infidelity.
Her story may be fairly summarised as follows. She was
born in Cork of respectable parents. Owing to her father's
financial difficulties she left her home in 1817, when scarcely
fifteen, to earn her living in Dublin. There she consulted
O'Connell concerning her father's affairs. He received her
at his house in Merrion Square " with much cordiality and
kindness." Yet she alleges that instinct warned her after a
few interviews that it was better to conduct her subsequent
business dealings with him in writing although she reflected
" that he was a most religious man, a married man with a
large grown-up family around him, and that his moral
character had never, in my hearing, been impeached."
After eight months, during which she was " engaged at a
boarding school of the first class " in Dublin, O'Connell,
according to her story, asked her to call and see him again
at his house concerning her father's affairs, and there, " in
spite of all my prayers, all my cries for assistance," seduced
her. O'Connell, she then alleges, swore that he would
liberally provide for her. He gave her a " trifling sum "
to provide for her journey to London where she " fortunately gained a situation of respectability." Finding she

---

[1] *The Times*, 26th November, 1835.
[2] *A Narrative by Miss Ellen Courtenay of most extraordinary Cruelty, Perfidy and
Depravity* perpetrated against her by Daniel O'Connell, Esq. (M.P. for Kerry),
London, 1832.

was about to become a mother, she returned to Dublin.
There a son was born (but not, one may point out, till
4th November, 1818) who she states was christened Henry
Simpson at O'Connell's suggestion. But he refused to give
her money in spite of her importunity and so she returned
to London. One point in her narrative is most curious,
for she states that she "never told any person of Mr.
O'Connell's conduct towards me save two or three female
friends" even when she and her child were subsequently
in extreme poverty in London. Her difficulties culminated
in her imprisonment for debt and the publication of her
notorious pamphlet. Unfortunately for her credibility she
had, however, in February, 1831, a year before the pamphlet
was published, written to the O'Gorman Mahon, who had
succeeded O'Connell as M.P. for Clare, urging him to let
O'Connell know of her design. She states in this blackmailing letter that she had been "strongly urged by many
persons who would assist her on the occasion to publish the
entire facts—it would make her fortune."

O'Connell, however, refused to be blackmailed and so
the pamphlet was published with much profit to its authors
if not to its authoress. Her sordid story set out in twenty-
seven pages of large black type is followed by ten pages of
notes in smaller type denouncing O'Connell's political
activities in the familiar style of his most venomous critics.[1]
In one of these notes she does not hesitate to assert that
O'Connell "had at the same time ten or twelve wretched
females, whom he had seduced, hanging upon him for
support, and who were *compelled* to visit him at *his own
house*,[2] in the midst of his grown-up family, or they would be
deprived of the wretched pittance, which he occasionally
doled out to them, as a compensation for their ruined
prospects, their estranged friends, their fall in society, their
blasted happiness and their lost honour." *The Times*
itself could hardly surpass this slanderous outburst. " The

---

[1] For a fuller discussion of this episode the reader is referred to Dr. Denis
Gwynn's interesting pamphlet *Daniel O'Connell and Ellen Courtenay* (1930) to
which I am much indebted.
[2] Italics in original.

lady doth protest too much, methinks," indeed, she contradicts her own story, for why should O'Connell have refused to help her when, as she alleges, he helped others in like case?

How anyone can have believed her preposterous tale it is hard to imagine, except that any tale designed to discredit O'Connell at that time was certain to be believed in England. Let us submit it to examination. There is first the incredible account of the alleged seduction of a girl of fifteen, in spite of her outcry and against her will, in O'Connell's own house where his wife and family then resided. There is then his refusal to provide for her and her child. One thing is certain, O'Connell was a most generous and conscientious man who never shirked his moral obligations. He was moreover in sufficiently affluent circumstances to meet any such demand. But above all he had every reason to avoid the public scandal which the publication of her story would most certainly entail. It is therefore absurd to suppose that he would have hesitated for a moment to help her had her story been true. There is only one conclusion possible, namely that Ellen Courtenay either suffered from an hallucination or was a depraved and unscrupulous adventuress who saw the immense possibilities of blackmailing O'Connell, and who was encouraged in her designs by others even less scrupulous. Her letter to the O'Gorman Mahon makes it almost certain that the latter view is correct. The late Sir James O'Connor was a competent and facile advocate, but good advocates do not always make good judges or even honest historians. At the time he wrote his book he was a disappointed man anxious to denigrate and criticise the accepted view of Irish history. O'Connell presented him with a suitable subject for such treatment which he could not resist. It is, to say the least, unfortunate that the story, which the judicial mind of a great historian like Lecky had obviously dismissed with contempt, should have been revived and endorsed by an Irish Catholic judge who could not have held that office but for the work of the man he vilified.

But there is one answer more potent than any other to these vile attacks—namely, the personal life and character

of Daniel O'Connell himself, concerning which there can
be no doubt whatever. The first and most important fact
which cannot be gainsaid is that he was a most affectionate
husband and father. His marriage was a love match. On
23rd June, 1802, he married his cousin Mary, daughter of
Dr. O'Connell of Tralee. She had no fortune and his
uncle opposed the match. Discussing his marriage with
O'Neill Daunt, his secretary and later his Boswell, in 1843,
O'Connell said : " I never proposed marriage to any
woman but one—my Mary. I told her I would devote my
life to make her happy—and she deserved that I should.
I thought my uncle would disinherit me. But I did not
care. I was richly rewarded by subsequent happiness,"
and he added a shrewd remark which is worth recording :
" It is unwise on the part of a lover to offer marriage at an
early period of his courtship. By this precipitation he loses
the advantage which female curiosity must otherwise afford
him, and in sapping his way to her heart discards a powerful
auxiliary." [1]

"A man cannot battle and struggle with the malignant
enemies of his country unless his nest at home is warm and
comfortable," he once said at a banquet in Edinburgh
responding to the toast of his wife's health, and, indeed,
his domestic life was supremely happy. In public he was in
perpetual turmoil and contention ; at home there was always
peace and sunshine, the love of a most devoted wife and the
endearing voices of children. He delighted to speak of this
domestic happiness, and at all the banquets in his honour
there was sure to be a toast such as " The health of Mrs.
O'Connell, the pattern of mothers, the pattern of wives—
a lady whose charitable and exemplary conduct sheds lustre
upon her sex and station " ; to which he would respond
with sincere emotion. " To the lady whose health you
have drunk " he said on one occasion " I owe most of the
happiness of my life. The home made delightful by my
family is, after the cares and agitation of professional life
a most blessed retreat. I am indeed happy in that home—
happy in a dear wife, happy in children into whose minds

[1] *Personal Recollections of O'Connell*, by W. J. O'Neill Daunt, vol. i, p. 133.

a fond mother early and carefully instilled a reverence for religion, the love of God and the love of country."[1]

On another occasion at a meeting in Belfast after his wife's death he thus spoke of his family : " I am a father, and I know what it is to respect as well as to love those whom, in paternal language, I call my angel daughters. They have never given breath to a word of offence against me ; their affection soothes every harsher moment of my life ; and whatever storms I may be engaged in abroad, when I return home, I have, as it were, attendant angels waiting about me, and cheering me on to renewed exertion. But that subject brings me back to a being of whom I cannot speak in the profanation of words. No, I will not mention that name. The man who is the happiest in his domestic circle may have some idea of what my happiness was. Yes I was her husband then, did I say I was ? Oh ! Yes I am her husband still. The grave may separate us for a time, but we shall meet again beyond it, never, I trust, to be separated more."[2]

One of O'Connell's daughter, Mrs. Ellen Fitzsimon, writes of her mother : " My mother was exactly the wife to suit my father in every way. She was devotedly attached to him and she sympathised with him as thoroughly in his public as in his private life. She knew that it was necessary for the success of affairs both of law and politics, with which his mind was occupied continually, that he should never be troubled about household affairs; and she, therefore, while regulating his family with the greatest exactness, took care never to harass him with any of her domestic troubles, as so many unthinking women are in the habit of doing. On the contrary she endeavoured to arrange matters so that he should never find anything but peace and repose at his own fireside. Thus, when engaging a governess, she was wont to stipulate that no chidings of the children should ever take place in their father's presence, but should be reserved for the schoolroom."[3]

---

[1] *The Life of Daniel O'Connell*, by Michael McDonagh, p. 118.
[2] O'Neill Daunt, op. cit., vol. i, p. 250.
[3] McDonagh, op. cit., pp. 120–21.

O'Connell's letters to his wife—letters which, of course, he never supposed would be published—are full of sincere love for her and their children. "The better side," wrote Lecky, "of O'Connell's nature never appears more clearly than in his charming but most unstudied letters to his wife and children. No one who reads them can fail to recognise in them a deeply affectionate nature, eagerly craving for sympathy, and disclosing to those he loved with an almost childlike simplicity all his moods and impulses of joy and sorrow, of triumph and disappointment. It is very noticeable how clearly his strong religious feeling is revealed in these letters which were certainly not intended to see the light. Not so many busy lawyers or politicians can have been so anxious to observe, and to oblige his fellow travellers to observe, strictly the Lenten fast, even when they arrived hungry at a wayside inn after a long day's journey; or so determined not to travel on a Sunday until they had attended early Mass."[1]

From amongst these love-letters to his wife—for they are nothing less—two may be quoted which are typical of the rest. The first was written from Limerick on 7th August, 1813 :

" My darling heart,

Your letter and Charles' account of you gave me fresh life and spirits, but I thought you would have written to me again, heart's treasure, and I felt lonely and disappointed at not hearing from you by this day's post. Upon consideration I have blamed myself for it, because I ought to have written to you every day, but I will do so in future my sweetheart love, and you must follow my example. Do then, my own Mary, let me have the happiness to hear that you are thoroughly well. Take the kindest care of my Kate, and, better still, more care of yourself for my own darling love. The business has become excessive upon this circuit—mine is increasing almost beyond endurance—but I never was in such good health, and have no anxiety but what relates to my own dearest,

[1] Lecky, op. cit., vol. ii, pp. 64–5.

dearest darling. I wish to God you knew how fervently I doat on you. Kiss sweet saucy Kate for me.

DANIEL O'CONNELL."[1]

The second letter, written twelve years afterwards from London, on 22nd February, 1825, proves that their domestic happiness was not of the kind that withers with time. He wrote :

" My own and only love,

It was Kate wrote the letter I got this morning, and I do most tenderly love Kate. Yet, sweetest Mary, I would have wished to see one line also in that handwriting which gives me recollections of the happiest hours of my life, and still blesses me with inexpressible sweetness and comfort when we, darling, are separate. All the romance of my mind envelops you, and I am as romantic in my love this day as I was twenty-three years ago, when you dropped your not unwilling hand into mine. Darling, will you smile at the love letters of your old husband ? Oh, no—my Mary—my own Mary—will remember that she has had the fond and faithful affections of my youth, and that if years have rolled over us they have given us no cause to respect or love each other less than we did early in life. At least darling, so think I. Do not smile either at the mere circumstance of not getting a letter making me somewhat melancholy. It is so cheering to my heart to hear from you—it is so delicious to me to read what you write that indeed I cannot but feel lonely when I do not read your words."[2]

Eleven years afterwards, when she lay upon her death-bed, we find him writing to his friend Richard Barrett. " God help me ! My ever beloved is in a state of much suffering and daily losing ground. I do most potently fear she cannot recover. She may linger. One week may— Oh God help me ! The purest spirit that ever dwelt in a human breast. She did not believe in the existence of evil.

[1] *Correspondence*, vol. i, p. 20.
[2] Ibid. i, pp. 100–1.

I am incompetent or too womanish, and too weak to do my public duty, and this is what she would condemn. But I think I can rally. She would advise me to devote my energies, even in misery, to Ireland."[1] When she died he wrote to Fitzpatrick : " I can never again know happiness and every day convinces me more and more of that fact."[2] It is frankly almost impossible to reconcile infidelity on the part of O'Connell with such letters as these in which he constantly poured out his affection for his wife.

But even if O'Connell could have been guilty of such duplicity, and the human heart is capable of strange deceptions, that shrewd Kerry woman, Mary O'Connell, would hardly have been herself deceived. Yet of her deep love and affection for him there can be no doubt. One example will suffice. On 14th July, 1817, the very year in which he is supposed to have seduced Ellen Courtenay at his residence in Merrion Square, we find his wife writing to him as follows :

" My own darling Dan,

I assure you my darling, you are our continual subject. When a kind husband or father is spoken of Ellen or Kate will exclaim, ' Mama, sure he is not as good a husband or father as our father.' You may guess darling what my reply is. You know what you deserve, and you are aware that in existence I don't think there is such a husband or father as you are and always have been. Indeed I think it is quite impossible there could, and if the truest and tenderest affection can repay you, believe me that I feel and bear it for you. In truth my own Dan, I am always at a loss for words to convey to you how I love and doat on you. Many and many a time I exclaim to myself, ' What a happy creature I am. How grateful I should be to Providence for bestowing on me such a husband ! ' And indeed I am. We will, love, shortly be fifteen years married, and I can answer that I have never had any cause to repent it. I have darling experienced all the

---

[1] *Correspondence*, vol. ii, p. 75.
[2] Ibid. ii, p. 113.

happiness of the married state without feeling any of its cares, thanks to a fond and indulgent husband. . . ."[1]

His love for his children was equally great. He delighted to have them around him. He was their counsellor and friend in all their childish difficulties, and when they grew up was ever ready with advice and sympathy. A letter of his to a married daughter who had been suffering acutely from nervous scrupulosity shows the intimate nature of this relationship and the good sense of O'Connell. He tells her to beware of despair, to throw herself into the arms of God by obedience and submission and to confide in His love. "Pray quietly," he counsels her, "and with composure of mind, once or twice a day; say coolly and deliberately 'Oh God! Thy will be done on earth as it is in heaven' and then attend to your family and children, taking your mind, without bustle and violence, from the thoughts that make you unhappy to your domestic occupation."[2]

His home life was what these letters would lead one to expect. To Mrs. Nichol, a daughter of Joseph Pease, M.P., the eminent Quaker with whom O'Connell was associated in the anti-slavery agitation, whom he met in 1838, he gave the following details of a typical day in his life. "He told me that, for twenty-five years of his life, he rose soon after four, lighted his own fire, and was always seated to business by five. At 8.30 one of his little girls came by turns to announce breakfast—gave an hour to that. At 10.30 he set off to the Courthouse; walked two miles there in twenty-five minutes; always reached the Court five minutes before the judges arrived. From 11 to 3.30 there was not a minute unoccupied. At 3.30 he returned taking the office of the Catholic Association on his way. He always went in—the regular meetings were only once a week—read the letters, wrote a sentence or two in reply, out of which his secretary wrote a full letter. Returned home, dined at 4; with his family till 6.30; then went to his study, went to bed at a quarter before ten, his head on the pillow always by 10."[3]

---

[1] *Correspondence*, vol. i, p. 51.
[2] Ibid. vol. ii, pp. 187–8.
[3] McDonagh, op. cit., p. 122,

Darrynane was however his real home. There he spent his vacations and was entirely in his element. It was to him what Avondale and Aughavannagh were respectively to his successors, Parnell and Redmond, a place of rest and refreshment where cut off from the political turmoil he could indulge his bent for country life and pastimes. " It was in the old ancestral home of Derrynane," writes Lecky in a memorable passage, " that O'Connell might be seen, perhaps, at most advantage. It was situated on that Kerry coast which in its wild and majestic beauty is scarcely equalled in Ireland, and hardly surpassed in Europe. Close to the house lay the open Atlantic with its gigantic waves, its clear deep waters, and its ever-changing hues, while the coast-line curved in graceful bays formed a long range of noble mountain heights. The delicious purity of the air, the mildness of the climate, where the myrtle, the arbutus and the fuschia can grow with true Southern luxuriance, the vivid, dappled, dream-like colouring on sea and land which give a peculiar charm to Irish coast scenery, could be nowhere found in greater perfection. It is colouring wholly unlike that of Southern Europe, but there are days when in its entrancing and most poetic beauty it could not be excelled on the Neapolitan or Sicilian shores. The population was purely Celtic and Catholic ; almost wholly Irish speaking, and O'Connell lived among them like a feudal chief. His house was filled with guests, and no one knew better how to exercise his hospitality. There was nothing there of the drunken revelry which so often characterised the rude hospitality of the Irish chiefs and with which the pages of Barrington and Lever have made us familiar. The chaplain and confessor of O'Connell had an honoured place in his house. There was a family chapel to which all the members of the household were daily called to prayer. The voices of little children were nearly always to be heard, for O'Connell loved to gather his numerous grandchildren about him. Even in his shortest holiday several hours of the day were usually spent in hard work in his library. He had never been addicted to the intemperate habits which were the prevailing vice of so many of his class, and to which his strong, impulsive animal nature naturally inclined him, and when the great Temperance movement of Father Mathew arose he supported it with all his influence, and himself took the pledge as an example to the people. But his high spirits, his countless anecdotes, his shrewdness and his wit made his conversation an unfailing delight, and his general unaffected kindliness of nature set all his guests at their ease. Forster, who visited him, described him as showing ' all the courtesy of a gentleman of the old school, which is indeed the tone of his bearing in his own house.' He was proud of his farming and would boast like an old squire of the superiority of his hay crop over those of his neighbours."[1]

He loved long walks. Accompanied by a favourite dog, he would breast the mountains, walking for miles over their stretches of golden gorse or purple heather until he had penetrated their loftiest and most austere solitudes, when he would lay himself down to gaze on the seemingly illimitable stretch of ocean below, so lonely with all its vastness, without a sail to be seen, its expanse broken only by the distant Skelligs rising like a battlemented fortress on the western horizon. Fox-hunting was impossible in a mountainous country like Iveragh ; but O'Connell thought it poor sport compared to his hare hunting, which was pursued on foot. " I am the only fellow who understands how to hunt rationally," he used to say. " The instinct of the beagle in tracking out the hare is beautifully developed in the Darrynane hills." Once a London paper derisively compared the " Repeal cry" to the cry of the Darrynane beagles. "Aye " retorted O'Connell, " but the fellow made a better hit than he intended, for my beagles never cease their cry *until they catch their game.*"[2]

Almost every alternate day, if the morning was fine, was devoted to this sport. O'Connell, and every guest who the night before expressed a wish to join in the hunt, were called before dawn, and as morning was breaking they were tramping up the steep sides of Coomakistha through the

---

[1] Lecky, op. cit., vol. ii, p. 312.
[2] O'Neill Daunt, op. cit., vol. i, p. 89.

luxuriant heather, followed by two huntsmen in red coats in charge of the pack of beagles, and a wild tribe of followers. O'Connell carried a long staff called a "leaping pole" to assist him in bounding from rock to rock, over tussocks and hollows, to keep in sight of the chase. Standing on a peak of Coomakistha, commanding a view of the open fields below where the beagles were scenting, O'Connell and his friends waited until the hare was started, and then with loud halloo they dashed excitedly along the mountain slopes—O'Connell usually leading the van—in the direction taken by the scudding hare—while the air re-echoed the musical cries of the pursuing pack. Meantime breakfast had been brought up the mountain-side in baskets on the backs of stout mountaineers, hot tea and coffee in jars, bottles of milk and cold whiskey-punch, abundance of cold meat and fish and bread and butter ; but it was the rule of the hunt that the meal must be postponed till at least two hares had been killed.

As the entire day, if the weather were favourable, was devoted to the sport, the plethoric post-bags were also sent up, and during breakfast, which was laid in some sheltered nook commanding a view of the Atlantic, O'Connell, whose meal on these occasions consisted simply of potatoes and milk, ran hurriedly through the numerous letters and newspapers, the latter representing all shades of political opinion, English and Irish, which he subsequently distributed amongst his guests, according to their nationality or politics, or poured forth an inexhaustible stream of jest and anecdote. The only thing that ever stayed his wild career after the beagles was the sound of the chapel bell ringing the mid-day Angelus. Then turning his back on the hunt he would take off his hat and recite audibly the appropriate prayer.[1]

" On days when he did not hunt," writes O'Neill Daunt, " the mode in which he usually disposed of his time was as follows : after breakfast the newspapers and letters occupied in general, from one to two hours ; he would then, if the day was fine, stroll out for a while to the beach, the garden, or to his turret in the shrubbery ; whenever I accompanied

[1] McDonagh, op. cit., pp. 367-8.

him on any of these walks, he has invariably pointed out among the surrounding rocks the course of some hunt, and detailed with a minuteness that evinced the interest he took in the subject, the various turns of the hare and the exploits of the dogs. He would then return to the house and spend the rest of the day till dinner in his study."[1]

To the English writer, Walter Savage Landor, he wrote from Darrynane in October, 1838, a touching plea for fair judgment : " Perhaps if I could show you the calm and exquisite beauty of these capacious bays and mountain promontories softened in the pale moonlight this lovely evening, when all which during the day was grand and terrific has become calm and serene in the silent tranquility of the night ; perhaps you would admit that the man who has been so often called a ferocious demagogue is, in truth, a gentle lover of Nature, an enthusiast of all her beauties, fond of each gentle and each dreary scene, and catching, from the loveliness as well as the dreaminess of the ocean and Alpine scenes around, a greater ardour to promote the good of man in his overwhelming admiration of the mighty works of God."[2]

At Darrynane he exercised all the rights and prerogatives of a chief. The following description, written by a school-fellow of his son John, shows him in this capacity : "After breakfast the Liberator held a court of police in the place fronting the parlour. About forty peasants were around him ; some came on horseback with their wives behind on pillions, and the scene was one of peculiar interest and novelty. Mr. O'Connell, having heard attentively their disputes, distributed justice all round, and each one seemed to go away well satisfied with the cheap law afforded them by the great impartial lawgiver of Darrynane. All this was in the Irish language, for on an average not three of the forty present could deliver his thoughts in any other tongue. All the disputes about property and other matters which arise during the year in Iveragh (or I may say in Kerry for I have seen people from Listowel arrive here) are kept in

---

[1] O'Neill Daunt, op. cit., vol. i, p. 163.
[2] *Correspondence*, vol. ii, p. 152.

reserve until the ' Counsellor ' comes amongst them once more. The peasantry on such occasions are always well clad, and the costumes of the women neat and picturesque."[1]

Although O'Connell spoke Irish perfectly his eminently practical mind had no sympathy with any project for its preservation. " The superior quality of the English tongue," he once said, " as the medium of all modern communications is so great, that I can witness without a sigh the gradual disuse of Irish."[2] In fairness to him it must be said that his attitude in this matter was characteristic of native speakers of Irish then and since. The strongest protagonists of the Irish language have always been those who have learnt it as a foreign tongue and it is they, strangely enough, who still propagate the fiction that it is the spoken language of the Irish people.

O'Connell's professional services were always at the disposal of the poor for nothing. Neither would he accept any fee from the clergy. In March, 1829, he wrote to a Franciscan father : " I am standing counsel for the friars, so that you owe me no apology, nor any thanks for attending to any affair of yours. My fee is paid by one moment of recollection of me occasionally in the Holy Sacrifice."[3]

Although his criticism of those who attacked him in public life was, as we have pointed out, frequently vulgar, violent and extreme, yet in private he was in fact one of the most charitably-minded of men. One day Daunt expressed to him the opinion that Charles II had died without true repentance for his sins. " Daunt ! Daunt ! " said O'Connell, " do not say that. We cannot presume to place a limit to the mercies of God. No ! No ! we cannot."[4] He was indeed the most liberal of men and his idea of the rights of conscience in religious matters was wide and generous. In his youth, as his early diary shows, he had been much influenced by the works of Radical writers like Godwin and Tom Paine, who apparently even affected his religious views, and, although he was certainly from

[1] *Diary of a Tour in Munster*, by Wm. M. N. Skelly.
[2] O'Neill Daunt, op. cit., vol. i, p. 15.
[3] *Correspondence*, vol. i, p. 179.
[4] O'Neill Daunt, op. cit., vol. ii, p. 59.

middle age a devout and fervent practising Catholic, he remained, politically at all events, a Radical to the end. No European statesman did more than he to promote the fusion of democracy and Catholicism. His breadth of vision and tolerance of mind was reflected in his attitude towards other religions. He held that no man's political or civil rights should be curtailed because of his religious beliefs, although he himself had sad experience of such tyranny. In his youth to profess Catholicism was practically to be an outlaw. To obtain the franchise and honours of the state it was not enough to abjure its most sacred mysteries and dogmas ; it was necessary to curse them on oath. His own father had to marry in a Protestant church in order to legalise the ceremony. Yet there was no sect, however small in numbers, or absurd in tenets, to which O'Connell would not extend absolute toleration. Not a single word insulting to Protestants as such, not a single adverse reflection upon their beliefs, can be found even in his Catholic Emancipation speeches, though they were delivered at a time when the most violent invective and abuse were showered upon Catholics and the most sacred mysteries of the Faith.

O'Connell was indeed no bigot. It was, of course, quite true that he had a strong Catholic party feeling which was naturally generated by his career. But he disliked no man on account of his creed. Men of every political and religious opinion were his welcome guests at Darrynane. A bigoted Catholic having once observed that it was quite impossible that any Protestant in Ireland should plead " invincible ignorance " O'Connell remarked to Daunt, " The fellow has no right to judge his neighbour's conscience, he does not know what goes to constitute invincible ignorance."[1] "As a Catholic," he once said, " I abhor and repudiate persecution. One of the greatest crimes which a Christian can commit is to persecute any human being on the score of religion."[2]

When a Protestant lady became a member of his family,

[1] O'Neill Daunt, op. cit., vol. i, p. 75.
[2] Lecky, op. cit., vol. ii, p. 221.

he thus addressed her on her arrival at Darrynane. "You are " said he, " a Protestant, and here at Darrynane, the nearest place of worship of your own persuasion is at Sneem, which is twelve miles off. Now I have taken care that you shall not want the means of worshipping God in your own way on the Sunday. You shall have a horse to ride to Sneem every Sunday during the summer, and a fresh horse, if requisite, to ride back ; and if the ride back should fatigue you, your carriage shall attend you." Her answer was, " I thank you, Sir ; but I have resolved to go to Mass." " Going to Mass is nothing," rejoined O'Connell, " unless you believe in the doctrines of the Catholic Church. And if you do not, it is much better that you should attend your own place of worship ; I shall provide with you the necessary accommodation."[1]

Writing to Archbishop MacHale, to solicit his assistance during the Repeal agitation, he described one of the beneficial consequences likely to result from that measure as being : "the abolition of all sectarian ascendancy." "There would be," he predicted, " no Protestant ascendancy over the Catholics, and no Catholic ascendancy over the Protestants ; religion would be perfectly free."[2] This glorious consummation was O'Connell's ardent wish ; to achieve it was one of the chief objects of his life and we of this generation in a free Ireland can proudly boast that it has been achieved. " Nothing," he once said, " can be more opposed to the spirit of Our Saviour than to persecute for errors in religious belief. Nothing can be more exquisitely absurd. Persecution may make a hypocrite, but it will not make a convert. If a man is already disposed to reject my creed, why I only give him an additional reason for rejecting it if I persecute him."[3]

Yet he had no doubts concerning the importance of religious belief. Once when travelling with Daunt the question arose whether errors in faith or errors in morals were the more dangerous to the soul and the more offensive

[1] O'Neill Daunt, op. cit., vol. i, p. 75.
[2] O'Neill Daunt, op. cit., vol. i, p. 74.
[3] O'Neill Daunt, op. cit., vol. ii, p. 310.

to God? Daunt contended that errors in morality were the worse; inasmuch as a man may believe wrong without knowing it; but a man cannot so easily do wrong without knowing it. Invincible ignorance is much more probable in the speculative errors of faith, than in the practical infractions of morality. A good Protestant would have a chance of going to heaven; whereas a bad Catholic would have none. O'Connell contended on the other hand that errors in faith were the more dangerous. Nothing short of a thorough and perfect sincerity—and moreover a cautious sincerity—could acquit the holder of erroneous faith from the guilt of heresy. Of course, every person thus thoroughly and cautiously sincere, was free from heretical guilt; but those who belonged not to the Catholic Church laboured under the grievous disadvantage of being deprived of true sacraments; or, in other words, they were deprived of those ordinary channels of grace and modes of reconciliation with God, of which all stand in need, inasmuch as all have at one time or another sinned mortally. Even though a Catholic should have sinned more grievously than a person without the pale of the Church, yet the position of the former was, he argued, " in one respect better—namely, that he stood a better chance of obtaining the grace of true repentance."[1]

He was greatly interested in the temperance movement of Father Mathew. " In my young days," he once said, " it was deemed an essential point of hospitality to make guests drink against their will—drink until they were sick. I myself was the first person who rebelled against this custom in Iveragh. After I returned from the Temple, I introduced the fashion of resistance, and I soon had abettors enough. It was fortunate for me that I never, while a youth, could drink more than three glasses of wine without being sick; so that I had my physical convenience to consult in aid of temperance."[2] Somebody happening to mention the great movements of the time in Ireland placed temperance last. " Aye," said O'Connell, " the

---

[1] O'Neill Daunt, op. cit., vol. i, pp. 227–8.
[2] O'Neill Daunt, op. cit., vol. i, p. 157.

temperance though last not least. I was greatly pleased with a remark in one of those vagabond newspapers, 'A nation who can conquer their own vices, never can be conquered by any other nation.' It was admirable ! It was in fact the purest and the noblest philosophy."[1] An Australian bishop happening to tell him that he had only seen one drunken man in Ireland, O'Connell said, "And I hope he was what they call a gentleman ? " " Yes," was the reply, " he was at all events better dressed than the peasantry. He was very tipsy, and was drinking the health of Father Mathew ! " O'Connell once marched at the head of a temperance demonstration through the streets of Cork, and himself took the pledge from the Apostle of Temperance. When, in later years, Father Mathew got into financial difficulties through his generosity, O'Connell at once sent a cheque for £10 10s od. " for the most useful man Ireland ever produced."[2] There is little doubt that the temperance movement contributed enormously to the decorum and dignity of O'Connell's monster meetings during the Repeal agitation.

But if O'Connell was tolerant in the true sense of that much-abused word he had no hesitation in exposing the errors of heresy in his speeches and with his pen. Besides his admirable tract on the Blessed Eucharist, entitled *The August Mystery*, he published two others not less able against the Methodists in which he vindicated the authenticity of the Vulgate, and with an amount of sacred learning, as copious as it was profound, and a simple, but lucid, chain of reasoning, demonstrated the impossibility of a Protestant making a single act of Divine Faith with the mere assistance of the Scripture, interpreted according to Protestantism.

On one occasion he was asked to meet a certain Count Maceroni who was a professing infidel. O'Meara, who was the host, asked Maceroni not to give vent to any of his atheistical views. The Count remained quiet enough at first but then slapped off some jeers at Christianity. O'Connell looked up at him and said :

[1] O'Neill Daunt, op. cit., vol. i, p. 234.
[2] O'Neill Daunt, op. cit., vol. ii, p. 144.

" Count Maceroni, I am now enjoying an excellent dinner and do not wish to be disturbed ; if, however, you choose to resume the subject when we have dined, I shall be ready to meet you upon it." " The Count said no more," narrates O'Connell, " until we went to the drawing-room, and then he renewed his attacks on Christianity. I said, ' Do you believe in Julius Caesar ? ' ' I do,' answered he. ' Do you believe in Caligula ? ' ' I do.' 'And yet you will not believe in Jesus Christ, although, looking at the matter as a merely historical question, the witnesses for Christianity are more numerous and unimpeachable than those for any historical fact whatsoever.' I very soon forced him to confess the historical fact of Christianity, and I then challenged him to show on what reasonable grounds he could discredit our Saviour's death, His Resurrection, and in short, the whole doctrines he came on earth to announce. For these witnesses were eminently trustworthy, as being in the highest degree disinterested. They had nothing of a temporal nature to gain for their evidence. No honour, no rank, no riches, no luxury ; on the contrary lives of toil, persecution and affliction, and they finally died the deaths of martyrs to seal the truths of their narratives. Could any rational man doubt such witnesses as these ? Yet such were the witnesses of Christianity. When the historical fact was once admitted, the divine character of the Christian religion must inevitably be received upon the self-same evidence. I promise you I never had a greater triumph than I enjoyed over my poor Count. How I used to hurrah ! whenever I drove him to confess the absurdity of some infidel cavil or other ! I actually extorted an acknowledgment from him that he had nothing to urge against my reasons, and I sent him home the most unhappy and terrified wretch breathing, lest after all his vaunting there should really be a devil.' "[1]

This amusing incident throws a clear light on O'Connell's controversial methods and his reasoned belief. There is no doubt whatever that, apart from a period in his youth when he was somewhat lax and possibly affected by Deist writers, he was a sincere and devout Catholic by conviction

[1] O'Neill Daunt, op. cit., vol. ii, p. 144.

and well as through faith. It was during that early period that he became a Freemason, and even the Master of a Lodge, but, as he afterwards pointed out, it was either before Freemasonry had been censured by the Church or before he was aware of that censure. During his subsequent life he was noted for his regular attendance at the services of the Church, and for his strict observance of her duties and penances. He was a monthly communicant, and when in Dublin attended Mass almost every morning, often, even in his old age, before breakfast. His favourite place of worship was the church of the Carmelite fathers in Clarendon Street—the scene of many an aggregate meeting during the Catholic Emancipation movement. Its Prior for many years, the Revd. Francis Joseph L'Estrange, was his confessor. In church he never, or very rarely, used a prayer-book. With bowed form enveloped in his ample cloak, the collar of which concealed the lower part of his face, and with downcast eyes, he remained absorbed in mental prayer during Mass.[1] "Among Protestant statesmen," writes Lecky, " there was a widespread belief that he only used his religion as a tool for obtaining the objects of his own selfish ambition. But whatever else may be doubted in the character of O'Connell, it is quite certain that this theory is untrue. No one who follows the details we now possess of his private life, who reads his unstudied letters to his dearest relations and his conversations with his most intimate friends, will doubt that at least from an early period of his married life he was a sincere and ardent Catholic. In the busiest days of his professional and political life he was exemplary in attending Mass and observing the fasts of his Church, and his conversation, though often violent, indecorous and scurrilous, appears to have been absolutely free from any taint of impurity or profanity."[2]

All through his most intimate letters to his wife and children there runs, as Lecky points out, a continual stream of reverent piety. At Darrynane the same atmosphere prevailed. An English traveller who received shelter there

[1] McDonagh, op. cit., p. 123.
[2] Lecky, op. cit., vol. ii, pp. 226–7.

was surprised to find the stormy agitator so full of simple faith and religious fervour. " He kept a domestic chaplain or confessor," he writes, " and it at first somewhat startled you to hear during the day the sound of children's voices from the drawing-room, and on entering you found, amid all the noise and childish laughter, the holy father walking too and fro as if totally unconscious of the juvenile racket around him with his breviary in his hand, muttering his prayers. In the observance of his religion O'Connell was seriously zealous and regular. At nine o'clock every morning the bell of Darrynane rang for Mass. From all parts of the house trooped the members of the family, visitors and servants to the chapel, and for one hour the whole place was silent as a tomb."[1]

At Darrynane in that little chapel the sacrifice of the Mass, by special dispensation, is still celebrated, and there, in the silence before the altar, perhaps more than anywhere else in Ireland, one may feel oneself united with the spirit and personality of Daniel O'Connell in the Communion of Saints. The small chapel, still as it was in his time, the great pew at which he knelt, the atmosphere of genuine piety and devotion, alike remind one of the great tribune ; there, indeed, in a true sense he still lives. It is interesting to recall that when travelling he frequently repeated the old Latin hymns of the Church, his favourites being *Lauda, Sion* and the *Stabat Mater*.[2] He was also much given to mental prayer. Of this a copy of the work *Preparation for Death*, quite worn and covered on every page by notes in his own handwriting, is unanswerable proof. He habitually prayed in Irish. When in London he heard Mass every day at the church in Golden Square. The late Father Mark McNeal was a young priest there at the time. One morning after Mass O'Connell went up to him and said humbly, "Father, will you do me the charity to hear my confession ? " Father McNeal, knowing who he was, was nervous to undertake the confession of the great man and replied : " Perhaps it is better that I should call Dr. Maguire

---

[1] *Correspondence*, vol. ii, pp. 294-5.
[2] O'Neill Daunt, op. cit., vol. i, p. 87.

(the Vicar General) to you." O'Connell smiled and said, " Now, my dear young man, I know what you mean. You need not fear. I have no state affairs. You will find my confession very short and simple."[1]

During a visit to Mount Melleray in August, 1843, Thomas Davis wrote : " By the way I find that O'Connell made a retreat here some three or four years ago, and the Prior assured me that so severe a retreat was unknown even in the Abbey, and was considered a hard and noble example by the monks."[2] Once while he was so occupied a message came that his services were required immediately in the House of Commons to ward off some danger that threatened his party. He quietly answered that he would benefit his cause far more by stopping where he was and committing it to God.

O'Connell in fact never forgot that eternity was before him. On one occasion O'Neill Daunt spoke to him of his future fame. "Alas, alas," he answered in a tone of great solemnity, "and of what use will future fame be to me when I am dead and judged ? " "Yet," said Daunt, " I think you certainly indulge in the expectation of fame; have you not often said both publicly, and to myself in private, that your deeds are making part of history ? " " I spoke of it " replied O'Connell, " as a fact ; not as desiring fame. If I know myself at all, I really do not think I ever did any one action with a view to fame."[3] On another occasion, when the people tried to take the horses from his carriage at Cork, he stopped them, crying out, " No, no, I will never let men do the business of horses if I can help it ! Don't touch that harness, you vagabonds. I am trying to elevate your position and I will not permit you to degrade yourselves."[4]

The tribute which was paid him by the people caused Lord Shrewsbury, an English Catholic peer, to insinuate that O'Connell's political activity arose from his desire to increase the " rent," as he termed this national annuity.

[1] This anecdote was told me by the late Mgr. Michael O'Riordan, who had it from Father McNeal himself.
[2] *Life of Davis*, by C. Gavan Duffy, p. 166.
[3] O'Neill Daunt, op. cit., vol. i, p. 238.
[4] O'Neill Daunt, op. cit., vol. i, p. 89.

O'Connell replied in a famous letter which is one of the finest pieces of reasoned invective in the English language and should be read in full by any one who wishes to understand O'Connell's supreme ability. After pointing out that while his claim to the " rent " may be rejected he will not permit it to be misunderstood he gives particulars of his personal and professional sacrifices for Ireland and concludes with these noble words : "All this I have done and suffered for Ireland. And let her be grateful or ungrateful —solvent or insolvent—he who insults me for taking her pay wants the vulgar elements of morality which teach that the labourer is worthy of his hire ; he wants the higher sentiments of the soul which enable one to perceive that there are services which bear no comparison to money and can never be recompensed with pecuniary rewards. Yes ; I am—I say it proudly—the hired servant of Ireland ; and I glory in my servitude."[1]

No account of O'Connell would be complete which did not deal with his remarkable powers as an advocate and orator. His quickness in reading character and seizing opportunities, combined with his complete and intuitive knowledge of the Irish nature, made him a deadly opponent in the forensic arena. It was an age of great advocates, but in range and versatility he had no competitor. He was supremely great as a cross-examiner, laying subtle traps for untruthful, exaggerating, or timid witnesses. With his eagle eye he detected every evasion and inconsistency, and was equally skilled in wheedling or browbeating the truth out of a reluctant witness. Absolutely fearless himself, no corrupt judge could intimidate him, no hostile jury could escape the lash of his invective. The spectacle of a Catholic advocate fearlessly vindicating the rights of his client and assailing a tyrannical bench with unceremonious ridicule was like a restorative to the downtrodden people. His perfect, and powerful, yet delicately flexible, voice filled the largest building seemingly without effort, while his gestures, so important in great oratory, were easy, natural and almost unnoticeable. His language although clear,

[1] *Reply to the Earl of Shrewsbury*, by Daniel O'Connell. p. 70.

nervous and fluent was always adapted to its purpose, and so lucid and spontaneous that his humblest listener could comprehend its meaning. " No man of his generation," writes Lecky, " could reason more powerfully, state a case more clearly, or sway the passions of a multitude with such consummate skill."[1] An acute French critic, Duvergier, wrote of his oratory : " I know of no living orator who communicates so thoroughly to his audience the idea of the most profound and absolute conviction," and this, after all, is the final test of great oratory. Yet he never wrote a speech beforehand, only the heads. In his youth he had learned, from listening to Pitt, to throw out the lower notes at the close of his sentences. At the monster meetings he played on the great audiences like a musical instrument, convulsing them with laughter, moving them to tears or the most passionate excitement. On such occasions he touched the whole gamut of human emotion. Constant repetition, he used to say, was necessary in politics, and so he never hesitated to repeat the same speech until it had sunk home.

His burly figure and somewhat large features, which his picture has made so familiar, were redeemed from vulgarity by his singularly keen and beautiful blue eyes which the prints do not show ; " the most kindly and honest " it was said, " that can be conceived." When he smiled his whole face was lit up. Being a practical politician he disliked literary politics and politicians. Like Parnell he was only interested in Irish history so far as it furnished material for his political arguments, nor, also like Parnell, was he always accurate in his political references. He was quite capable of indulging in gross exaggeration if it suited his purpose. In oratory as such he had no interest. "A great speech is a fine thing," he would say, " but after all the verdict is *the thing*." Yet he had clear political foresight as is shown by his opinion that international arbitration was the only means of avoiding war, and his prophecy that England would some day need Ireland's aid. Naturally humane, of war he had a conscientious horror. " One murder or one robbery," he said, " will horrify and I cannot conceive how

[1] Lecky, op. cit., vol. ii, p. 64.

robbery and murder are one whit better for being multi-
tudinous ! Yet this is war."[1]

He had a wonderful memory and his conversation was
replete with amusing anecdotes. Yet he never betrayed a
confidence, even of his opponents. He had also a marvellous faculty of bestowing attention upon different subjects
at the same time which was no doubt due in part to his legal
training. Combined with these intellectual gifts went an
enormous physical energy. "Activity," he said, " is with
me a habit," and a list of his public engagements during
the Repeal agitation, when he was already old, proves that
this faculty persisted almost to the end. But this active
politician, this wily lawyer, was also a dreamer, a lover of
nature, almost a poet. One evening at sunset, pacing the
beach at Darrynane, he said to O'Neill Daunt : " Come,
let us turn. Now," he continued, facing the sea, " look at
those majestic mountain waves. How often have I walked
down here to watch the white breakers dashing in and
breaking in foam on the rocks."[2]

Thus Daniel O'Connell emerges from the crucible of
history after one hundred years ; a man of immense intelligence, enormous energy and protean personality, fused
into greatness by a fearless and fervid faith and a fine
courage. His character was in truth largely responsible
for his triumphs. This it was which enabled him to see the
political power that lay dormant in the neglected and
despised masses of his people ; the enormous and over-
mastering strength of any national demand behind which
the people stood in organised and determined array. When
he started the agitation for Catholic Emancipation dry rot
had already set in amongst the well-to-do Catholics who
were anxious for social recognition by the Protestant
ascendancy. Many of these Catholics were loyal to the
Faith, and well-meaning, but they were prepared to conform to anything for the sake of peace. They would have
left to their children a fatal heritage of weakness. Others
were only Catholics in name and would have fallen before

---

[1] O'Neill Daunt, op. cit., vol. i, p. 184.
[2] O'Neill Daunt, op cit., vol. i, p. 201.

any threat to their security. O'Connell came just in time to save the common people, who were still outside the influence of Protestantism, from a similar fate. He took up their cause, led them out of the wilderness, taught them their power, made them feel that they could shame the Catholics of social standing who had failed them. If he had been a weak man he could not have done this. But, as we have seen, he was a man whose character and ability towered above all others of his class, who was not afraid to meet the " ascendancy " on their own level, and who above all refused, by condoning violence, to subordinate moral principle to political expediency. How he would have overwhelmed the arrogant Yeats in the molten lava of his invective !

When he commenced his task his party consisted of himself. He had to face the traditional ascendancy and the rooted bigotry of three hundred years. Moreover, whatever education the great mass of the Irish people had received was imparted,

> " While crouching 'neath the sheltering hedge
> Or stretched on mountain fern."

The first difficulty he had to overcome was to be allowed to sit in Parliament at all. He then had to form a party and to unite a people whom a brutal and persistent persecution had left nothing more than Horace's *nos numeri sumus*. We of this generation can but poorly realise how gigantic a task it was to put national life into a race whose history was written in blood and whose hopes had been so often cast down by disappointments and betrayals. But we can at least do homage to his greatness and learn from his example. His own people knew him as " the Liberator." That noble title epitomises, not only his achievement, but his character.

INDEX

A.

Abbot, Charles, 130.

Abercromby, Sir Ralph, 66.

Address to Pope Pius VII, 88, 89.

Age of Reason, 72.

"Aggregate Meetings," 105.

Ahearne, Francis, 31, 32.

Allen, William, 26, 42.

American War of Independence, 51, 54. 55, 59, 83.

Anglesey, Lord, 141.

Arbitration Courts, 109, 111, 153.

Artois, 29, 33, 36.

Augsburg, Peace of, 86.

August Mystery, The, 294.

B.

Baert-Duholand, 237.

Balzac, 70, 251.

Bellarmine, Cardinal, 27

Bentham, Jeremy, 56, 83, 156, 162.

Beresford, Archbishop of Armagh, 143.

Bolívar, 101, 102.

Bourbon, House of, 91, 92, 93.

Brougham, Lord, 211, 213, 215, 218, 232, 234.

Bulwer Lytton, 108, 211.

Burdett, Sir Francis, 138, 139.

Burke, Edmund, 6, 7, 62.

Butler, Alban, 33, 34.

C.

Caleb Williams : or Things as They Are (Godwin), 75.

Canning, George, 127, 128, 129, 206, 208.

Carlyle, Thomas, 212, 230.

Casey, Charles, 45, 46.

Castlereagh, Lord, 119, 127, 129, 132.

Catholic Association, 65, 95, 98, 106, 107, 153, 188.

—— Committee (Irish Catholic Board), 125–128, 130, 135.

—— Relief Bill (1829), 115, 116, 123, 143–149.

Challoner, Bishop, 42, 43.

Chartists, 104, 111.

Chiaramonti, Cardinal, later Pope Pius VII, 82, 83.

Civil Constitution of the Clergy, 61, 62, 64.

Clarendon, Lord, 228.

Cobbett, 209.

Coercion Act of 1833, 162.

Colleges Bill, 201–204.

Collins, Michael, 151, 154, 155.

Confessions, Rousseau, 75.

Convention Act, 105, 107.

Conversations–Lexicon, 249, 250, 263.

Cooper, George, 239.

Cornwallis, Lord, 119.

Council of Three Hundred, 110, 111, 153.

Courtenay, Ellen, 276–279, 284.

Cuius regio eius religio, 86.

Cusack, Christopher, 26, 48.

D.

Daniel, Rev. John, 43, 46.

d'Avèze, Count Joseph, 267.

Davis, Thomas, 151, 152, 172, 173, 183, 186–198, 200–205, 298.

Davitt, 158, 167.

de Beaumont, Gustave, 259–263.

Declaration of the Rights of Man, 59, 60, 62, 85.

de Feuillide, J. Gabriel Capo, 266, 267.

de Hauranne, Duvergier, 95, 243, 244, 259.

MADE AND PRINTED IN IRELAND BY BROWNE AND NOLAN LIMITED
THE RICHVIEW PRESS DUBLIN